R.C.

W

The Work of the Film Director

LIBRARY OF FILM AND TELEVISION PRACTICE

The Work of the Film Director

by

A. J. REYNERTSON

FOCAL PRESS LTD.
London & New York

ISBN 0 240 50712 6

Printed and bound in Great Britain by
Richard Clay (The Chaucer Press), Ltd.,
Bungay, Suffolk

Contents

Contents   9

Introduction

Before you venture further in your exploration of this book on film directing, you may want to consider, first, what might cause a man to enter an endeavor such as the making of a motion picture. Perhaps it is the promise of wealth: certainly much money has been made from the profession of film directing. Or it may be a mild infatuation with that elusive mistress, fame: to a certain extent, this too can be fulfilled. Griffith and Eisenstein are fairly well and widely remembered, and for the now, Fellini, Bergman, and Kuresawa would certainly not be overlooked in any contemporary gathering.

But your exploration might be for other reasons. Perhaps you feel the need to create a film with a "mission." Then again, your films may be conceived and fashioned as items of commerce or of entertainment. Perhaps another motive moves you to more modest goals: to preserve some observation of man or of nature, or to record a family growing up, a child, a son or daughter.

Whatever your need, the "motion picture," the "movie," or "film" is of itself a means—a very good means—of linking human understanding, the technology and tools, and the present and past techniques of the film making process can be learned in the same sense that the potential film maker can become aware of their possibility and can master their performance. But the use to which these tools can be put, or the derivatives or the mutations to come, cannot be known. One cannot "learn" to become a film director; but people do become film directors. And that is why this book, *The Work of the Film Director*, was written. It is concerned with time and design, and with realizing this design; with sound, and with sound and film together as they become a "motion picture"; with internal composition, and with external composition too; with ideas in their physical form, as they are presented on a screen and as they are carried as content within the forms upon that screen; and with actors, both as human beings, and as the embodiment and reality of the characters necessary to tell the story. And, most important, with the director and his audience, for this is where the essence of the effort of the work of the film director lies—between himself, his story, and his audience.

S.B.   B.-E.

1

Directing Today

THERE IS A luminous haze surrounding the term, "director," especially when it is attached to the even more dazzling term, "film." In some way, it seems, every film must have one. Somehow, magically, this Merlin mixes lenses and synchronous motors, silver halides and iron oxide, with ideas, perceptions and human beings in the alchemy of making motion pictures. Sometimes his formula doesn't work, and the wizard comes up with tinsel and brass. But occasionally that rarest of events occurs: the heart of another human being is touched, a soul is moved and some small change has taken place in the universe.

> We would sit in one room and talk out the whole script for weeks. You couldn't even separate lines of dialogue. Once or twice the other writers would come up with an outstanding line on his own—Diamond's "Nobody's perfect!" at the end of *Some Like it Hot*, for instance.
>
> —Billy Wilder [1]

Each hopes for an audience; these makers of the modest home movie and the Hollywood epic. Their films may differ in size and complexity, but not in their essential goals. The newest owner of an easy-loading eight millimeter, holiday special is, oddly enough, trying to accomplish the same thing as the most profit-conscious Hollywoodized film mogul, or the self-conscious otherworldly experimentalist. Each takes a place in a broad spectrum. All, in fact, have some idea or feeling which they are trying to convey to others. They are involved in an ancient human activity, which, when it is successful, when it closely touches man's insights to that hazy evanescent vision called "truth," has come to be known as art.

Not only *must*, but every film *does* have a director, *is* directed, whether consciously and purposely, or not. Because it is in the mind of the "director" —by whatever name he is called—that the idea in a film form first takes shape, it is his imagination and taste which guide and control, coax and inspire, reject and select what goes into and what comes out of the machines with which films are made. His is the basic responsibility—whether or not he chooses it or recognizes it—of communicating concepts, ideas, emotions and experiences to other human beings, his audience.

Of the many forces affecting the relationship of the director to his work, none is more important than the director himself—his characteristic, distinct pattern of perception and response. While this personal factor is at the core of any human endeavor, in film production its results are documented in a tangible, enduring form. The director's conception of his work, his understanding of the human tragicomedy, his "philosophy of life," shape his approach to the idea of the film, and determine the fate of the film's concept, the depth of meaning brought to the audience.

FILM AS AN IDEA

But before anything can come into being—a film included—it must exist as an idea, and as a plan. This plan is essential. Because the production of even a modest film is expensive and time-consuming, the film-idea is usually written down and a plan for its development thought out and recorded before production begins. The document which results serves, in its most complete and useful form, as a clear, incisive representation, in words, of the idea to be created in images and sounds.

Directing a good picture is, according to Fred Zinnemann, "mainly a question of getting a good story."[2] This story is embodied in a plan of action, usually called a script, which allows production to proceed in a purposeful way.

But however useful and valuable the plan is, it remains, at best, a potential. Bertolucci was quite aware of this when he said:

> Many things came to me at the moment of shooting that were different in the script. This happened because, when I wrote the script of the film, I did not know that I would direct it—another director was supposed to do it. I was hired only as a scriptwriter. . . . Thus, for me it was a question of taking in hand this script that I had written without going into the real problems, which I left to the director who would have shot it.[3]

No more than the written version of a play can substitute for its performance can words on paper, making up a script, stand in place of the completed film. Rather, a well-written script, intelligently used, can serve as a source of inspiration, as a guide and as a goal.

Different directors use scripts in different ways. One director will use the script (or idea or outline—whatever form the plan for the film takes) as a mirror from which to project his own point of view. In his hands, the script becomes a vehicle for the expression of his ideas. Into it, he injects much of himself and his underlying ability to develop meaning for his audience. He is an improviser, rather than interpreter, to a greater or lesser degree he projects himself, his attitudes and his views into the story he is communicating to others. He does not translate—he transforms it. For better or for worse, he acts upon it, changes it readily, adding sequences or discarding what he feels is unsuited to his purpose, or is dramatically invalid. To him it is virgin material; through him it achieves fulfillment.

Another director might look upon the same script as something inviolable, a document to which he feels an obligation. This man conceives as his mission the faithful, literal presentation of the script's verbal concepts in visual and aural terms. Although the story he tells will be formed by his hand, or even to some extent embellished, basically he looks upon the script as something to be plumbed for meaning. Such a director allows the material to act upon him, to evoke and dictate his reactions. Exactness, detail and faithfulness are the criteria of his success.

Sometimes nearer one of these approaches, sometimes another, but usually between extremes, are the areas in which most directors work. The typical director creates and translates, improvises and interprets. At what moments he acts upon, or reacts to, his material, varies from film to film, or within the same film, or even within the making of a single scene. A director might approach one script quite actively, another passively. It is even possible for him to feel the paradox of looking at the material both ways simultaneously. And though this may seem an untenable position, in practice many directors find the horns of this active-passive dilemma are the framework of their directorial existence; that in essence they must alternate and balance between the two, lest they become impaled on either. They find that from the tension of this dilemma comes their ability to refresh their inspiration and to find and express deeper meaning.

FROM IDEA TO FILM

From the story implied in the script, the director develops a plan, a design; he organizes the physical elements from which the film is to be made, selects detail, manipulates time and other factors which must be shaped to trigger an emotional and intellectual response in his audience. Whatever greatness or smallness of story reaches the audience, reaches it because of this. Above all in significance is the director's relationship with the target of effort—his audience. Here, too, the human factor is paramount. Though it is only through mechanical means that the director can communicate with his audience, the communication itself takes place in human terms, that is, in the realm of human emotion and intellect. To achieve this communication the director must have "audience sense," a knowledge of people and an understanding of them as individuals, and as members of his audience. His goal is a communion of minds—of his mind with that of another individual. In part, he must find his audience. But he must also create it during the showing of his film. Finding an audience is finding what touches the emotions of other human beings; creating it is guiding these emotions along paths which lead to the conclusion desired. In speaking of the audience, Godard said:

> In my early days I never asked myself whether the audience would understand what I was doing, but now I do . . . At the same time I feel that one must sometimes just go ahead—light may always dawn in just a few years' time.[4]

The Mechanical Element

Although the work of directing is based on intangible and unmeasurable human values and judgments, the goals of directing are achieved through the measurable and tangible means of mechanics, optics, electronics and chemistry. Thus the director must have an understanding of machines as well as men, because it is through machines that his work is recorded and transmitted to the audience.

Just as there is a gap in perception among human beings, because individuals do not have identical systems of perception, there is a gap of perception between men and machines. No machine "sees" or "hears" in the way that human beings see and hear. The director does not work in terms of scenes and sounds as he perceives them in reality, or even as he sees and hears them in his imagination, but in terms of images and sounds as he knows they will be recorded, channeled, modified and transmitted by machines. The medium shapes as well as carries the ideas. While this is to some extent true in all arts, it is particularly intense in film because of the mechanical character of its image and sound transmission. If freedom from the overbearing technological nature of the medium is to be achieved, understanding of the technology must be attained.

The Human Element

Directing is not a mechanical process, however, but a series of highly personal relationships with those who operate machines. The director not only wants correct exposure, the semblance of motion from the camera and cameraman, not only visual effectiveness and arresting composition. He wants to extract story, dramatic and filmic value, meaning. From the actor the director not only looks for patterns of speech and motion, for characterization; he wants value, story, meaning. Production is a human activity and, like all human activities, it is subject to the biases, emotions, prejudices, to the fears and joys and defense mechanisms of the human beings engaged in its performance. Ultimately it is the force within the human being who operates the machine that counts, not the machine itself. It is in this area of human motivation that the director has his greatest opportunity, for from him those engaged in the production of a film take their cue. He must create, shape and channel the efforts and accomplishments of his co-workers. He is chief interpreter, overseer, disciplinarian, critic, censor, foreman, arbiter, conciliator, inspirer, provoker, energizer and father-confessor to everyone from the cable carrier to the actor. King Vidor, an American director whose work spans many years, said during an interview in 1963:

> I think the job of a director is a mixture. I've spent a period in my life being a painter, a cameraman; direction is a mixture of writer, frustrated actor and musician. All this preparation never shows on the set. You simply say "Put the camera over here. Be very good," . . .[5]

Carl Dreyer, a European master of his craft, said, in speaking of work with his technical crews:

> . . . within this collective, the director must remain the prime, inspiring power, the man behind the work, who makes us listen to the poet's words and who makes feelings and passions flare so that we are moved and touched.[6]

While every director has his own idea of what the directing process is, one thing about it is certain: directing is decisions—hundreds, thousands of them, simple ones and complex ones, each made to solve a specific problem and thereby carry the meaning of the film forward. The director's skill in making these decisions establishes the limits within which the film will come into being.

EARLY FILM MAKING

The road to success for today's fledgling director has been paved with the work and the experimentation of others who have gone before him. Much of the road has been smoothed, and technical changes make constant improvement easier and more convenient, while at the same time minimum standards of acceptance have risen along with sophistication, allowing a wider variety of subject matter, treated in more and more complex ways. But the road was not always so wide, nor so smooth. Directors and audiences—in another day, a simpler world—were content with much more modest paths. Familiar, accepted subject matter, simple, direct story-telling methods were enough. Indeed, the presence of subject matter or technique themselves were advances over what had occurred earlier, for in the first films subject matter was anything that moved; technique consisted merely of adequate exposure.

Among the earliest of makers of this kind of film were two Frenchmen, the brothers Lumière, who, with a perspicacity which has proved characteristic of many a film maker since that day, produced around 1895 a short film entitled, *Lunch Hour at the Lumière Factory*. Since the actors in the film were Lumière employees, it can be safely assumed that the budget for this infant effort was small. Although this film often has the honor of being called the first motion picture ever made, it was in reality little more than a picture of motion. It consisted simply of a shot of the Lumière employees leaving the factory.

More films followed, from France and around the world. They had no story, no plot, no characters, not even any planned action, but to the audience of their time, these first films were a miracle. At last man had a way of recording motion, or creating a synthetic visual reality, a way of reproducing to his senses the moving world in which he lived. Anything that moved became the subject of a film, and audiences flocked in. Before the novelty wore off, another Frenchman and an American, working independently, brought to the motion picture the elements that would hold an audience beyond the time when novelty would be gone.

MÉLIÈS AND PORTER

// The Frenchman, George Méliès, was the first of his countrymen to perform the work of directing in any present-day sense of the term. He was an innovator; he told stories with films. Méliès seemed addicted to fantasy and magic (he was a practicing magician)—one of his early films was called, *A Trip to the Moon*. Being an inventive and original person, Méliès did what others of his time had not yet learned to do: he built sets in which to make films, used actors in costume, staged action within scenes and made a series of little story films whose purpose it was to entertain.

In the United States, Edwin Porter was also making story films, but he made them in a different way. One of his earliest films, and one which immortalized him, was called *The Great Train Robbery*, the first in a long and venerable line of this genre of film. A thrilling and suspenseful sequence of a daring robbery of a passenger train, the film not only introduced new subject matter, but it was performed and photographed out of continuity. While Méliès had focused his camera upon a scene and directed all of the action to happen within that camera's viewpoint, Porter, in effect, set the camera wherever the action occurred. Continuity came later. It was built up from a series of independent shots after the shooting was completed. With Porter, the camera became more than Méliès' recording tool: it became a tool of selective vision. The place for the camera was chosen on the basis that at the particular moment in the story, this was the best place from which to view the action. Thus in a way Méliès and Porter represented two extremes in directing, extremes which are found in the work of directors today. //

FILM FINDS AN AUDIENCE

From these modest beginnings, production of films spread throughout the world and became an activity of particular interest in the United States.

Because of certain business conditions in New York City, theatrical center of the country, the work of making films found a financial support which went a long way toward establishing the activity as an industry. The first successful tools for making films were invented and became known in the United States at an opportune time. Substantial audiences existed, particularly in the New York area. A firm, syndicated control of theatrical activity was easily transferable to films and there were many theater buildings in which films could be shown. The vaudeville houses projected short films as "fillers" between vaudeville acts and soon audiences came to see, not the vaudeville but the shadows on the screen, the magic shadows of people like themselves. Turn-of-the-century science fiction, trips to the moon and adventurous train robberies soon gained a popularity which would eventually draw away the audience so generously given to films by vaudeville. But while the audiences gradually changed allegiance from one form of entertainment to another, the composition of the audience remained substantially the same. Predominantly in the middle income range, they were affluent enough to spend time and money for entertainment but not so wealthy that they could afford the flourishing legitimate theatre. Such people were (and are still) interested in incidents of crime, violence, poverty, morality, fashions of the day, interested in the bizarre and the unusual, and in stories about the problems they themselves face. They wanted, as do all people, reaffirmation of and yet escape from the values of their own way of life. During the next fifty years of film, this large and relatively stable audience formed a strong supportive economic base, providing constant demand for what the American film producers supplied. So well did the producers satisfy this market that, in spite of the absence of language barriers in silent films, foreign films only rarely competed successfully for this audience.

Early in film history the director arose as the principal creator. In more primitive days of the art, the director performed all of those tasks which were later to become so specialized and differentiated: he was writer, producer, photographer, cutter, sometimes actor, make-up man, costume man, property man and probably errand boy, all in one. As the years went by, and film making grew more complex, portions of the director's work were delegated to others; nevertheless, throughout the history of film, from its inception until the present day, the director has continued to be the person in whom responsibility for creation is vested.

GRIFFITH

One director who stands out in history as a major creator and innovator of his time is David Wark Griffith. With his work, the film found its identity as an art form.

Today, Griffith's films seem antique, somewhat ponderous, opinionated, sometimes puzzling and inarticulate. Their techniques and means of telling the story seem mundane. What the more sophisticated audience takes for granted today, however, and what is so familiar now, was little known, or at least little practiced, before Griffith. When he used the camera as a dramatic tool, or as an actor in the story, when he used it to move with the action, or placed it in the best spot from which to view the action, Griffith was certainly not working without precedent. All this had been done before. But never before had a single man used all of these techniques—and many others —combined, in single works and for such powerfully unified dramatic effects. Griffith, in other words, used specific techniques consciously for specific effects, skillfully and comprehensively. There was little accident in what he achieved. Though none of what he did seems startling today, it took a Griffith to make common a collection of skills only randomly employed by others. This man, who did so much to make film the art and entertainment form we know, died unknown, unheralded and unemployed in Hollywood in 1946.

Griffith began his career adopting the techniques of his predecessors, but improving upon them and intensifying their dramatic effectiveness. When Griffith used cuts, fades and dissolves; when he manipulated time, extending and condensing it, showing actions which happened far apart in time and space as if they had occurred simultaneously; when he devised even rarer transitional devices seldom used today—the spot iris and the mask; when he intercut two or more stories simultaneously, introduced suspense, tension, symbolism, complex structural form, Griffith was building upon the work of others. It is not so much a question of whether Griffith's films were great films—although one of them was great—it is that no one before Griffith had quite grasped, or at least so thoroughly explored and used, the potential of the medium; no one had realized its scope, its breadth, its huge number of expressive variables, the impossible things it could accomplish, the dreams it could make real.

Like all successful experimenters, Griffith has had his detractors, those who have forgotten what went before, and in what environment of simple exploitation and commercialism he lived. Even working within this limitation, Griffith was able not only to stamp his own personality upon his work, but to bring an artistic identity to a medium which before had been looked upon as little more than novelty.

LAUGHTER AND SOUND

After Griffith's time, the director became an individual of special importance in the production of a film, and while there are dozens of such individuals who might be discussed and the contributions of each of the men outlined, in effect none of them went beyond what Griffith had done. Each director made his own contribution, however, intensifying some aspect of the work and lending to it whatever creative or inventive genuis he had. Some of these men were great showmen, and their fame and fortunes grew from their ability to select subject matter and to promote films which caught the public eye. Others were the great craftsmen of their time and each developed one aspect of the directing process with intensity. Better stories were used, structure became more complex, and there was a greater awareness of the pictorial. Also, visualizations of mood and atmosphere became more imaginative, and spectacle was elaborated. With this movement also came the new world of the visual gag. The twenties were, among other things, the great years of comedy. While the comedy directors did not change the directing process, introduce new techniques or make startling discoveries, seldom have the techniques of directing been better applied with more delicacy and finesse.

The ten years following World War I were relatively arid for the development of film technique. This calm was interrupted by the thunder of sound films which came late in the twenties. For a while, terrific physical limitations of sound reproduction equipment threw film technique into chaos. Once again, as if experiencing a second childhood, the camera became a recording tool rather than a means to interpretation and took a static view of the action which was so arranged that it could be performed in front of the camera. This was a difficult period for directors, as well as producers, cameramen, cutters, actors and the new sound engineers, a period during which all of these craftsmen tried to regain the great losses which had occurred with this new blessing.

Oddly enough, it was during the Great Depression that followed that the film makers regained their balance. Many of the directors and actors of silent films faded into obscurity. Others took their place and many of these are still at work today. These new directors made up lost ground and found out how sound could become the blessing it was intended to be. They became directors in the fullest sense of the word.

The great days of discovery were now over. The tools and materials of film making improved technically and there were, as indeed there still are, many experiments and attempts to refresh old techniques. But no really revolutionary elements, other than sound, have been introduced since Griffith's time. In a sense, directing found a stability in Griffith's work which enabled those who followed him to master their craft. In the years since sound, directing has undergone a period of refinement and control which has weathered the introduction of color, 3D, widescreen and even television. In spite of the profoundly industrial nature of the major theatrical film effort in the United States, a few directors have managed to perform successfully the many tasks involved in transferring an idea to the screen. When directors have been given or been able to assume sufficient power to do their job in its fullest sense, they have often created works of deep significance to the progress of human culture.

Since the days of the Lumières, film production has become an exceedingly complex activity. While with complexity much has been gained, in a sense some measure of control has also been lost, and with it, much of the adventure of experimentation. Without control and without experimentation the film as an art form will ultimately fail to reach its audience. The tremendous growth of the small-gauge film industry (sixteen millimeter and eight millimeter widths) since World War II, even apart from the new medium of transmission in television, together with the reconstruction of European film efforts, should be providing the opportunities for ever-enlarging numbers of people to learn the directing craft. Unfortunately, at least in the United States, that small group of masters practicing their craft are, like most masters, inaccessible to the student and have little time or energy with which to instruct others in the work they do.

EXCELLENCE AND EXPERIMENTATION: FILM IN THE FUTURE

Much of the process of directing must be self-taught, since it is as much a process of internal spiritual growth as it is a mastery of technological skill. Until recently, there were few means available by which the student could provide himself with an appropriate learning experience. But today, the availability of handy small-gauge equipment has brought the work of directing within reach of almost everyone who has an interest in putting ideas on film. Within the last decade, the number of people making films— the number of directors—has risen sharply. Every purchaser of small-gauge equipment, whether or not he realizes it, is assuming the responsibility of directing. Although for some time the technology of raw stock exposure, camera operation and splicing occupies all of his attention and energy, eventually he grows aware that he can convey ideas through his use of the equipment. He becomes a director. He can choose to follow and perhaps improve upon the techniques and methods of those who have gone before him. Or he can, if he wishes, attempt to recapture some of the spirit of spontaneity and discovery in which the film industry was founded. He can try new methods which need not, at least for the present, have any obvious commercial value.

For most commercial film makers—that is, those who depend upon film production for their livelihood—such luxury of attempting the unknown is impossible, although a few commercial directors have successfully juggled their way into making more risky films, using John Ford's technique:

> I must make films whose success is assured in advance in order to have the right, and the opportunity, to make others that are commercial risks but more worthwhile. On their success hangs my freedom of action. In this way I have been able to make some films I wanted to make, and to make them according to my tastes and weaknesses. But I haven't been able to make ten such films.[7]

In commercial production, known and proven techniques are the keynote. This is the goal toward which all major effort must be directed. Because their films are products, such producers strive for excellence in forms which are well understood, and therefore accepted, by their potential audiences. Seldom have they the opportunity to innovate, to experiment, to gamble with ideas or techniques which may or may not be welcomed by their audience. Development and perfection of existing techniques is the sphere of their activity, and rightly so.

But for those without immediate commercial pressure—or interest— experimentation and innovation is, or can be, a major part of their film production activity. From these persons can come a resurgence of spontaneity, a rebirth of that intimate relationship between director and idea and audience which can bring audiences further along the road of human understanding. They know that quality of idea is independent of cost and size of equipment, and that cost, and size, not quality, are all that need separate the theatrical from the so-called non-theatrical director. The division could more profitably be labeled in accordance with its overriding purposes and aims than with its means. With one group, the aim is the perfection of an already tried and existing form. The purpose of the other group is by nature revolutionary, its habit is to turn up new ideas, new ways of doing things, to hazard the chance that something untried might work. Both groups are equally necessary to the health of the most profoundly influential form of communication in the world today.

2

Time and Design

EVERY HUMAN ACTIVITY is performed with purpose, whether or not that purpose is known to, or has been articulated by the performer. In film making, also a human activity, the purpose is conceived by someone—the director—it is carried into being with someone—the members of his production crew—and is presented for someone—the audience. Until the purpose and audience are known design cannot begin, because design is purpose executed, and organization to that end. It is plan, attack, approach, sometimes simply attitude. It is the means to the end—affecting an audience. It is control and variety, challenge and interest, balance and imbalance, use of the film medium and proportion. In film, the successful design is firm and yet flexible; it allows the sudden accident which leads, oddly, to a more unified, better controlled design. It rejects the irrelevant, the distracting, the disintegrating. In design there is freedom because there is control.

THE DESIGN CONCEPT

In practice, designs for film may be formal or informal, that is, written out, sketched and noted, or existing simply in the mind, memory and imagination of the creator. Each system has its advantages and drawbacks. Formality can breed both unity and rigidity, clarity and deadening stability, integration and inbred elaboration, while informal designs can result in immediacy, intimacy, spontaneity, the sense of life and movement, while they confuse, diffuse, bring little order out of chaos. Neither approach is intrinsically more worthy than the other. The approach, the use, grows out of the subject being treated and the conditions of production. Often both attitudes guide the director, with formality and detailed thinking characterizing the earlier part of his work when the materials of the exposed film have yet to be created. Informality and improvisation may be found in the later work, when touch, rhythm and sensitivity impart final coherence and meaning to the exposed film.

The design gives the final work structure, makes it organic, holds the

24

parts together as a whole, making them work together and making them greater by their integration. This is not to say that there exists any regular or recognizable structure apart from the individual structure of the particular story being told. Structure, like the design itself, grows out of the subject treated. It exists both in inter-frame and intra-frame relationships. It grows from the temporal and spatial relationships which result from shot juxtapositions and from the contents of the shots themselves. Structure suggests the inner nature or form of the event. It is arrived at by examination of the event itself. Structure in film, as in architecture, gives soundness and durability to the work, making it more available to more people over a longer period of time.

But a film is not a fixed object. It has movement, duration, and therefore sequence. If its sequential structure holds together, if as it moves and lasts its parts lead the beholder continuously, the film is said to have continuity, or logic. By logic is implied a certain flowingness in idea, association and symbolic significance. Logic is the sense of rightness, though not necessarily expectation of the usual, and many kinds of continuities are logical. Those based on time are the most common, but those founded in psychological or emotional or intellectual concepts are equally valid. So long as the flow of event is maintained, uninterrupted by an awareness of the medium or its workings, then continuity has been achieved.

This is the essence of telling a story. With continuity, a story, an event of interest to human beings, can be told. The director is a story teller. He creates film experiences and film events so that others may see and know the stories as he sees them. Such stories, when they are successfully told, are more than communication and more than mere accident or random selection, though they contain these elements. They are among the highest products of human activity—art.

FILM AS EVENT

Time is a component of all arts. Even in those arts in which it is not the primary component, time plays a part. Consider architecture. A building has an implicit time element in that time is consumed in examining the structure in its entirety—the whole cannot be experienced at a glance. Whether brief or lengthy, the interval between the moment of the onlooker's first attention and his moving on to the next experience is of consequence to the artist. In arts which in themselves have duration—dance, drama, music and film—this interval of art experience is relatively long and to its creator the way it is used is very significant. Music is a familiar example. A musical composition has duration, a life in time. In fact, time is one of two elements with which the composer works, the other being tone. Whatever meaning the composer wishes to convey to his audience during a musical event, is conveyed by his manipulations of time as expressed in tone. So in film. The organization of images and sounds, in time, is the primary method used to convey meaning.

To the audience, the timing and sequence of sounds and images is as important to understanding the story as the content of the images themselves. Meaning often lies in the time factor itself, the sense of potentiality in an event or scene—that feeling for time continuum in which events emerge from previous events and lead into still other events. This potentiality, which might be called the "quality of becoming," exists because time exists. Of course, any event also possesses a "quality of being," independent of its function in a continuum (fig. 1). The two qualities of being and becoming are inseparable. But though events individually can have value, their meaning is derived from their relationship to the whole. Thus in a way, art reflects life which itself embodies the two factors of being and becoming, as a successful day or an unhappy day becomes part of the continuum of a human lifetime. In film, scenes or shots assume meaning beyond their immediate value because of their internal tempo and their place in the organized sequence of shots which comprise the film.

Fig. 1. "Being" and "becoming" in a sequence of shots.
[The Bed, *James Broughton*.]

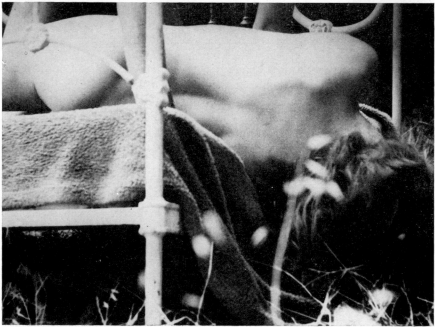

"Real" Time

Time—that is, tempo and sequence—is significant to an audience. When the audience commits itself to watching a film, it knows not only that an interval of time will pass, but it expects that within that interval, tempo and sequence will be used purposefully. The director, therefore, must impose his own deliberate use of time—his time design—upon this inevitable audience awareness. If he fails, the audience feels that its time has been consumed, not used. But if he succeeds, he creates within the film an illusory time experienced by the audience. This illusory time, though of course composed of time in its literal, measured sense: minutes, seconds and fractions of seconds, is flexible and tractable. It has no limits of duration or content, except those imposed by the director.

The physical situation in which directing takes place, however, is another matter. The actuality of production is rigid and filled with restrictions of both the human and mechanical kind. There are the simple but unavoidable limitations involved in moving actors and equipment in time through space. There are mechanical limits and limits to the skills of the cameraman and the actor. There are all the difficulties inherent in the complex process of obtaining finely synchronized relationships while employing the large numbers of people and machines necessary to stage many of the elements from which the film is made. These are the realities of directing a film. Through them, often in spite of them, the skillful director achieves his illusory time design.

Synthetic Time

Within the over-all time design, time may be used with internal regularity, or pattern. Occasionally, such patterned time is imposed upon the inherent irregularity of human behaviour and of nature in order to achieve an effect. An example is the "crowded metropolis" sequence in the 1930's documentary *The City*. This film shows the rush and congestion of city dwellers as they eat, work, try to cross streets and finally find refuge in equally congested Sunday "outings." Segments of human action are selected to intensify an overriding rhythm which is superimposed upon the action. In some shots, the action itself is artificially speeded. This is done by under-cranking (slowing down) the camera so that the pictures, when projected, take on the unnatural staccato hurriedness of a silent comedy film. In other shots, actions are broken up with cuts and reassembled to create an over-all external movement. While artificial in the sense that it reflects no actual event, it gives an emotional experience that even now, long after the film has otherwise become dated, strikes the city dweller as being true in a sense that no literal documentary could. Such rhythms and tempos tend to be more successful when they emerge from the ideas presented. Comparing the hectic rhythms of this section of *The City* to the sensuous, flowing rhythms of *Song of Ceylon* will suggest the breadth of interpretation and portrayal of human action that is available to the film director.

Time design is free to change from moment to moment with relatively little external or arbitrary restriction. Rarely, a film is made in which all or part seems to approximate real time: Hitchcock's *Rope*, which also used the device of a continually moving camera rather than cuts; Zinnemann's *High Noon*, where the real time of waiting for the killers to arrive is literally approximated, although the complex parallel actions occurring within that time segment made it seem more illusory than real to the audience.

Often, film time is independent of any literal representation of time. Actions which are lengthy in life may be accomplished in moments in a film, and a moment can be stretched into minutes or even hours. Throughout the planning phase, and continuing up to the actual shooting situation, the concept of the film's time can be formed and reformed. Time is unconfined at this stage in the work; only the basic relationship of tempo to emotion need be considered. Depending upon the proposed length of the film, thinking is in terms of hours, or, occasionally, minutes—but only on extremely rare occasions in segments of time less than a few minutes. The impact of the whole film, in terms of time, is of concern now. Ultimately the film maker will deal with single minutes, with seconds, and even fractions of seconds—but not yet. The aim at this stage is to begin to create some general impression of a time segment which is appropriate to the script and potentially meaningful to the audience.

By the first day of shooting, plans become firm, and feelings about specific rhythms and tempos more exact and refined. The ideas of the script become events and the script will begin to take on a lifelike quality it did not have before. No longer is it a collection of words on paper—it is beginning to be a film.

The use of time in the completed film is in some ways similar to that in music and drama. Film time is somewhere between the two—freer and more variable than musical time, yet more controlled, more capable of precise shaping than dramatic time. Both the freedom and the precision are possible as a result of the conditions under which a film is made.

After the Plan

Beyond the planning stage, the work of directing is accomplished in two separate but interlocked and interrelated steps. During the first, images and sounds are created and placed upon the motion picture film—this is the shooting period. The second step is editing. In shooting, time may be used with the freedom and variety which characterizes all dramatic media. Here the plans begin to become a reality. But the reality does not become fixed or complete until the editing stage, where the film is arranged and assembled from selected, fixed materials, and where precision and control approaching, and at times exceeding, that attained in music is possible.

Although the twin stages in the directing process—creating and arranging materials—are sequential, they are considered simultaneously. This is necessary because in the finished product the results of the two steps are merged, the two aspects of the total design being dependent upon one another for success. If they are to become one, they must be conceived together. Before and during the shooting situation, the material must be designed in a way that will enable it to be assembled, or edited. Guided by knowledge of the powers and limitations of the editing process, remembering the special kinds of material necessary in editing, the director keys the immediate, internal tempo of his directed scenes to his conception of the total time design of the film. For him, a moment in time is part of a whole; as each moment of the scene occurs, he envisions the completed work and creates the moment accordingly.

The product of this shooting period becomes the raw material for assembly, during which the images and sounds that have been recorded will for the first time become a whole. When such raw materials have been properly made, a film with style, effectiveness, and meaning can result. If the material is poorly made—it may be effective in its part but incapable of being assembled into a whole—then style and meaning of the total work can be lost. Often it is impractical, if not impossible, to redo ineffectively or defectively conceived or executed work, not, at least, without a substantial expenditure of time, money and effort. In commercial film production, this extra expenditure is sometimes, but not often, available to the director. In documentary production, and even when film footage is shot by an individual for his own enjoyment, many events cannot be repeated at any cost. If a particular shot does not exist in the exposed footage, there will be little, probably no, opportunity to recreate it once the shooting situation is past. Other alternatives must be used. The entire scene in which the shot was to appear may be discarded. This is a drastic step, but sometimes necessary. If the story is so constructed that the scene cannot be deleted without calling attention to its absence, or if there is action within it that is important to the story, then another solution must be found. Altering the scene as a whole is sometimes a solution—shortening it or attempting to convey the crucial information some other way, sometimes using material intended for another scene if it can be made to fit. Dissolving within a scene, adding a sound or voice, using a discarded shot intended for another portion of the film may be necessary in the effort to maintain continuity. If alternatives cannot be used without damaging the story, there may be recourse to "cheating," creating scenes synthetically, without sets or actors. This may involve various optical effects, animation, laboratory tricks, miniatures, or model shots. Synthetic material, when it is a part of the original design of the film, can help materialize the story. But as a substitution for directorial oversight, it is at best an artificial solution, rarely an effective one. Ultimately, the defect must be faced. It is impossible, after all, to wish footage into being. In spite of an almost unlimited opportunity for creativity in the film making process, the production of a film at some point abuts an unyielding reality. The finished film must be made out of the footage that is there.

This burden of absolute completeness in shooting a film is something unknown to the conductor or composer, the painter, the writer or even to the stage director, each of whom has an opportunity to do and redo up to the last moment before presentation of the finished work. Such an opportunity exists in film only as the director rehearses the actors and crew in creating the scene. Here he has all the power of a stage director to manipulate the internal timing of a scene. But once he leaves one shot to go on to the next, there is no going back to modify, change, adjust or replace. This film system has advantages as well as disadvantages. Once an effect has been achieved and recorded it can, if necessary, be repeated exactly thousands of times—without deterioriation through time, loss of patience, poor health or the immediate psychological condition of the actor. While the product of the first stage of the directing process is finished in the sense that it cannot be altered but only rearranged, it is also internally fixed and stable. Though it seems a contradiction, this stability means flexibility, because it means the footage can be manipulated during editing.

MAKING THE TIME DESIGN

Designing the time factor in a film, the tempo, rhythm, flow of action, is like other design tasks. An over-all design is conceived, followed by shorter range patterns out of which the whole is to be made. Generally the fundamental rhythm appears first to the film maker—the basic sense of movement and progression which the specific film idea contains. Once this has been sensed, or discovered, then variations may be introduced. In using these variations, however, the effect of time upon an audience must be understood. A time design is cumulative in its effect upon an audience. Throughout the work there is a pressure that propels it toward some final ending, resolution, goal. When this culminating moment is reached it carries an impact enriched and deepened with the accumulated memory of all the moments which preceded it. The final scenes in such films as *All Quiet on the Western Front, The Man in the White Suit, A Place in the Sun, The Third Man, The Asphalt Jungle, Citizen Kane, 8½, Orpheus, Don Quixote*—and countless others, have a meaning and impact for their audience far beyond the immediate scenes themselves: their effectiveness derives from the total film experience and film memory of the viewer. While it is true that constant change and fluctuation characterize the time pattern—so much so that a too detailed analysis will seem to destroy it—such change and fluctuation always drives toward a particular end, and it is this sense of drive and purpose which gives the design its unity and its fundamental rhythm. Contrasting rhythms may be useful for the sake of inducing tension and relief, but there is always the risk that they will become too attractive and too lengthy, thus forming a purposeless diversion from the main event.

Use, or misuse, of time can mean the success or failure of a film. Other errors may be accepted; major errors in rhythm and tempo cannot. Let a scene or sequence develop and progress too slowly, and the audience becomes bored, restless and loses interest. Attention wanders from the screen, or, worse, there is a shift from a personal, subjective participation in the ideas being presented to an impersonal, objective, sometimes antagonistic and derisive examination of the scenery, the acting or whatever else might divert the attention. This is a shift which all directors work to prevent, or at least control. Once it occurs, the work of the preceding sequences of the film, which induced the audience's empathy and captured its imagination, is lost.

A substantial part of audience attitude is the immediate result of directorial manipulation of film time. The effects of such manipulation cannot be overestimated. The human sense of time and rhythm, based as it is on physiological and biological elements, is not something that can be ignored or presumed quiescent.

For all its importance, however, time manipulation is difficult to achieve successfully: difficult to design with any amount of precision in the pre-production planning stage and difficult to carry out within the often antagonistic rhythm of the shooting situation.

SIZE OF THE IDEA

Creating an illusory time design for a film begins with the literal and mechanical sense of time discussed earlier. The reality with which the director begins is that all films ultimately have a defined length. They are three minutes or thirty minutes or three hours and forty-seven minutes long. The exact length of the ultimate film, of course, is something which need not, under normal circumstances, be of concern. Ideally, the length of the completed work is a function of the idea, and the treatment of that idea. The completed film is as long as it takes to tell that particular story. However, ideal conditions seldom exist, and there are occasions when a more or less exact time slot must be filled. The slot is more exact if the film is for television, in which case there is a definite minute–second time limitation. The slot is less exact, but still a factor to consider, if the film is of standard feature length. Audiences have come to expect something about an hour and a half to two hours long, except for the so-called spectacular which, provided the audience has a sufficient supply of food and access to restroom facilities, apparently has no time limit whatsoever. Most educational films are contained within certain time limitations simply because they are designed to be shown within a school class hour. A business film may be produced to be shown in a stockholder's meeting or a briefing conference, and hence it too will probably be limited. Obviously, there are many external reasons for setting the lengths of films, or at least of defining certain limits within which they must occur.

Even within such externally imposed limits, there usually exists some room for variation. Here the internal factors which define film length come into play, factors which are totally a function of the idea of the film itself and of the audience for which it is intended. Ideas come in various sizes. Some are capable of being explored within minutes—they are straightforward, simple, uncomplicated. Others are complex, with much that is unanswerable within them. The first task of the director, then, is to discover the size of the idea of the film which is to be made. As guide there is the script itself, and the director's good judgment. Unfortunately, there are no rules of thumb or arbitrary measures for determining the best length for any film. But at some time, usually early in the creative process of designing and preparing for production, some feeling of an approximate running time emerges out of consideration of the complexities of the script, the depth and weight of the idea, the production facility, perhaps the limitation of budget, the time slot if that is a factor, and the character of the audience.

This estimation of the "size" of the idea is expressed in probable running time of the completed work, usually in whole minutes but sometimes in feet or reels of film. Determining probable running time is important for several reasons. First of all, budget estimates are based, at least partially, upon the probable running time of a film, since the cost of a completed film is often related to its length. Then too, probable running time gives a rough sense of the amount of work undertaken, although it should not be presumed that film length relates directly to work length. Some short films are exceedingly taxing to produce in terms of time, energy, and creative effort; others are not. However, with a fairly accurate sense of the over-all size of the idea, the director can prepare himself emotionally and physically to do the job.

Other production decisions hinge on estimates of running time—the amount of raw stock to be purchased, equipment to be rented, technicians to be hired, time to allot for actual shooting, time to allot for editing, and so on until all the thousands of items can be determined which must be assembled during the making of even a comparatively simple film. Running time thus expresses not only a judgment about the story, but it allows the physical elements necessary to production to be estimated realistically and with workable accuracy.

Stages in the Event

With an approximate size in mind, relatively large blocks of action can be apportioned, and an estimate made of the proportion of one block to another and to the whole. From the first readings of the script, the probable

B

number of large segments in the film can be determined, as well as the proportions between the first establishment or introduction of the idea to its progression and development in time, and thence to its summary, resolution, climax, or review. If the film is relatively long, each of these main sections may have distinguishable subsections. There will develop some sense of time length for each major sequence relative to the whole, then for each scene in each sequence, and ultimately, perhaps, for each shot of each scene. A typical script would include sequences in a variety of locations, each with its own time factor. For example, in early readings it may seem best to use three or four minutes to tell the sequence in the bedroom, about nine minutes for the subway, and twenty minutes or more for the story of the early life of one of the characters. The proportions are still quite flexible at this stage. A further reading of the script might call for a reevaluation of part of it. The importance of what happened in the subway might now seem to have been under-estimated and the childhood scene overestimated. There will be adjustments —trimming, paring, expanding, developing, until each of the parts is pro-portioned properly to the others and is appropriate to the whole.

Although the use of time can in no sense become exact during the planning stage, a fairly concrete conception of how a shot is finally to be used must become a part of its plan. The length of shots—apart from their content —can affect audience perception of a scene and imply a dynamic action which is never shown. To accomplish this successfully the ultimate use of the shot must be in the mind of its creator, who considers both its internal and external time relationships when making it, as in this sequence from Buñuel's *Viridiana*, where the unspoken conflict between the determined religiousness of Viridiana and the son's equally determined idea of work-accomplishment is resolved by implication:—

		Shot length (seconds)
1	Low angle, medium long shot, steeple. Pan and tilt down to house and yard, workers in medium long shot. At 9 seconds a figure crosses the camera close from left to right and the camera moves left to right with the son as he crosses into a two shot, overshoulder a worker, at 15 seconds. They converse.	24
2	Long shot Viridiana calling the beggars to Angelus. They move into a circle around her. The camera is static. They are assembled in place by 6 seconds, when one beggar moves away, right to left.	8
3	Medium shot dump truck discharging its load.	$1\frac{1}{2}$
4	Two shot, close, low, Viridiana and beggar praying, camera static.	$5\frac{1}{2}$
5	Full shot, low, Viridiana and beggars praying. Camera static.	$2\frac{1}{2}$

		Shot length (seconds)
6	Medium close shot log being sawed.	3
7	As in 5.	$2\frac{1}{2}$
8	Two shot, two beggars, one close in foreground, one in background, praying. Camera static.	$3\frac{1}{2}$
9	Medium close shot worker sawing, vigorous movement.	1
10	Close shot Viridiana praying, camera static.	$1\frac{1}{2}$
11	Close shot liquid splashing in mortar tub.	$\frac{3}{4}$
12	Two shot, medium close, beggars praying. Camera static.	1
13	Medium close shot worker pounding stone wall.	4
14	Two shot, close, low angle, as in 4.	4
15	Close shot wheelbarrow dumping rocks on ground, harsh sound.	1
16	As in end of 2.	4
17	Close shot mortar being thrown violently at wall.	$1\frac{1}{2}$
18	As in 10.	$\frac{3}{4}$
19	Close shot mortar tub, another large splash.	$1\frac{1}{2}$
20	Close shot beggar praying.	$1\frac{1}{2}$
21	Close shot tool pounding violently.	2
22	As in 20.	$5\frac{3}{4}$
23	Close shot rocks being shaken.	2
24	Medium close shot another beggar praying, near end of Angelus. Camera moves to left to take in blind man.	4
25	Close shot logs being thrown on a pile.	$1\frac{1}{2}$
26	Close shot Viridiana.	2
27	Close shot logs falling across frame.	2
28	Long shot Angelus as in 2. End of Angelus. The beggars get up and leave in all directions.	20

The shots in this final edited sequence are, of course, not in the same form as when they were made. In production, the individual shots would be longer and more complex, but made to be cut and arranged in this way.

Impressions gained during the initial thinking and planning of a film tend to persist throughout the production process. Decisions made now lead to other decisions to be made later. For these reasons this first period of work is important. To accomplish it successfully will demand a good sense of story value and of proportion. What, for example, would have happened to the story idea if the subway scene had been underplayed and the childhood overplayed? The story might become unintelligible or unbelievable to the audience, or, the idea would be altered because of a shift in emphasis and implication.

Points of emphasis in the story are created and defined partly by the proper apportioning of time. But again, as with total running time, there is no rule to apply. Take, for example, a film which is to be about eighty minutes in length. The script for such a film could be about 120 pages. One way to attack the problem of apportionment would be to plan to shoot one and one half pages of script for every one minute of final running time. With this method, a running time of 40 seconds could be assigned to each page of script, and the total length of any scene computed on the basis of what percentage of a page or how many pages were devoted to describing the scene. But, early in this process, it would become apparent that no such system is feasible, for a simple and quite basic reason. Between the script and the film there exists a gap that must be bridged. It is a gap both in the manner and in the contents of the communication involved.

Script Length and Film Time

The two media—images and sounds on the one hand and words on the other—have quite different powers and characteristics in the way they communicate information, in the kinds of information communicated and in the emotional effect achieved by the communication. These differences must be understood clearly if the script is to be useful as a plan for the film. In a script, information and ideas are conveyed with one system of symbols—words, abstractions or representations which stimulate a personal creation of reality. To become a film, the meaning of these words must be re-embodied in an organized combination of photographed images and recorded sounds. Between the words and the sounds and images which realize their meaning there is no quantitative relationship. The following script selection, for example, occupies a relatively large amount of script space, but the information contained could be conveyed in film virtually without use of screen time, since the selection consists largely of a description of the physical environment for a sequence in the film:

> MEDIUM SHOT of the town square. The square is neat, although the grass is somewhat wild. There are trees, bushes, flowers, and walks through it. In the center of the square, to which all the walks lead, is a large commemorative bronze statue. The square is surrounded by old buildings which are the core of the town. Ross scans the buildings: on his right is a hotel; almost directly ahead is the church; next to it the town hall; and on his left, the prefecture of police. [The film takes place in France.] Further down the street ahead is a theater, a museum, and other buildings. Several statues stand in the square: in the front of the church is one of the Virgin Mary; in front of the government building is a statue of Joan of Arc; a nude is in front of the hotel. Around the large center statue is a fountain, and birds are sitting on and around the statue; one is taking a bath in the fountain. As Ross walks toward the square, a horse-drawn taxi goes by on the main street. The occupants glance at the soldier, interested, as the taxi

passes. Across the square, the wagon which carried the two boys is parked in front of a small shop facing onto the square. Ross walks into the square and toward the hotel. Over the hotel door is a large weatherbeaten sign saying: "l'Hôtel Grenadine."

The amount of action taking place in the above sequence is relatively small and therefore the time necessary to convey the major amount of information could be small. Much of the description is actually intended to inform the director of the setting for the action to follow. Most directors would not feel it necessary, or even desirable, to convey the described images to their audiences in the same sequence and with the same time relationship as in the written description of the scene. It is clear from the description, in fact, that parts of it are even intended to be the framework for latter scenes in the film, but are included here because of the narrative style of the written script. The narrative styles of films, even those following a relatively close chronological development, rarely parallel such script descriptions.

The following dialogue sequence illustrates a further difference in quantitative relationship between script and film:

Anadine goes out a side door of the museum to a small fenced-in garden. He picks up a pair of shears from a ledge outside the door as he goes by, and walks toward some flowers. Ross follows him.

Ross

(patient, but still anxious. Politely:) Yes, of course, Monsieur Lemaître at the hotel said that you would know . . .

Anadine

(snipping a flower) Monsieur Lemaître! (he snorts, snips another flower) . . . I am sorry monsieur . . . I do not know the where-abouts of your people . . . However, if you must join them . . . Lacôte is three kilometers away . . . you will find your army . . . they will know . . . And now, pardon . . .

Ross

Thank you . . . thank you very much!

The description of action which precedes the dialogue would of course in most instances become the action in which the dialogue was given. They would be simultaneously, rather than sequentially, given. In estimating the length of such a scene, the director would have some idea of the length of the dialogue, and then add to it some amount of time to represent moments of silence where action was performed but no speech given. The two examples above occupy approximately the same amount of script space. What they represent in terms of film time is entirely different.

Occasionally, written descriptions leave the actual extent of time to be devoted to the scene almost entirely up to the director's discretion. This is often the case in documentary or factual scripts. The following scene, from a fictional script, could occupy only a few seconds, or could be extended into several minutes of screen time, depending upon the director's idea of priorities in the sequence in which the scene appeared:

> Ross runs very fast to the stairs and goes down the first flight. Moving very quickly, he runs down two or three flights of stairs. On the next to last flight, he stumbles and falls down the steps onto the landing below. He rises quickly and starts down the last flight without pause and without slowing his speed of descent. He has met no one on the way down, but the sound of voices and confusion grows louder as he nears the bottom floor.

Even when the script is relatively specific about the actual shots to be used, the time factor is almost completely within the province of the director:

> OVERSHOULDER from Ross POV [point of view] as he drives a jeep down the street. He takes the main road out of town—which passes by the dump. SEVERAL SUBJECTIVE ANGLES of Ross' drive through town at high speed. One shot includes a CLOSEUP of a gasoline truck burning. Soldiers around it are trying to get near enough to other trucks to move them out of the way. Other soldiers are attempting to put out the flames. Another shot is a LONG SHOT toward a farmhouse. SOUND OVER of flames—then suddenly the SOUND of one large esplosion as the scene lightens. This is followed by other EXPLOSIONS of varying size and intensity. Several townspeople run out of the farmhouse at the first explosion, shouting to one another. The jeep passes by the farmhouse and moves away down the road out of town.

A script writer may take many pages to describe settings, visual impressions, or character relationships. In a film, the setting may be seen in a few seconds, the relationship between two characters may become clear with a gesture or glance or the tone of voice. On the other hand, the writer can convey abstractions and generalizations in extremely brief form: e.g., "money is power." To convey this idea in film could take an extended series of images, perhaps with sound effects and even dialogue. This would take time. Fortunately such generalizations seldom appear in a script, although any script, no matter how well written, contains many elements which have no set or literal time factor. The time factor they ultimately consume in the film is a matter of interpretation.

TIME AND "AUDIENCE SENSE"

But if quantitative measures do not apply, then what can serve as a guide? How can an estimate of film length be made, and how can this total available time be apportioned among sequences and scenes?

The guiding factors are dramatic ones, the feeling for action, the developed sensitivity to what is appropriate, to proportion—the sense of timing and basic rhythm or flow of action in the story. The basic action may be slow and languorous, or it may be swift. It may change from one tempo to another. The location of changes in tempo and their rate of change must be determined. Suspense should be considered—the artificial stretching of time and attention to achieve a temporary psychological stress. Perhaps the action should be telescoped or shortened, or parts of it deleted altogether. And still other matters enter into the process of developing a time design—structural form, impact and the audience's understanding and reaction. Time flows differently in the exposition part of a story than it does in the development, and as the film develops and moves toward increasingly meaningful climaxes and toward the ultimate one, the use of time both creates and clarifies structural landmarks. Then comes the denouement, its length and tempo growing from the preceding material. It is with a sense of drama, an "audience sense," that the basic structure and the details of the time design are created.

INTERNAL TIME

Putting aside considerations of speeding or slowing apparent motion by means of camera manipulation, the first, and almost only limitation in time design is physical. Internal time, time used within any one shot, must be within the tolerable limits of human capability, of movement of a live actor. But since human beings move within a relatively narrow time range in performing any action, this internal time limitation is simple to determine. At first the estimate can be made by pacing out the action to be performed and saying the lines aloud. With experience, such time estimates can be made in the imagination. Of course if it is necessary to the story, time distortions can be introduced to almost any degree away from the normal. However, unless done mechanically (by changing the speed of the camera, for instance), such manipulations must stay within the physical cability of the actor. Because of such human limitations, this part of the time design usually closely approximates real time. Distortions are relatively minor; departure from the norm limited. Nevertheless, within this limited range exceedingly rich and subtle variation can take place.

Emphasis upon the internal time of shots tends to focus attention on the action being portrayed for the camera's benefit, rather than upon the film itself as an event. The tradition or style of directing which accentuates this "portrayed-for-the-camera" concept goes back to Lumière's factory shots and the earliest days of film making, where the miracle of the illusion of photographic movement itself was enough to make a film. This tradition continues to the present with such masters of the technique as Jean Renoir and Max Ophuls. It is even in a way employed by the more recent *cinema verité* school of film making which attempts to let the film making process interfere as little as possible with the action being filmed. Thus, films as different in style and content as *The River* and *Le Plaisir* on the one hand, and *Primary* and *Chronique d'un Eté* on the other, share this predominant attention to the internal action. The difference between such film treatments is in degree rather than in kind, as becomes apparent when two documentaries such as *Night and Fog* and *Triumph of the Will* are compared.

When the internal qualities of the action are developed, the camera acts principally as a tool of recording and observation—intelligent, sympathetic, omniscient. Generally it follows action or the action is staged for its benefit, but always there is a close relationship between camera and subject. The technique often demands a constantly moving camera, such as the intricately complex shots created by Max Ophuls, which sometimes took days and weeks to rehearse and were always made to perfection with trucks, dollies and cranes. The *verité* school also tends toward the constantly moving camera but, taking a more simple, direct approach, uses a hand held camera to follow its subject in an unrehearsed, artless, hopefully unselfconscious manner. The tailored artfulness of Ophuls perfected the technique of coordination between camera and action. So perfectly is this done that the audience does not notice the absence of normal editing cuts. A cut from long to close shot is replaced with movement of camera or action, or both. "Editing" such films consists largely of stringing together, with cuts and dissolves, a series of lengthy shots each of which contains within itself a variety of long, medium and close shots. Whether this studied technique is any more artificial than the *verité* hand held technique is a matter of personal interpretation.

EXTERNAL TIME

But film scenes are made of many individually recorded shots. Internal time limitation ends with the shot itself. Then external time, illusory time, begins, and unlike internal time, it is free, limitless, or, more accurately, is limited only by taste, purpose and imagination. Since this external time is built up from the tempo of the individual shots, and the way in which they are put together, the tempo of a whole scene need not be, and rarely is, restricted to the limits of reality. Much artificial extension or compression of time is possible if the individual shots are properly made, an extension and compression impossible to accomplish within the individual shots themselves. The greater part of the film maker's power to manipulate time for effect lies in the unseen, unnoticed, physically non-existent gap between shots.

The subtle modification of apparent time between shots—one of the great powers of film making—carries with it one of the major problems of the cutting process, that of maintaining a purposeful and meaningful continuity. Continuity is governed by the strong human psychological tendency to order events which are presented in sequence and to attribute relationships (such as the cause-effect relationship) to events which are juxtaposed. This phenomenon occurs even in the absence of any ordering among the shots. Randomly photographed human gestures, assembled without regard for the content of the shots themselves (such as in a film called *Movement* made by Welland Lathrop in 1962), are given "story" qualities by audiences who impute some design or purpose in the collection. The absence of a discernible intended continuity in a film places a burden of interpretation upon the audience, which will thereupon attempt to order what appears to be randomly juxtaposed events. For a short time, this will satisfy. When continued beyond tolerance points, however, the audience will begin to fail to make order out of seeming chaos, and become confused and bored.

There is a broad middle ground between obvious, literal relationships among shots, and more abstract, obscure, ambiguous ones. To be more obvious or more abstract at any particular moment in the film is a choice the director must be constantly making. When he chooses obviousness, he runs the risk of losing an audience which is called upon to contribute nothing to the understanding of the film. In choosing abstraction, he must take into account that he is moving along an edge of confusion, where an audience is asked to contribute too much. To err in either direction, to err by using too much of one or the other extreme, is to invite failure to convey something of value.

CONTINUITY

To exist, time creates a continuum. The sense of continuousness or continuity is of primary importance to the time design for a film. Action within any individual shot is internally continuous. But beyond the confines of the shot, a purposeful continuity—a flow of action—is something which occurs by virtue of the contents of the shots themselves. Any two shots can be physically spliced together, but a purposeful continuity will exist between them only if their internal nature is such that, when one shot follows the other, there appears to be a physical and/or philosophical relationship between them. Some such relationship must be established every time one shot follows another, hundreds, perhaps thousands of times in one film. Mainly because of this problem of continuity the typical conditions of film production seem to frustrate the realization of any careful and elaborate plan for the use of time. The problem is best illustrated by comparison of the action in a stage play with the action of a film. Though at times a film and a stage play appear to contain like action, the portrayal of this action is achieved in two quite different ways. On the stage, dramatic action is continuous, interrupted in performance only by act or scene divisions. But the action of a film is interrupted at every cut. It does not become continuous until long after the shooting period. Until the film is completed, continuity is only a plan, not a reality.

There is still another barrier to achieving continuity. Not only is the action continually interrupted (being recorded in short segments as each of the shots is separately made) but it is usually recorded out of sequence. Thus there is a double violence: the violence of interruption, and the violence of discontinuity. The film director must be prepared to achieve his plan in spite of these disruptive conditions of production. The task facing him can be compared with that of a conductor who is asked to record each bar of a symphony individually and at random.

Fortunately, the consequences of such interruption and discontinuity in film work are not all bad. Hazardous as these events are, they have their virtues. One that has been mentioned before—once photographed, the action of the shot will not change—allows unlimited experimentation without danger of destruction of an already achieved effect. Opportunity for objective evaluation is another virtue. The product of the intensely personal and immediate tensions of the shooting period may be calmly viewed later when judgment is uncolored by pressure. There is also the virtue of flexibility, of making minute modifications within these interrupted moments, and of reworking or masking defects which might flaw the action. And finally, because the parts of the whole are still parts and there are no rules for their assembly, there is the power to create new rhythms and new continuities.

The range of manipulation of external time is almost unlimited; there are no limitations except what the audience can understand. Centuries may pass in a single hour, or a minute in two hours. The director is empowered by the characteristics of his medium not only to expand time far beyond the ability of any actor to do so, but to compress it to nothing. He can so subtly mold time that audiences are unaware of any change from actuality. If the director so desires, he can completely ignore time and appear to lose reference to it entirely. He can distort it, putting effects before causes, or show as simultaneous, events which in reality occurred in sequence. These new powers more than compensate for the disadvantages of the working situation and the disadvantages themselves can be minimized by a skilled director. In anticipation of the inexactness and physical limitations of the shooting situation, and to allow for minor errors in calculation, the experienced director makes "cushions," certain kinds of duplications, variations and binding materials which enable him to control time and put together a cohesive and effective film under almost any conditions.

3

Realizing the Time Design

BECAUSE OF THE uncertainties inherent in the shooting situation, particularly where actors are involved, and because the time design itself is arrived at by intangible rather than measurable means, some provision must normally be made to take up the slack of miscalculation of planning and error in performance.

Such devices are useful not only in manipulating external time between shots, but, because of the fractionalized nature of action, they are a useful means of seeming to modify the internal use of time.

SECOND TAKES

The most obvious of these devices is making more than one try at recording the action of the shot. When a film director calls for more than one recording of the action, or "take," as each try is called, he is doing what the stage director does during the rehearsal of a stage play. He works with the actors, perfecting pieces of action which, when combined, form a larger continuous action. The director calls for as many takes as he feels are necessary.

Each take is made with the camera in the same spot, and the action from take to take is duplicated as nearly as possible. The purpose of alternative takes is to attempt perfection, and to provide choice. In the second and succeeding takes, modifications improve or change the tenor of the action so that it will more nearly realize what the director has imagined is right.

But although alternate takes supply a choice of performances of one action, they give the director only limited power to manipulate time from one shot to the next. Neither do alternate takes, once they have been made, provide any means for correcting or changing or intensifying tempo within an action. This must be accomplished by other means, such as cover shots, overlapping action, inserts, cutaways and reaction shots. These devices give flexibility and control in the second stage of the directing process. They provide footage which can be used for transitions—cuts, dissolves, fades and other optical effects. And, because they are alternate views of an action, they make possible a choice not only of what to use, but when to use it. The director during editing can do more than choose the exact moment at which the image should change. He can select from one of several images, or work back and forth between two or more images if this will achieve the desired effect.

He can determine the best beginning and ending for the action.

This control is only approximate in the shooting stage, but in editing it is exact to within one twenty-fourth of a second, i.e. one frame. With the five "cushions," cover shots, overlapping action, inserts, cutaways and reaction shots, modifications of time and tempo become possible.

COVER SHOTS

The term "cover shot" or "covering" refers to the practice of recording all or part of a scene from more than one point of view, making two or more strips of film with the camera in two or more positions relative to the action. Examples of this are: a long shot and a medium shot of the same action; two different closeup angles of the same action; one angle of a complete action with another angle of part of the action, or other variations in camera angle in relation to the subject. By providing more than one angle of an action (or part of an action), the director gives himself a means of modifying action. Each cut and change of angle in a scene can redirect audience attention, refresh audience interest and clarify and intensify the meaning of the scene.

When shooting the cover shot, the director usually makes sure that the action between the "master" or basic shot and the cover shot is duplicated with reasonable exactness, so that all or any part of the cover shot can be used to replace any portion of the master shot. Thus anywhere in the cover shot the director can change viewpoints without destroying the illusion of continuity.

As a correction device, the cover shot can also be used to replace any part of the master shot which contains errors. These may include faults in actor movement, gesture and line delivery. Also, camera movement can be corrected by substituting the cover shot for that portion of the master shot which is defective.

But the cover shot has an even more important function as a means for modifying the internal tempo of scenes. The "timeless" interval between shots, where the cut to another angle occurs, is used to extend or delete time intervals in the larger action. Cutting to a cover shot at a later point in its development, and then back to the master shot will in effect compress the time scale.

The audience, because of the masking effect of the cut, sees this as a continuous action. More rarely (because it is more difficult to accomplish), intervals can be added by extending the action in the cover shot which, again because of the cut, is perceived by the audience as a continuous, but slightly longer action than was actually the case. Of course there are reasons other than covering a mistake or making minor time adjustments which prompt the director to choose from a selection of long shots, closeups, high or low angles—matters of emphasis and spatial orientation. These are to be discussed later. At this point the cover shot is of interest only as a means of manipulating and controlling time.

Overlapping Action

The close duplication of action in alternative takes and in cover shots provides choice as well as the possibility of correction. Alternative takes give varying performances of the action, whereas cover shots give different views of that action.

A third technique of shooting, important because of the problem of interruption and discontinuity, involves the exact duplication between shots of relatively short segments of the action. This is called overlapping action. Its purpose is, simply, to provide a segment within which two shots can be joined. This joining segment makes it possible to select the exact point at which one shot will end and another begin, a job which cannot be done until the editing process. At the time of shooting it is impossible, at the normal rate of 24 frames per second, to determine which frame is "the" frame at which to end the action of one shot and begin that of the next. Moreover, even were such selection somehow possible, the action of the two shots would not match, either in physical detail or in flow of movement. These two factors are essential to a "smooth," that is, flowing, as opposed to staccato or choppy action. It is outside the realm of human capability for an actor either to hold an exact position while camera and lights are being changed to another angle, or to continue a flow of movement at exactly the same tempo as before an interruption.

Then too, shots which adjoin one another in the final film are often recorded days or weeks apart, making an even closely approximate duplication impossible.

Thus, in shooting, this potential point in time exists within the segment where the action is duplicated. Afterwards, the two strips of film with almost identical action may be joined anywhere within the overlapped segment without the interruption becoming apparent.

By means of overlapping, fragments become scenes and give the illusion of a continuous flow of action.

How does overlapping work in shooting? As an example, consider the situation in which a man walks across a room to a door in one shot, and in the next shot, with the camera taking another angle, the man opens the door and leaves the room. The two shots are designed to be used in sequence. Most of the action of the scene is not duplicated—in one shot the man goes to the door and in the next he leaves the room. The director has already decided that the shots will be joined at some point during the time when the man approaches and opens the door. But at what exact point that is he cannot yet know. To give himself room in which to make a choice, he asks the actor to repeat, in each shot, that part of the action in which he approaches and opens the door.

This repeated action, which may be long or short, is overlapped on the tail of one shot and the head of the next shot.

Without the overlap there would be no way of joining the two sections except end to end. If the ends did not match, and in all likelihood they would not, then the action would be interrupted. If the mis-matched ends were joined, the audience would get the impression that there was a flaw in the action.

To delete this section entirely would usually make the action even less complete. It would have a beginning (crossing the room) and an end (leaving the room) but no middle (opening the door). Such a gap would not only destroy the illusion of continuity but also the flow of rhythm and tempo.

Only one other alternative would be available: to insert another segment of film between the two segments which did not match. The added shot would distract the audience and disguise the discrepancy. But this is not always possible—suitable footage may not be available—nor is it always desirable. Of course, if it is part of the plan to cut to another object or event at this point, there is no problem.

But if a continuity of physical action is the intent, such cutting away is destructive.

There are other reasons why overlapping action is useful. Illusory time can be expanded or compressed by including or excluding duplications which the audience will not notice. Stylized repetition of action can be achieved, if this is part of the design, and space in the film material itself is provided for the mechanics of making fades, dissolves, or any other optical effects.

Overlapping action, then, must be used whenever a continuous action is interrupted in the shooting situation, either by plan or by accident.

Since these interruptions in the recorded action are necessary and advantageous to the production process, long before the shooting period begins it is decided where approximately the action is to be interrupted. Such points of interruption are usually marked on the shooting script.

Interruptions are essential also from the actor's point of view. Were an actor's attention consumed with such trivial matters as whether he put his right foot on the floor exactly seven inches from the door or twelve inches from the door, he would not be able to apply himself to the more important matters of characterization, evocation of emotion or line delivery. Rather than distract the actor so, the director changes the relationship of the camera to the action, and the change makes minor discrepancies unnoticeable. Without the change, the otherwise continuous action would seem to jump. Hence the term, jump cut.

The exact placement of the camera relative to the action is determined by the spatial design of the film (see Chapters 5, 6). Any noticeable change in camera angle so distracts audience attention that discrepancies of continuity and consistency in time and space become invisible.

COMPRESSION AND EXPANSION

Continuity in films rarely involves showing complete actions, in spite of the fact that the actions may seem complete. An act will seem complete if its key parts are shown within an expected period of time. Both the particular parts selected to be shown and the sense of time contained within them contribute to the audience's feeling that the action it is seeing is continuous in nature. In fact, however, the director often selects only portions of the action for the camera to record. He may, for example, show an actor preparing to leave an automobile in one shot, and in the next show the actor closing the door of the automobile. Assuming that the angle was changed between the two shots, the deletion of physical action will be accepted by the audience, which will not realize that it has not seen a complete action. The amount of deletion which can be made depends upon the tempo of the story, the editing style, the tension level of the audience, the familiarity of the audience with the action being portrayed, and the amount of distracting material, either from within the scene or from a shot interposed between the two parts of the action.

A typical example of time compression, creating illusory time out of real time segments, occurs in the first section of Buñuel's *Viridiana*. While the actors' movements within the shots are all in actual time—internal time has been in no way modified—in external time there is a great over-all reduction between the shots. Shortly after Viridiana has arrived at her uncle's farm, she and her uncle are seen walking down a lane, talking. The sequence begins, as is characteristic for this film, with a shot of their feet and a tilt up to their heads as they converse. A cut directly to the next scene excludes a long time segment, which is from the moment of her arrival ostensibly to that evening, as Viridiana prepares for bed. The time gap is made understandable, however, because Buñuel cuts to a shot of feet pumping an organ, and even by this early point in the film the audience has learned that a shot of feet is an introduction shot to a segment of action. The tilt up to the hands playing the organ which follows prepares the audience for another time gap. The next cut finds Viridiana in her bedroom, undressing. The shot ends with a tilt down to her legs and feet. A cut with a slight tilt up on the head of the shot again finds the uncle playing the organ. The next cut is to a shot of the maid outside Viridiana's door; the maid walks to the key hole, bends down, and looks through it. So far, the major time compression has taken place between the afternoon and evening shot, but with the elements of the scene now established, more time is to be deleted in the next few shots. From

the shot of the maid looking in the keyhole, Buñuel cuts inside the room to
Viridiana removing the cross, thorns and other paraphernalia from her
suitcase. As the shot ends, she turns from right to left and exits frame left.
The cut to the final shot in the sequence finds the maid also moving from
right to left—but she is already downstairs. The time gap has been bridged by
paralleling the movements of the two characters. The maid proceeds to tell
the uncle about Viridiana's cross, nightgown, etc., revealing much more
information than she could possibly have gained from the momentary glance
shown in the previous shot. It is implied, of course, that in real time she spent
some minutes at the keyhole. Even the physical movement of her leaving the
keyhole and going downstairs is markedly condensed, since she arrives so
quickly at the bottom of the stairs. A comparison of the implied action, and
the action as shown, will show the amount of condensation taking place:

Implied action	Action shown
Viridiana arrives at the farm, talks to her uncle while walking to the house.	Viridiana and uncle shown walking down lane.
An unspecified amount of time passes between the daytime of the preceding scene and the interior night of the following scene. Presumably Viridiana has, at the very least, been shown her room, and has dined.	Viridiana undresses.
The uncle meanwhile, decides to play the organ. Apparently it is he who dispatches the maid to spy on Viridiana through the keyhole, since he later engages the maid's help in seducing Viridiana and since he seems unsurprised that the maid has, in reality, looked through the keyhole.	Uncle plays the organ.
The maid goes upstairs to Viridiana's room and approaches it, while, inside, Viridiana prepares for bed, undressing, putting on a nightgown, taking out her prayer items, and preparing her bed on the floor of the room.	Maid looks in keyhole. Viridiana, already in nightgown, takes out prayer items.
The maid goes downstairs to the room in which the uncle is playing and reports on Viridiana's smooth skin (only to be seen while she was undressing), nightgown, prayer items, and the fact that she is going to sleep on the floor.	Maid reports.

From the continuous stream of implied activity of the first column, Buñuel
has selected only those moments which are of particular value to him in

telling the story. While he does not in general disregard time sequence in cutting these moments together, he completely disregards time quantity. Only the last cut in the sequence, in fact, could be interpreted as disregarding time sequence, since in real time the maid would still be looking in the keyhole in order to observe Viridiana lie down to sleep (implied but never seen) while in the same real time segment she would have to be moving toward the uncle's room. To include all the details of the implied action, even disregarding the large passage of time between the first two shots, would have been not only tedious, but would have denied the scene its tension and sense of discovery.

Such compression, in the sense of deleting parts of continuous actions, occurs more often than not in making films. To show the intervening parts of action is often to slow action. If for some dramatic effect it is desirable to implant a feeling of slowness or exactness, of extended time, often all that need be done is to show a complete action in all its detail. Portions of actions can even be repeated to further extend time. Skillfully done, this will not be apparent to the audience. Of course, any noticeable repetition will be perceived by the audience as either an error or a form of stylization.

OTHER DESIGN DEVICES

There are other methods by which a flow of action can be constructed from materials which in reality have no continuous action between them. These are inserts, cutaways and reaction shots. In addition to being time expanders and compressors, these devices can give emphasis, make analogy, reveal detail and establish relationships. They are among the most useful and yet ill-used of the materials of film making. Inserts and cutaways have been used since the earliest days of film making to direct the audience's attention to some dimension of the action other than the direct line of action shown in medium or long shot (fig. 2). Originally inserts were used as explanation, but as film making technique became more sophisticated, they came to give emotional as well as informational effect.

INSERTS

An insert is a shot designed for insertion, during editing, at whatever point in the action appears best. It may be a point of emphasis, where a close shot will make a dramatic accent; or it may be a moment when a long establishing shot is needed to remind the audience of the relationship of the action to the larger scene. Or it may be a moment in which the audience briefly takes an actor's close view of a scene detail—the page of a book or, in the example used before, a shot of the door handle or the man's feet moving across the floor. An insert can bridge action, lengthen or telescope time, call attention to a specific object or event, heighten tension and suspense, and clarify and define the flow of action. For the few moments it is on the screen,

Fig. 2. Direct line of action (*left, top center and bottom*). An insert (*right, top*) one of many possible and useful in amplifying detail of the action. Cutaways (*right center and bottom*) useful in enlarging the action and in adding tension to the sequence of shots.

the insert can break the pattern of audience as observer and call it into action as actor, participant in the action.

Inserts are often used as a mask, to disguise flaws in conception or execution of the action. At times, inserts are shot "here and there" during production, just in case they should be needed later as a way out of an editing predicament. Such inserts are photographed so that they will fit into the action at any one of a number of places, and this usually means that the insert is only loosely related to the shots on either side of it. This may not be the best use of inserts, but it is sometimes a necessary one. Ideally the insert should be planned just as carefully as the action around it. It is then tailored to do a specific job. In such cases, inserts can be among the most absorbing and dramatic moments in a film.

CUTAWAYS

A cutaway is similar to an insert—a shot not directly in the flow of physical action which is occurring, but related, and contributing, to it. Like the insert, the cutaway has the same tension, tempo and feeling as the master scene. Unlike the insert, which occurs in the same location as the larger scene (being a different view or portion of view of the same event), the cutaway is typically a shot from another event, usually occurring simultaneously with the master scene, but in a different location. The primary relationship between the cutaway and the master scene, therefore, is one of tempo and feeling, rather than spatial orientation. Because cutaways are a means of sustaining the flow of action and intensifying its meaning without being bound within the physical limitations of the scene being viewed, they are extremely important in carrying out the time design, both as bridging devices and as a way of controlling time.

An example will illustrate the usefulness of the cutaway. When, during a frantic chase in a dark and deserted warehouse, the director cuts away to a police car swerving around a corner, tension and suspense are intensified. Time is either stretched or telescoped, depending upon where in the master action he cuts back to the warehouse. Mismatches in recording the warehouse scene can be eliminated. But what is more important, a new dimension in time and story can be achieved—an enlargement of meaning emphasizing emotion by destroying the isolation of the scene and relating its actions to other actions elsewhere. In the scene with the man approaching the door, a cutaway might consist of a shot of another man approaching the door from the other side, or perhaps someone listening through the wall of the apartment, or a shot of the doorman downstairs on the street floor as he admits a woman to the apartment house.

Whatever its content, the cutaway, like the insert, must be planned carefully to be effective.

REACTION SHOTS

Inserts and cutaways can be used in almost any scene, regardless of the kind of action being recorded. A reaction shot is more specialized. Reaction shots are used in scenes which portray interpersonal relations between two or more human beings, or in scenes where the actor's reaction to an object or event is important. As the audience views the action, it becomes eager to see what effect the events of the film are having upon the characters. At times this interest in reaction can be greater than in the action itself. To know how life affects others seems to be a basic interest of humanity, a way of measuring one's self with another and of feeling with another. Reaction shots can be used to capitalize upon this interest.

Like inserts and cutaways, reaction shots can be used for either comic or tragic effect. In point of fact, much of the audience's interpretation of action as being comic or tragic is based in the kind of reaction shots used. If, as the man walked to the door, the image had changed to a shot of a woman in the same room crying, this reaction would give the audience a different feeling than had she been laughing, or had looked relieved. This is a feeling quite independent of the action itself as performed by the man. Reaction shots are especially critical in dialogue sequences, where characters are reacting to one another's words as well as actions. Often the reaction of the listener more easily reveals the meaning than the action of the speaker. It is even possible to change the content of the dialogue by deleting words and using reaction shots, or to change the apparent tempo of the dialogue through reaction shots.

Reaction shots are equally useful in the warehouse scene described previously. In his flight through the building, the man suddenly comes against a door through which he must pass in order to escape. He finds it locked. The closeup of his face as he realizes that the door is locked is a reaction shot. In other scenes, the reaction of a witness to an accident, of members of a rioting crowd to the arrival of police, of a boy to his new puppy—all add a powerful dimension of meaning, as well as scope for manipulating time, which did not exist in the larger action. Meaning can be further enlarged and a sense of irony added to a scene by use of contrasting reactions of different persons to the same event.

By isolating and calling attention to single human actions, or reactions, the reaction shot brings the element of humanity to a story.

Because reaction shots can be moments in which the flow of physical action is interrupted—they show reaction more than action itself—they have a definite effect upon tempo. But the effect is not always one of slowing tempo. Often the reaction shot quickens apparent tempo because the emotion the audience experiences with the shot increases its understanding of the action quickly and forcefully. A classic example of this is found during the final scenes of Lang's *M*, where the underworld characters are shown advancing on the child molester. Suddenly they stop, and, in graded sequence, raise their hands above their heads. The audience never sees the police, but it is quite evident from the reaction of the underworld characters that police have appeared on the scene and are in control of the situation. To show the police advancing at this moment would have deflected attention from the underworld characters, whose actions and comments on M's predicament have been built in steady concentration over the last few moments. It would have shifted attention and interest to another group of persons not of central interest to the scene. Thus Lang achieves a powerfully rising unity in the scene while he suggests, by means of reaction, the pressure of unseen forces.

Whether, at any particular moment in a film, action or reaction will prove more effective depends largely upon the principal subject of the scene, and the way it has been developed.

Camera Movement and Time

In the discussion above, the actors and the action have been moving in relation to the camera, but during any one shot the camera has been viewing the action from a fixed or stationary position. In every film many shots are made in just this way. But, as often as not, the camera is moving in relation to its subject, and thus there is still another factor which bears upon the plan for the use of time. In considering this aspect of camera use and

Fig. 3. A combined tilt and pan from a high camera angle introduces compositional change and internal time into a shot.

camera movement, it helps to think of the camera as an eye suspended in space, able to take any view of the action and to move anywhere in space while the action is being performed.

Basically, the motion picture camera can move in two ways. It can pivot on its axis or pivot point, independent of its support, or the entire camera body can move through space, together with its support. Any of the pivotal motions can be combined with any spatial motions. Thus the variety of possibilities for use of camera movement in any situation is almost unlimited.

PIVOTAL MOVEMENT

Most camera movements have been given names which have come either from the type of movement being performed, or from the device supporting the camera which enables it to move. There are two pivotal movements. That in the horizontal plane, a turning motion from side to side, is called panning, which is an abbreviation of the word "panorama." Such a shot gives a panorama effect—an arc of vision scanning horizontally across the scene. The movement can be broad and sweeping, or confined and narrow; it can be slow, or fast, or its tempo can change while the movement is being made. The movement can be with, or against, any motion taking place within the shot. It can be from left to right, or right to left, or, it can change direction in the middle of the shot, or pause in the middle of the motion before it continues. Panning, or a pan shot, as the resulting shot is called, has the effect of changing the scene without use of a cut, changing the point of attention, or emphasis, changing relationships, composition and tempo. It can accomplish these things alone, or, as is often the case, when it is used in combination with the second type of pivotal movement, tilting, movement in the vertical plane. Tilting can be varied just as panning can. Extent of motion, speed, direction and relationship to internal motion, i.e., motion within the shot, can be varied individually or in any combination. The tilt shot gives the effect of looking up or down, changing attention, emphasis, relationships and tempo, as does the pan shot.

Fig. 4. A dolly around gives a sense of anticipation to a static object, transforming an object into an event.

SPATIAL MOVEMENT

Other movements are possible when the camera is mounted on a wheeled support or platform, and the body of the camera with its support can move as a unit. Dolly shots, trucking shots and crane shots, all signifying different kinds of camera movement, get their names from the supports used to move the camera. A dolly is a small wheeled platform on which a camera and its tripod can be mounted. A dolly can vary in size from the simplest arrangement, a skeleton platform supporting the tripod and with a wheel below each tripod leg, to a relatively heavy and large vehicle that can support not only the camera, but two or more camera operators and their equipment. The size and construction of the dolly affect the stability of the camera, and therefore the smoothness of its motion. But all dollies, large or small, perform the same work: their wheels allow movement toward or away from the action, around it, or along one side, or in any combination of these motions.

Trucking is an extension of dollying. The truck is a large self-propelled vehicle capable of moving greater distances than the manually pushed or pulled dolly. But the basic effect on the screen, though larger in scope, is similar. Dollying and trucking motions are usually toward or away from the action, or accompanying the action. But the camera generally remains within a narrow range of height in relation to the action.

To accomplish greater vertical movement, a motion picture crane is used. With the crane, the camera is able to move vertically in space and, if need be, to rise twenty, thirty, forty or more feet above the action. In addition to its vertical movement, the crane arm can swing the camera around in an arc. Also, the platform on which the crane is mounted usually has wheels and is therefore capable of movement. Although the crane is the most versatile of the devices used to move the camera, it is not the most flexible. Its large size, great weight and complexity confine it to the large sound stage, or the mammoth exterior shot. For the same reasons, trucking shots are generally used only on exteriors. The dolly shot can be made in any place where a suitably smooth floor or ground surface can be found or constructed.

Tilting and panning shots can be made where there is room enough for the camera body to move. They are the most flexible and therefore the more frequently used of camera movements.

Each of these movements, whether limited or extensive, has a definite effect upon the audience's attention and attitude. When used in combination, the effects compound. With these means the director has a complex and yet relatively controllable tool of interpretation and creation. Not only the velocity of camera movement, its angle and direction, but also the timing of the camera movement relative to the action are ways not only of changing the spatial relationship between camera and action, but of varying and manipulating time. Revelation, concealment, suspense and relaxation can all be achieved by use of simple or compound camera movements. The precise moment in the action at which the camera starts or stops any motion comments on the action. So does the kind of movement chosen in relation to the action: when the actors move in concert with camera movement and when in opposition. Such choices are made with one purpose in mind—the goal of meaning.

Thus the camera, the eye in space looking at the action from any point of view, can move with it or against it in any of the three dimensions of space and, of course, always moves in the dimension of time. Time is not only

Fig. 5. Camera movement alone can add
the dimensions of time and tension to an
otherwise static object. Moving toward
the carving, the camera reveals it; moving
away would conceal it. Control of focus is
used to direct audience attention during
the movement.

consumed in making a moving shot; the audience's perception of time is
affected by the moving view it gets of the action as a result. This time factor,
considered separately from the spatial factors involved, provides another
instrument with which to plan and execute the time design.

Film Sound

FEW MOTION PICTURES have been either conceived, or presented, as totally silent. For the first thirty or so years, in what are called the silent days of film, public showings of films were almost always accompanied by organ or piano music. Music served both as musical score and as sound effects track. Printed titles interspersed within the body of the film indicated commentary or dialogue, but these were never satisfactory in that they interrupted the flow of action on the screen. The loss of visual flexibility experienced during the early days of sound film caused some film theorists to conclude that sound was an unnecessary adjunct to images in motion, and, indeed, that sound was destructive of aesthetic effect. Much experimentation was performed in the name of "pure cinema," as the adherents of silence called their work. Their films are valuable as a means of expanding the boundaries of the art. But the exclusive use of one or another film element does not of itself represent most effective use of a complex and many-faceted medium, any more than a man who has learned to walk on his hands has proved that legs are not essential.

Freedom in use of synchronous sound recording and camera movement during sync sound shooting came with the improvement of sound recording equipment. Transistorized electronics and sync pulse recording, together with improved lightweight camera design, have made it possible to physically move both camera and sound equipment without difficulty. Such freedom has meant that sound, as a dimension of film, has assumed broad use as one of the basic film dimensions. To some directors, sound has an importance far beyond that usually attributed to it. Fritz Lang feels that

> Sound is rarely used dramatically these days and yet the world is becoming auditive, Easternizing itself. Our civilization is moving away from the visual toward the auditive. The visual is the only sense that gives us detachment, objectivity, rationality. All the other senses are irrational, discontinuous and disconnected, especially sound.[8]

Just as the concepts of space and time are interwoven in the whole fabric which is the film's design, so the dimension of sound colors and shapes the patterns which emerge. Sound defines and sharpens the viewer's sense of space, giving him, by variations in its amplitude and pitch, a means of measuring distance and spatial volume. Variations in timbre create the illusion of size and physical condition. Sound also affects the perception of time and motion; repetitions of sound, particularly if they are rhythmical, can create an impression of the passage of time which is far slower or swifter than the passage of real time.

Sound can perform all this even when it carries no symbolic significance. When meaning is added, then it can perform even more, influencing ideas, emotions and attitudes. The particular emotional cast of a piece of music, for instance, when it is used to accompany action, can shape attitude toward that action. Imagine a man walking down a city street. Over this image hear, first, a jazz piece with a wailing, mournful horn then, with the same image, hear calliope music, or a full symphony orchestra bearing down on the final chords of Beethoven's fifth symphony. The action is unchanged, but in each case, our attitude toward the meaning of the man's movements, and even our perception of the movements themselves, will be modified by our emotional reaction to the sounds we hear. Words from within the scene or superimposed upon it, or sound effects such as feet shuffling on the sidewalk or sirens blowing, or the sound of wind: each would carry its own suggestion of meaning as well as information about the time–space situation of the action.

Like the visions or images which are described or suggested in the script —the locations, settings, actors, decor, lighting and camera angle—and like the implied movement found there in terms of story progression, actor and camera movement, editing rhythm and tempo, the dimension of sound grows out of, and ultimately must embody, the meaning of the film idea.

Script Words and Film Sounds

As with time, the printed words of a script only suggest sound. Words cannot describe with any reasonable exactness the particular nuance in an actor's delivery of a line, or the particular quality of certain sound effects. Nor can they indicate the exact moment in the flow of action where the sound effect should occur, its duration, or the exact nature of the music which will play so large a part in the meaning of the film. Words describe line delivery and musical quality in terms of subjectively desirable effects: such terms as "sadly" or "slowly" or "disturbed" explain character motivation. Musical ideas may appear in a script as "jazz background," "melodic theme" or "piano soloist playing Bartok," each suggesting also the emotional tenor of the scene. Sound effects, if mentioned at all, are seldom indicated with more than a label and an approximate intensity: "loud gunshot," "church bells tolling" or "woman's scream." Except in cases where elaborately written descriptions of sound occur for some specific reason, these simple suggestions must serve as the only clues as to what the nature of the final sound track should be.

In the first, generalized approach to the script, sound images begin to form in much the same way that visual images do in working out the spatial design for the film. A particular vocal quality relative to each of the characters, the tempo and punctuation of the sound effects, the emotional quality of the unwritten and unheard musical score are gradually envisaged. These imaginings are often an integral part of visual imagery, the visual and sound image being conceived as one. At other times, the sound image may be created first, and at still other times, the specific sounds to be used in a scene are conceived later—sometimes much later, during the editing process. The exact moment of imagination is unimportant; that at some point the imagining be precise and complete, is. Rene Clair, in speaking of the early uses of sound in film, said:

> The makers of the first sound films registered very nearly every sound [which] could be captured by the microphone. But it was soon observed that directed reproduction of reality created a completely unreal effect, and that sounds had to be selected as carefully as photographed objects.[9]

Conceptions of sound can no more be vague than conceptions of action. Vague and inappropriate conceptions can deflect or destroy audience understanding. Just as an overly quick movement on the part of an actor, too much light on the setting, or some other visual detail can destroy or at least change the effect of an image on an audience, so can a faulty sound perspective, too much or too little volume, or an inappropriate sound quality destroy or alter the meaning not only of the sound track, but sometimes of the visual image with which it has been associated.

The sound track is usually conceived as a completed product. During planning, it is mentally recorded, rerecorded and mixed until it is in its final conceptual shape, just as the operations of acting, photography and editing are performed, mentally, for the action track. Though conceived as a unity, the master sound track, like the master action track, is composed part by part. The elements out of which this master track is to be made are recorded and collected one by one. Speech, sound effects and music, the three basic track elements, are usually recorded individually on separate strips of film. Later they are rerecorded, distorted, modified, corrected and timed, and the various tracks, after being edited to some specific relationship with the picture, are then placed upon a single master printing track, with all the proper blending and relative volume levels. This ability to record the three different kinds of sounds separately and (except for synchronous dialogue) independently of the visual image, gives both control and flexibility. Each sound can be individually shaped and changed at will and only with final rerecording does the sound take on its final quality and its final relationship to the picture.

The director works with both sound and picture to create a whole. From the script he makes his plans, during production he attempts as closely as possible to realize them, and during editing he creates an exact combination with exact timing of the materials which have resulted from his efforts.

SOUND EFFECTS

Few sound effects tracks are given the attention they deserve. While the style of using sound effects will necessarily differ from one film idea to another and with the intent of the film, the ability of the sound effects track to create mood and atmosphere, induce emotional reactions, convey information and enlarge upon the meaning of the scene is rarely exploited. An early and yet highly sophisticated example of the possibilities inherent in a carefully selected sound track is Lang's *M*. Though it was made four years after *The Jazz Singer* with relatively primitive equipment, there is a complexity and inventiveness in the use of sound that is unusual not only when compared with other films produced around the same time, but even against many films produced today. In *M*, sound is used not only to create a scene, a feeling for the environment of action, but actually to motivate characters and story. The key sound is the murderer's whistled tune which identifies him to the audience and ultimately also to the beggar who betrays him to the underworld. Other sound effects such as the children mechanically counting in the first scene, the ominous tapping of the child's ball as she walks down the street, the mother's call of "Elsie" over the emptiness of the stairwell and the deserted basement, the similarity of the speeches in the police and the underworld plans of attack, and the offscreen sound of the police raid on the underworld, all account, in spite of their technical crudity, for much of the still-present effectiveness of the film as a whole. Like music, sound effects can invade an audience's subconscious mind, modify the perception of action and perform symbolic functions. Effects, like music, change perception of time and the audience's conception of the place of the action. Sound effects can carry the same kinds of sub-rational, as well as the more ordinary rational, meaning as does music. In function, effects amplify, diminish and superimpose meaning just as do other parts of the master sound track.

Most commonly, use of sound effects is confined to that of motivated sound, sound which could reasonably be expected to occur in the scene being viewed, although there is no reason to do this from the point of view either of the audience's threshold of credibility, or of the effectiveness of the film in general. Though motivated sound literally arises from the scene being viewed, this is not to imply that it can have only documentary, and no expressive, qualities. In *The Queen of Spades*, for instance, the motivated sound of the skirt scraping on the floor comes to be associated with the dry, mildly abrasive quality of the woman herself. Later the scraping is used out of context, and recalls for the audience their earlier emotions associated with the sound. The effects tracks of *Dr. No* and *Goldfinger* emphasize hard, metallic sounds which, though fully motivated, impress themselves so insistently upon the viewer that when leaving the theatre he finds himself sensitized to these grating elements in his environment. Interpretive sound effects, those introduced without reference to any visible source, can be equally effective. In *The Man in the White Suit*, a distinctly characterized bubbling sound becomes the sign that the inventor has spawned a new idea. A major impact of the film rests on this association. In the last scene, the inventor walks off into the distance, after having been ruined by the instability of his latest bright idea. As he all but disappears from view he stops, the characteristic sound is heard and, as he continues to move away with lighter step, the audience knows he is not defeated but that he has conceived another incredible invention.

Whether sounds seem to arise naturally from the scene being viewed, or have obviously been superimposed upon it, they create a strong bond of communication and identification between audience and film. Unlike music, sound is a normal part of human life, accompanying human beings everywhere they go and in everything they do. They themselves make sounds as they move and live. The objects they create make sounds and other animals and the elements make sounds. Sound is so much a part of life, in fact, that absolute silence, like loss of movement, is associated with death.

In life human beings to some extent create their personal psychological environment by hearing sound selectively. In a film, the director has the same control not only in the selection of sounds to be heard, but control over the particular qualities of sound, and over the relationship of sound to sound and sound to image.

SELECTION

Whether an over-all point of view toward the master sound track for an entire film is being conceived, or the particular elements to be used for a single scene are being created, the sound design usually begins with the factor of selectivity. There is a broad range of choice, from complete selectivity to complete non-selectivity. All sounds which would in life emerge from the event being filmed can be ignored completely—even to the extent of throwing away synchronous dialogue and synchronous sound effects and inserting in their place other sounds from other sources. Total silence, or dialogue overlaid from another sequence, could be used. Moving from this extreme of total selectivity toward non-selectivity, all sounds which would naturally emerge from the scene within the camera's view could be ignored, but sounds which could be expected to originate from the immediate environment outside the camera's view could be included. In an office scene, for instance, even if typewriters were not actually visible one could reasonably expect to hear the sound of typewriting. Any degree of selectivity is possible. Every sound both within the camera's view and outside it can be included, exercising no selectivity, or, exercising complete selectivity and creating a track independently, without regard for the expected or the "real," expressing, perhaps, some inner psychological state rather than a semblance of external reality and made of fabricated sounds entirely outside the range of normal human experience. Most sound tracks lie somewhere between the two extremes. The best is one that enhances the meaning of the story and has within itself sufficient variety and interest for the audience.

Along with changes in attitude during the last ten or fifteen years toward the use of camera, scripting and editing technique, has come a changed attitude toward the use of sound. These trends have had two extreme effects: first, a relative disregard of the sync dialogue track and, in its place, the use of tracks reflecting some other aspect of reality than the literal one of the immediate present; second, the use of the "all-inclusive" track, which attempts the equivalent of complete non-selectivity. Formerly only the documentarian or the experimentalist "dared" freely associate sound with image, or discard more literal tracks for more interpretive ones. Now the sound track, even in sync dialogue sequences, no longer need follow the movements of the actor's lips. Audiences can accept a much wider separation between track and picture (just as they accept a wider separation in continuity of action between cuts) and still make sense out of the film. The freely associated track has been more successful than the all-inclusive track in that such obviously highly selected sounds tend to call attention to themselves, and are invested with a meaning which the audience feels a responsibility to interpret. The all-inclusive track, on the other hand, gives not only a sense of carelessness (all sounds are equally important, therefore none is important) but can lead to a serious vacuum of interpretation or understanding if the viewer's ear happens, quite naturally, to pick out some particular sound on which to focus. Human hearing, like human seeing, is a tremendously interpretive and selective process and it is probably difficult, and it may be impossible, to meaningfully interpret or understand more than one sound at a time. A maelstrom of sound can prove extremely disconcerting to the film goer who is accustomed to listening with any care.

Deciding upon the area of the selective–non-selective scale in which to work thus involves a consideration of this important by-product of the relative power of the sounds to call attention to themselves. If the sounds do not coincide with the images being presented, then their function tends to be highly commentative. With a more non-selective, "realistic" use of sound, as long as it is not carried to the extreme, audience attention tends to focus upon the scene as a whole, or some aspect of the image.

The selection process ends when the sources for the selected sounds have been determined. Sound effects are commonly available from two sources, stock sound effects available on records and tapes from sound effects libraries, and effects recorded live either on location or in the sound recording studio.

From stock, thousands of cuts of sound effects are available, with great varieties of every kind of sound. These include such diverse items as a cash register ringing, bells of every kind, old and new automobile engines, the automobile engines of different manufacturers, motorcycles, machines, screams. If a suitable sound can be located in this way, an effects tape or record saves the time and expense of recording the effect live. However it often happens that only approximate effects are available. The recorded duration of the sound may not be suitable, or the sound may only approximate the sound which had been imagined. Furthermore, if some kind of distortion is to be introduced, this is most easily done when recording the effect live.

In live recording the nature, quality and duration of the sound can be controlled exactly. The exactly desired quality of an effect can often be found simply by going into the field with a good tape recorder and picking up the effect live on location.

Modification

When determining the content, or nature, of the sounds to be used, any modifications or distortions to be employed when recording them are also considered. Again, there is a scale from which to work which ranges from recording as nearly "natural" as is possible with modern recording instruments, to a degree of distortion so severe that the nature of the sound source being recorded can no longer be recognized. Much recording is done at one end of this natural-to-modified scale with the highest fidelity possible in the particular working situation. Modifications, when they occur, are usually introduced to counteract deficiencies in the sound being produced, in the recording situation, or in the recording mechanism, so that the final track is as accurate as possible. When needed, however, controlled distortions can be created for any one or all aspects of sound. Pitch can be raised or lowered, amplitude increased or decreased and harmonics accentuated or minimized through the use of audial filters. Changes can be made in recording speed, or in acoustical situation. Amplitude distortion is commonly used to achieve optimum audibility, a sense of closeness or distance, and to provide crossfades and superimpositions between the various parts of the master track. It can be applied individually to the speech, effects and music tracks, or to all three.

Special effects such as echo chambers and reverberation devices might be chosen on occasions. It is even possible, should it be necessary to introduce distortion within the duration of a sound, to move toward or away from the natural sound while it is being recorded.

Basically, there are three ways in which the selected sounds can be modified: by variations in pitch, in timbre and in amplitude.

PITCH

The term pitch refers to the frequency of a tone in cycles per second, or hertz (Hz) or, in subjective terms, to the relative position of a tone on an imaginary scale which includes all tones within the range of human hearing. Tones of greater frequency are perceived as being high pitched, or high on the relative scale; lesser frequency tones are perceived as low pitched. The approximate range of the most acute human hearing is 20 to 20,000 Hz.

The normal pitch of any sound can be manipulated quite easily in film recording mechanisms simply by recording or rerecording the sound at a speed other than that at which the sound will be played during performance. Normal playback speed is twenty-four picture frames per second (or thirty-six feet per minute in sixteen millimeter work, ninety feet per minute in thirty-five millimeter work). A sound recorded at a speed slower than normal playback speed, and played back normally, will seem higher in pitch than previously; a sound recorded at a high speed, and played back normally, will assume an abnormally low pitch.

Probably all owners of tape recorders are familiar with the process of manipulating pitch through speed. They are aware, also, of the side effects: distortion, and, if the variation from normal is great, loss of intelligibility.

Another means of pitch manipulation available with professional film sound recording mechanisms is the sound filter which cuts out a limited range of frequencies from any sound passing through. Since all but the purest of tones consists of a group of frequencies, rather than a single frequency, the sound filter can be used to modify pitch. High-pass filters, for instance, allow higher frequencies to pass; low-pass filters inhibit these higher frequencies, producing a tone more purely "low" than before.

Within normal hearing range, reaction to the pitch of a sound is largely subjective, based upon factors of experience. What is heard by the listener as a "pleasant" or an "unpleasant" sound will depend upon personal preference and upon any associations which have been established in the listener's mind. While there are no well defined relationships between pitch and emotional reaction, some generalizations can be made about typical reactions, in much the same way that generalizations can be made about typical reactions to color.

Other factors being equal, very high frequency sounds tend to seem more tense than the generally more relaxed lower frequencies. High frequencies can be heard as "thinner," harsher, more penetrating, lighter, more pure, more distant, more free and flexible sounding. Lower frequencies can seem full, soft, enveloping, heavy, varied, closer, more stable and less capable of change. Since all sounds have the dimensions of amplitude and timbre, as well as pitch, the effects just described vary with these other factors. And, since perception of pitch is relative, both the audial and the visual

C

context within which any sound is heard must be considered in anticipating the effect the sound will have on the audience.

TONE

Characteristic tonal quality, or timbre, results from the pattern of overtones, or harmonics, which is sounded with almost all tones. These combinations of vibrations identify the particular source of sound to the listener. A certain pitch sounded on a violin is easily distinguishable from the same pitch sounded on a flute because the timbre, or harmonics, is different. A doorbell sounds different from a churchbell, even when both sound the same pitch. Timbre varies with the recording situation as well as the sound source. The sound of feet walking in a recording studio sounds different to the listener from the same feet walking in a subway station. The listener's perception of a sound is changed by the acoustic characteristics of the recording situation. Just as different surfaces reflect different quantities and qualities of light, so they reflect in a number of ways the various frequencies which make up a sound. Thus timbre can be manipulated either by changing the source of the sound, or by controlling the acoustic characteristics of the recording situation.

Sounds with few overtones, when used in great quantity, tend to be less pleasing than those which are richer in character. But purer tones are effective as points of emphasis or accent. Every audience comes to the theatre with some predispositions and prejudices for or against certain kinds of tones. But, since aesthetic responses to tone are almost all associative, it remains for the director to provide whatever associations he wishes his audience to have.

AMPLITUDE

Amplitude, the relative loudness or softness of a sound, is the most easily manipulated of all sound characteristics, and the easiest to manipulate independently of other characteristics. Amplitude can be varied at the sound source, in recording and/or at the time of rerecording. Very quiet sounds can be boosted to greater levels, and loud ones reduced in volume, the success of the procedure depending upon the amount of change necessary and the quality of the recording and rerecording mechanisms.

Extremes in amplitude have their limits, so far as human comprehension and comfort are concerned. With too little amplitude the sound is inaudible; with too much, it is disturbing. Loud sounds are generally associated with objects that are forceful, intense, dynamic, massive, close and/or powerful, while quiet sounds can connote hesitation, impartiality, stability, smallness, distance, weakness and/or delicacy.

But the total effect of any particular sound must be defined in terms of all three of its characteristics, relative to other sounds and to the images which make up the context of the sound. A high, pure, quiet sound will differ in effect from a low, pure, loud sound. For maximum effectiveness and maximum meaning, all of the qualities of the sound must be accounted for, together with the modifying effects of the recording situation. Reverberation or echo, change of direction (sound perspective), and change of dynamics can all change an audience's subjective reaction to any sound.

Modification, like selection, affects the over-all interpretation that an audience will give to a scene. And, as with visual distortions, which are easily measured by the spectator from his sensory experience outside the theatre, audial distortions, even when comparatively slight, are immediately noticed. They are accepted as deliberate and not accidental, and as having some special meaning in relation to the story.

RELATIONSHIPS OF SOUNDS

The juxtaposition of sounds—their relationships to one another and to the accompanying images—is as important to the meaning of a film as is the juxtaposition of images. Changing relationships of either sounds or images changes meaning. A sound which seems to be a subjective component of a scene being viewed can assume an objective, commentative function, merely by shifting its position in the film relative to the scene. The audience's perception and understanding of the scene can thereby be changed. Contrapuntal sound, where the rhythm, meaning or direction of the sound runs counter to the image, can convey a sense of satire, irony, or can call attention to the underlying meaning of a scene—a meaning which may be quite different from the more superficial meaning immediately attached to it. The opening sequence of *Dr. Strangelove* attests to this. Counterpoint can take place among the components of the sound track, as well as between sound and image. The final, combined sound track, the master track, might be looked upon as a musical score, with voice, music and sound effects being the various instruments. Like a musical score, the master track can parallel the imagery, as the numerous background sounds of *Primary* do, or contrast with it, as does the tense understatement of *Night and Fog*. It can be incidental to the imagery, merely describing or lending a sense of completeness, the common function of synchronous sound. It can be imitative, often in some rhythmical way as in the crowded metropolis sequence of *The City*. It can comment upon the image by taking a contrapuntal point of view of it, such as in *Very Nice, Very Nice*. It can reinforce by its evocative, dramatic value as in the four early James Bond films. It can provide an over-all feeling through the use of themes, or leit-motifs of speech, music or effects, as the bells of *Belle de Jour*; and, finally, it can be the dynamic element, seeming to urge or lead the imagery to action, as does the whistle of *M*. At various moments throughout any film, the master track may shift between these functions.

Sound has often been used, particularly in more recent films, as a bridge between sequences occurring in different time segments. Formerly, sequences taking place in the past were often introduced by means of dissolves in which it became quite clear that some imaginary thought process was being visualized for the audience. More recently cutting between past events and present events, and indeed in some cases to future, imagined events, has become common. Images of the past are brought forward by the present, and often it is impossible to distinguish between past and present. The present seems a chaotic jumble of memory, imagination and perception. In such cases, sound often is used to make the psychological tie between two differing time periods by means of overlapping. Such is the practice, for instance, in *Belle de Jour*, *Juliet of the Spirits* and *Petulia*.

The technique is relatively simple. The sound associated with the image of the present slightly overlaps the cut to the past or imaginary sequence, or, conversely, if the past or imaginary sequence continues to affect the present, its sound continues slightly beyond the cut to the present time segment. Usually the sound for such overlapping, whether it consists of a sound effect, speech or music, is selected with a view to its applicability and relevancy to both time segments.

Determining the exact relationships of sound to sound and sound to image is a process which occurs during editing, where the work proceeds in terms of one twenty-fourth of a second (frame by frame). The fact that any sound or combination of sounds can be superimposed over any image gives unlimited flexibility while it imposes the responsibility of control. The task is one of realizing the film's meaning in terms of mutually existing sounds and images, or, more accurately, of realizing the idea in terms of the sound film.

MUSIC

Music in film can never be ignored or discounted, even when the audience is not consciously aware of it, and even when the music is so low as to seem almost inaudible. Not only is music among the most effective of film making tools, it is among the most flexible, at least when used to create and direct emotions and psychic states of being. Its appeal is non-rational so far as the film audience is concerned. Should the audience become aware of the musical component of a film, or analyze it rationally, then that component has failed in its work. Music in films is a major carrier of non-rational meaning. As such, it may be used to amplify the emotional content of a scene, to diminish or counteract emotional content, or to superimpose meaning through some symbolic attachment to image.

As in all stages of film design, selection, modification and fixing of relationships are guides in the work of creating the musical score. Of the three, modification enters least into work with music. Most music is recorded with as high fidelity as possible. If it is distorted to any extent, it tends to become a sound effect.

MOTIVATED MUSIC

Music in film can arise from several sources. The scene itself may suggest music. A character in the scene may be using a musical instrument, a radio might be playing, or, in the case cited previously of the man walking down the street, a previously established calliope could provide the musical source. This motivated use of music gives the audience a sense of naturalness, because the music seems to be part of the scene itself. But although the music source seems natural, the music itself can be made to perform functions more complex than simply adding to the reality of a scene. Depending upon the quality of the music and the context of action, the music can simply give the sense of reality (because the sound is expected), it may enrich and enlarge upon the emotions the audience is experiencing, it may counteract feelings and perhaps comment upon the scene in some ironic or critical way, or it may give meaning to a scene which has no particular meaning of its own. In *Casablanca*, for instance, the pianist in the bar in one scene picks out a tune called *As Time Goes By*, which is introduced in the film at a somewhat nostalgic moment. Later, the song itself becomes a romantic comment on the action, which portrays a kind of displaced European life in North Africa before World War II. If the scene in the bar had been a melancholy one from the point of view of the action being played, and if the piano music were also melancholy, then the emotive content of the scene would have been amplified. But perhaps the piano music is not melancholy, perhaps it is to be a light melody played over the melancholy action. Depending upon the music, this might intensify the melancholy feeling by means of contrast. Or, it might tend to neutralize the feeling of melancholy or give an ironic comment—the exact result would depend upon the prominence and choice of music in relation to the action. If the melody had been one the audience recognized, not from some other part of the film but from some life experience, and were something to which some significance or meaning had been attached apart from the meaning of the scene, then the music would tend to add that meaning to the scene being viewed.

In this use, musical themes might become unifying, structural elements in the film's design, as is the case in Buñuel's *Viridiana*. Music (always motivated) is one of the important devices used by Buñuel to provide not only a background for the particular scene but a symbolic measurement of parts of the action. In the whole first section of the film, for instance, religious music is used whenever the uncle plays the organ, or is using his record player. In the scene in which he carries Viridiana upstairs, drugged unconscious and wearing his wife's wedding dress, the religious music provides an irony of relationship with the action, giving it a tone of consequence and yet unnaturalness. Later, after the uncle has died, the son begins to play the organ very harshly and badly until the maid asks him to stop. This, in effect, completes one segment of the action. No further music appears until the feast of the beggars.

The religious feeling is again used in one of the last sequences, where the accused leper beggar puts the Hallelujah record on during the feast, and then dances to the sound of the music, dressed again in remnants of the wedding clothing. In the feast, the final mood is built both with sound effects and music, as well as with the camera work and the action itself.

The scene opens when the feast is already in progress, the tablecloth, glassware and expensive china and silver filling the banquet table. As the feeling intensifies, the baby begins to cry, the clanking of the dishes and silver becomes pronounced, hard and metallic, the beggar woman begins to play the guitar, and the talk of the beggars grows louder. The track is matched with an abruptly shifting camera, focusing first on one beggar and then on another in urgent closeups. As the scene moves on, the noise grows harsher. The action reaches a preliminary peak with the obscene "picture" and the "last supper" freeze frame. The momentum continues to build when the accused leper places the record of the Hallelujah chorus on the record player and the dancing begins. All the old objects are used again, and now the leper appears in a mockery of the bride, wearing the aunt's bridal costume. The audience has been adequately prepared for the culminating tension of the rape scene which is to follow shortly and which, given this buildup, comes with a sense of shock, but without surprise. The profane use of religious music, mixed as it is with the secular peasant dances, has marked a second segment of the action. The progression becomes complete in the final scenes of the film, where the son is entertaining the maid in his room with the sound of a loud, popular tune in the background. The music is harsh but, in a way, joyous, singing of love far different than that of religious fervor.

Interpretive Music

Absence of literal musical motivation—even for what later becomes a widely remembered film theme—is common. Musical motifs from *High Noon, The Third Man, Spellbound, Born Free, The Bridge on the River Kwai, Dr. Strangelove, Never on Sunday, La Dolce Vita, Goldfinger, The Graduate, Lawrence of Arabia* and *Mondo Cane*, to name but a few (and none of them musicals), are all as well known as the films from which they come. Where there is no motivation, no visible or logical source, music on the sound track takes on an interpretive character. Unlike motivated music, which seems natural and expected to an audience, interpretive music is more obviously imposed upon the scene from without. It may vary from the kind of interpretation which almost becomes imitation (such as the locomotive rhythms of *Pacific 231*, or the galloping rhythms of *High Noon*) to a more subtle and abstract, but equally effective, interpretation (such as the jazz score of *Litho* or the open desert feeling of *Lawrence of Arabia*). Use of interpretive music has been so frequent that audiences have become accustomed to it. However, a slight miscalculation in taste and the audience will immediately become aware of it with a rough jolt, and sometimes a laugh. Full symphony orchestras playing over images of a lifeboat supposedly lost at sea can be ludicrous—if this is the effect intended, then it is successful. If this effect were undesirable, it might have been better, if music were necessary, to have used a more modest, smaller combination of instruments, or perhaps a single instrument. It may even be to greater advantage to decide against music and settle simply for an appropriately chosen sound effect, or for silence.

The director must also be aware of the possibility of change in styles which would ultimately render his use of interpretive music obsolete. Rossellini's *Open City*, for example, was in its time a startlingly documentary approach to a theatrical film. Seen today, it betrays its genesis in theatrical style in only one respect, its use of interpretive music. Again and again, during the film, whenever there are moments of great tension and drama, the sound track is taken over by totally unmotivated but profoundly dramatic music. This florid-sounding music dominates the sound track over scenes of explicit documentary character. Such interpretive use of music is mixed with a motivated use wherein expected music occurs—such as the sounds of church music during scenes in church. In this free intermixture of motivated and interpretive music, the interpretive music sounds by today's standards unnecessarily artificial, while the motivated music is all but unnoticeable.

Interpretive music, properly used, can perform the same functions as motivated music. It can amplify, diminish, comment or superimpose meaning. In Bergman's *All These Women*, interpretive music is used to set the feeling of a silent comedy. Visually Bergman uses the techniques of Chaplin and other silent comedians (including traditional slapstick and the throwing of cream pies) to make a 1920s dialogue film. The sound track repeatedly includes jazz music commonly associated with the 1920s, thus helping to set the style and tone of the entire film. By contrast, the only motivated music in the film, that of the cello player, is relatively serious.

There are stylistic differences not only between films (some call for a mixture of interpretive and motivated music, some for all of one or all of the other) but also differences in style between directors. Some prefer interpretive music regardless of the story. They feel that a full music track, whatever the logical source, is as important a tool for expression as a full action track. To these directors, music is an essential component. Usually their films have no documentary or realistic aim, but tend to be symbolic and interpretive themselves, such as Fellini's *La Dolce Vita*, *8½* and *Juliet of the Spirits*, all of which make extensive use of interpretive musical tracks.

But to other directors, music is one of many kinds of sound. It is an element of choice, not a necessity. Hitchcock said:

> . . . when you put music to film, it's really sound, it isn't music *per se*. I mean there's an abstract approach. The music serves as either a counterpoint or a comment on whatever scene is being played . . .[10]

So long as the music that is used is effective, it makes little difference to the audience whether the director belongs to either of these stylistic schools.

CREATING THE MUSIC TRACK

The bulk of the work to be done in creating the musical score, if there is to be one, is done in consultation between the director and the person or persons who will supply him with the music. Although the director conceptualizes the nature of his musical score, at least in some vague fashion, before shooting begins, it is usually not until final editing that the music for a film becomes fixed in any way. Speaking of his film *Stray Dog*, Kurosawa said:

> I remember the difficulties we had with the music. Hayasaka and I went from one used record store to the next trying to find just the right music for the scene with the showgirl where the radio was playing. The record had to be old and scratched and the music had to be right. I remember we were so happy when we finally found that ancient rendering of *La Paloma*. During the scene the dubbing was so difficult that I remember my sound man actually cried with rage and frustration.[11]

Since it is easier to modify musical tempo than the tempo of human action, the music is usually adapted to the action as it is finally portrayed, rather than the action being adapted to the music. Working from and with the edited film, over-all timing can be specified exactly, as well as the rhythms or beats of individual scenes or moments. The score may be a complete one running throughout the film, or it may be partial where music is heard in some places in the film, and not others. The exact time limits of these scenes (or of the film as a whole) can be determined only after final editing. Unfortunately this can be used as an excuse to wait until the final cutting process to visualize the score. The film is designed in terms of space, time and motion, and then any gaps that occur are "filled in" with music. While this is not the best way to operate, it is surprising how often it seems to work—or at least, passes unnoticed.

However, determining the nature of the music (if not the music's exact timing and tempo) during the planning and shooting stages of film work gives greater means of expression, greater insight into the potential of the scene and greater control of the chosen medium of art. The effect of music on film can begin quite early in planning for a film, as Richard Brooks describes:

> I found a piece of music about three years before I did *Blackboard Jungle.* Driving home late at night from a poker game I heard this piece of music on one of those small stations and the rhythm interested me very much. I didn't remember its name. When I was planning to write *Blackboard Jungle* I asked the music store if they could get it for me. They finally came up with the record: "Rock Around the Clock." So six to eight hours a day while I wrote the script I played this record in the office. I felt that this record was indicative of young people's attitudes. When we began to shoot the film I played this record quite often on the stage through the dialogue so that the body movements would have this feeling, then dubbed some of the dialogue later.[12]

STOCK MUSIC

Music is derived from two sources: "stock" or "canned" music (material composed and recorded apart from the film), and music that is composed and recorded especially for the film.

Stock music presents the same problem of selection and adaptation as was suggested for stock sound effects. From the extensive libraries of stock music which are available (containing the well known recordings generally purchased by the public, or in the case of the lesser known libraries, containing specially collected music for film, radio and television use), must be found music which, although composed for some other purpose, will suit the design of the film. Factors in selection here are: basic appropriateness of rhythm and melody, the tone and feeling of the music and the suitability of the instrumental combination. The physical factor of quantity sometimes plays a part.

The final score may consist of one work, or selections from dozens of works which, through the processes of music editing and rerecording, become a single musical score. Success in using a stock musical score depends upon the amount of time, taste and patience which can be devoted to this part of the film.

Sometimes the selections can be found quickly; more often ten or twenty or thirty hours of listening is necessary in order to find the right five or ten minutes of usable music. And throughout all the hours of listening, the original musical concept must be retained and not changed by the force of the music being heard at the moment.

Once the music for the film has been selected, however, recording it is a simple matter. It consists, in the case of stock music, merely of a transfer from record or tape to magnetic motion picture film.

Composition for Films

Music composed and recorded specifically for the film presents a different set of problems than that of stock music. Here the work involves a communication of ideas and attitudes to another individual, the man who will compose and perhaps conduct the performance of the music. With composed music, of course, is the opportunity for maximum effect. The loose but workable fit of stock music disappears. In a composed score, every note and every measure can be made to fit exactly the action which has been photographed and edited. The effects desired, the selection of instruments, themes and styles of music, the meaning of the story and function of the music at any particular point in its telling, these factors are determined by the composer and the director working together. Such a score, like the stock score, can be either "spot composed," which means simply that key points in the film have music written for them and other portions of the sound track take over during other times in the film, or "through composed," which means that music is written for the entire film.

Once the musical score has been composed, recording it becomes a matter of performance and technique. All aesthetic decisions apart from those involved in performance have been made. Consequently there are few decisions left for the recording session. The instrumentalists assemble, rehearse and perform under the auspices of the composer-conductor. Usually this operation takes place in a recording studio which has been constructed especially for the purpose of recording sound. It is "silent" in the acoustic sense, and technical problems in attaining high fidelity are minimized. Since these are optimum recording conditions, attention can be directed toward the content and quality of the sound being produced. Occasionally, music is recorded in the field, perhaps at the location where the instrumentalists may be employed as performers.

Improvised Score

There is one additional source of music that should be mentioned in passing—the improvised score. The edited film is projected to a group of instrumentalists, who then improvise music to accompany the film. The music is in most cases jazz, Indian ragas or other forms of improvisation. Here, none of the aesthetic decisions has been made previous to the recording session. The intent of the film can be discussed with the musicians, the story outlined and specific kinds of musical background described. Sometimes specific instruments can be selected to predominate. Neither the director nor the musicians know what will emerge from the session. Hopefully it will be something useful. Here the director depends heavily upon the skill, sensitivity, sense of timing and taste of the particular group of individuals gathered to produce music.

In improvisation, the group is ready to record after a few discussions and a little warming up. Usually all of the music produced by the group is recorded—even the first run-through. Improvisation being what it is, it is impossible to know in advance when the best performance will be given. It may be the first attempt, the last, or perhaps none of the attempts made on that particular day. But if all attempts are recorded, there is a better chance of getting the effect desired. With consistency in volume levels, microphones and filtering, there is the further possibility of being able to choose the best parts of each attempt, combining them later in the editing room to make a single score.

Depending upon the length of the film and the skill and experience of the musical group, the director may request a complete run-through—attempt to get a score for the entire film. Or he may call for recording the music sequence by sequence. Exact timing with the film is the problem in any case, since there is always some lag in reaction time, and because smaller nuances are generally ignored for the larger units of flow. The smaller the unit of time for which the improvisation is made, the greater the accuracy of fit with the film. The larger the unit of time (within limits), the greater the sense of a complete composition and of flow between parts of the composition. Some balance must be struck between the two extremes.

Occasionally, a group will be asked to perform without having seen the film. The group may, in fact, be purposely kept ignorant of the story, and simply be given segments of time within which to work and the moods with which to fill that time. Another method would be to show the film once— there is no best way of achieving intended results. The methods used must be tailored to suit the personalities of the persons who are to perform and the complexity of the musical composition desired.

PRE-RECORDED MUSIC

In the foregoing discussion, music has been post-recorded, that is, recorded after the image has been photographed. Under certain conditions, however, music may be pre-recorded, before the image, often to be played back during the shooting period. The purpose of playing the music back on the shooting set is usually to provide a sound track reference for the actors. Perhaps they must move in rhythm with the music, either in ordinary movement or in dance. Perhaps, if there are words with the music, they must appear as if they were singing, or, if they are an orchestra, they must look as if they were playing the music.

In any of these situations, the music is first recorded in a sound recording studio, under optimum recording conditions which would not be available on the sound stage. To actually record music while dancers were performing would mean to record feet shuffling and other noises which might accompany the action. To record a song during its delivery on a sound stage would mean

Fig. 6. Optimum recording conditions allow the performer to concentrate totally on the production of sound. [Dr. Doolittle, *20th Century-Fox.*]

recording all the bad takes caused by missed notes, poor delivery, grimaces, mispronounced or slurred words, and so on. It is much easier for a singer to deliver a song well if he does not have to be concerned with how he looks at the same time. Playing these pre-recorded sounds back during shooting gives the effect of the scene having been recorded synchronously. Of course, it is not necessary that the sound-producing voice be from the same individual being photographed.

In the pre-recording situation, it is the director's responsibility to act as an intelligent audience. The dancers or actors will want to know if their movements were visually appropriate, and if they were indeed synchronous. The director is there to tell them when they have been successful. While he may make suggestions and offer some guidance, the director serves mainly as a mirror to the actor's work.

WORDS

The third element of the master sound track, and sometimes an element which overtakes even the picture track in importance, is words. Because they are so closely associated with the human thought process, they are a main carrier of information and attitude between human beings, and because their meanings are personal and individual, words are always an important factor in a film's effectiveness. They must be selected with care, produced with feeling and related to the image in a meaningful way.

Presumably the job of selection was performed as the script was written. In words, above all else, the script is usually most precise. The exact words which should appear on the sound track have been selected and structured, whether they are synchronous dialogue said by a character, or a non-synchronous monologue spoken by a narrator. The great bulk of these words which have been collected and grouped in the script does appear in the final film. But, on occasions, there is need for re-casting a line, rearranging a few phrases or deleting or adding words for clarity or effect. Whenever such changes are made, extreme care must be taken to make the additions or deletions in the same style as the script, else the changes will stand out for what they are.

Occasionally, because he is working either with extremely skilled or with completely unskilled actors, the director begins the shooting process without having fixed the dialogue to be given. With extremely skilled actors, especially actors who have worked in ensemble, it is possible to create dialogue sequences in a semi-improvised manner. The characterizations are known, the situation and at times an ultimate story goal are described. From this some sensitive actors may be able to create a dialogue sequence while the camera is photographing them. The technique has the advantages and dis-advantages of improvisation. There is a possibility of spontaneity, freshness and vigor but also of repetition, vagueness, unpredictability. With com-pletely unskilled actors, it is often more possible to achieve a "natural" per-formance if the actors are allowed to create their own lines. Obviously such a technique will only be useful if the unskilled actor has some talent for this, and if he completely understands the nature of the scene.

Although selection of words is for the most part determined by the script, the production of words, their duration, emphasis, inflection, and tempo, and relating the words to other sounds and to images, has yet to be accomplished. The amount of control and manipulation possible varies both with the person producing the words, and with the physical conditions of the recording situation. Various recording situations place differing amounts of stress upon those who are trying to work within them. The number of distractions in the form of other tasks to be performed simul-taneously with the production of words, the distractions of other work being performed by other people within the same work space, the difficulty of obtaining good acoustical surrounds in which to record, the pressure of time and expense with its inherent restriction of opportunity to correct errors—all of these vary markedly with the time, place and manner of recording.

Like other master sound track components, dialogue or narration can be created before, during or after the recording of images. That is, it may be pre-recorded, synchronously recorded or post-recorded. Pre-recording and post-recording most often involve the use of a sound recording studio, or, with increasing frequency, field recording. Synchronous recording generally takes place on a sound stage, or on location in the field.

PRE-RECORDING

Except in the case of animation films, where the master sound track is usually completed before work on the image track has begun, there is little pre-recording of words, either synchronous or non-synchronous, in the production of professional films. There is no reason to pre-record synchronous dialogue. Indeed, the technical difficulties of producing a sync effect in this way would be so great as to invalidate any reason which may arise to try the technique. Only rarely is it necessary to pre-record non-synchronous material. The occasional field-recorded or studio-recorded interview might possibly require it, or perhaps where a suitable narrator or actor would not be available at a later time.

When it is necessary to record a narration before the picture has been photographed, the first consideration is for maximum flexibility and variety in terms of line delivery, pacing, inflection and the recording of alternate lines. This is especially important when the narrator will be unable to appear later to make pickups, a process of redoing parts of the narration track for either technical or aesthetic reasons. It is important to anticipate areas of possible difficulty before the time has come to record, and to plan alternate recordings to ensure editing flexibility.

Whether recording in a studio or on location, "room sound" should be collected: this is a recording of the quality of "silence" offered by the particular acoustic environment in which the words are recorded. A totally dead sound track will not match properly with recorded silence; instead the "open" mike background noise must be obtained. (Known also as a buzz track.) Later this track can be used to space out the pauses between words or phrases, and thus time the words closely to the action.

Since the nature and timing of the action to be performed can at this point only be imagined, work with a narrator will consist mostly in helping to understand and convey the meaning of the words, and to create a style of delivery suitable to the final film.

The only other instance of pre-recording which occurs is in the pre-recording of a song or other musical composition. The reasons for this technique, and its problems, have been discussed in the section on music (page 75).

SYNCHRONOUS RECORDING

Whether recording synchronous dialogue on a full sound stage, or a sound effect on location, it is to the director that the actors and sound technicians turn for help. A well conceived plan is the director's best insurance that he can provide such help.

SOUND STAGE RECORDING

The heaviest responsibility occurs when the crew is working on the sound stage, for the director is as much director of the sound recording operation and the sounds being recorded, as he is of the image recording operation and the images being recorded. Because he is the only person on the set who has a complete idea of the final film—other members of the crew can at best be expected to know only their particular function in the film—they always turn to him for guidance and instruction.

If the shooting set-up is large and complex, responsibilities are usually delegated to those who serve as crew chiefs. These are the sound recording engineer, director of photography and production designer. Capable, talented people make the best crew chiefs. They can, at times, serve as a source of inspiration and refreshment. Their ideas and suggestions might help to create new possibilities in the scene and reveal new meaning in the film idea. But even in a situation where the creative work is being performed by several individuals working in close agreement, ultimate decisions, ultimate responsibility and therefore ultimate authority must lie with the director alone. Without such a single source of authority and responsibility, the film risks loss of unity.

Sound stage recording covers a variety of recording situations according to the amount and nature of sound being recorded with the action. These include shooting silent, silent with sound to be post-recorded, and synchronous dialogue recording.

There are few occasions that call for a truly silent scene—that is, a scene which will be silent in the final film. Presumably no speech, no music and no sound effects would occur in such a scene. For an especially tense or dramatic effect, at times a totally silent scene may be used within the context of a sound film. Such scenes have a strong effect on the time design of a film. They call attention to themselves in much the same way that a moment of absolute silence would call attention to itself in daily life, which is lived with a constant background of sound. Because of the severe contrast, tension is introduced. For these reasons such scenes must be handled carefully. Used too much, they seem self-conscious. They can alienate an audience and result in giddiness and objectivity. An entire scene or sequence could be rendered ineffective, and possibly the whole film. When recording such scenes, special attention must be paid to even minute actions from the actors, to the length of the scene, and to its place in the stream of sound which will ultimately surround it. If the scene is to take its place in a flow of action (even though the flow of sound might be interrupted), it must be particularly well matched to the surrounding scenes in terms of tempo and spatial arrangement.

Except for dialogue sequences, the great bulk of most films is actually shot silent, with the sound being post-recorded. Many documentaries, almost all educational and experimental films, and large portions of fictional films are made in this way. Even within the dialogue sequence, silent footage often is photographed. Reaction shots of one character listening to another can be recorded silent, the off-screen dialogue being added later in the editing room.

Because of the great flexibility and control possible with present day recording methods, the problem of matching sound quality in this kind of shooting has been minimized. But problems of rhythm, timing and intensity remain. The effect of any scene being recorded is strongly modified, in terms of tempo and meaning, by the sound that is added later. When actors are not actually speaking in a dialogue film, the sound track tends to take the place of the actor's voice in conveying meaning. Here music becomes particularly powerful. Not only does it provide a basic rhythmical element, but it tends to carry the spectator's emotion in whatever direction the music is going. A large portion of what is perceived as film acting is actually performed by the music track. Of course, well chosen sound effects can be as powerful as music. No special problems are involved in recording a silent scene to which sound is to be added later beyond this anticipation of the effects of the sound track upon the meaning and rhythm of the scene and upon the audience's visual perception of it.

DIALOGUE

This is not the case in sync (short for synchronous) dialogue work. Technically speaking, this is the most difficult of the typical film sound recording situations. Part of this difficulty arises because the source of the sound, the actor, is human, with all the variability and unpredictability inherent in that term. This human sound source is a moving one involved in a dramatic situation, performing the difficult and demanding task of being someone other than himself, emotionally charged and working in the impossible situation of a sound stage with all its paraphernalia, and all this in the midst of frequently indifferent, impatient and blasé technicians. Moreover, the actor knows that whatever he says or does is being recorded. Every error, no matter how small, becomes history.

Thus the problems arising from the sync dialogue shooting situation are of two kinds: technical and human. The technical problems are fairly well provided for by the quality and placement of the sound recording mechanisms and the skill of the recording engineer and his crew. Although the director must always be aware of what the sound crew is doing, and how its actions are affecting the sound recording, the principal weight of attention can be diverted to the solution of the more difficult and more important human problems.

LINE DELIVERY

The first item of attention is the reading of lines given by the actors. The actor's reading and pronunciation must be correct and his enunciation clear. The pitch, rate and intensity of the delivery must be appropriate to the characterization, and of a nature capable of being recorded. Too low or too high a pitch may be distorted or muffled on the final track because of natural limitations in sound recording equipment. Too rapid a delivery may result in the editor being unable to separate words for purposes of editing. Even the audience may not be able to grasp the lines. Too much volume or too little may result in sounds beyond the range of the recording. Although most present day recording systems have automatic volume controls, extremes of loudness or softness may still result in distortion or inaudibility.

As well as being recorded with satisfactory quality, the actor's lines must be consistent. Continuity is as much a problem in sound recording as it is in picture recording. It is almost as difficult for a human being to repeat literally a specific line delivery between several takes as it is to duplicate motions exactly. Tonal quality and rhythm must be approximately matched, even if they cannot be duplicated. To allow room for cutting, dialogue is repeated (overlapped) much as is the action. Where necessary, the recording of the previous or following shot can be played back on the set in order to refresh the memory. This is a costly process, because it is time consuming, but it saves by allowing close matching of sound quality.

Timing is another factor. In addition to the internal rhythm of the lines relative to lines preceding or following, there must be a correct relationship between the actor's movements and the delivery of lines. Unless the actor has been previously coached, or if the actor has developed his own conception of the character he is playing, the timing of movements as well as line delivery is developed during the sync recording process. Again pre-production planning is the guide. Again the plan must be flexible, yet firm—reasons for departing from the plan and reasons for remaining faithful to it must be weighed carefully.

Reading lines with consistency and good timing all affect the work of the sound crew directly. Microphone placement, for instance, is determined partly by the typical volume of an actor's voice, or his delivery of a certain line. To achieve consistency in sound quality, which includes consistency in sound perspective, microphone placement must be a planned operation. As an actor moves about the set, the microphone must follow him. If placed on a boom or a wireless (radio) microphone is used, the microphone becomes fully mobile (fig. 7).

If the boom is used, the boom operator must rehearse the scene with the actor to assure good recording quality. The director of photography must guard against microphone boom shadows and the intrusion of the microphone into the camera's view. If the microphone is planted somewhere on the

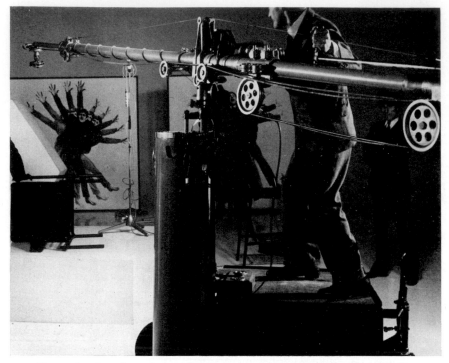

Fig. 7. A microphone boom of the type used in large production recording situations. [A Hard Day's Night, *United Artists.*]

set, the actor must learn how to speak so that it obtains an optimum recording of his voice. He must not shuffle his feet or rattle papers near the microphone unless this is part of the plan. Even when these logistical problems are solved, there are other decisions to make which do not influence the sound recording directly, but which affect the audience's understanding of the story.

SILENCE IN SOUND

A sync dialogue scene is not all sound. There is silence within it, and this silence can be as important and as meaningful as any words the actors may utter. The placement and duration of such moments of silence—which have such a strong effect on the rhythm of the scene—are a part of the audial design for that scene. They may be moments of absolute silence, or interruptions in speech where music or effects will take over.

Many moments of silence with relatively sparse dialogue can affect action in two ways. A low proportion of sound to a high proportion of action can give an increase of tension in a dramatic scene. In a scene which is basically slow or relaxed, it can accentuate both the slowness and the sense of relaxation. If the silence is intermittent, and not typical, then a regular or irregular rhythm is added, depending upon the frequency and patterns of the silence. Such use can become identified with a certain character, or a certain idea, and thus become thematic or symbolic. It can be used to suggest ideas not seen in the picture itself, but experienced elsewhere in the film. A momentary and non-patterned use of silence can convey the effect of listening —a character listening, or the camera listening, or even the audience. Shifts from an objective to subjective experience of the scene, similar to the shifts from objective to subjective use of the camera, can result from such silences. In a dialogue scene, the person listening may actually be of more interest to the audience and have more meaning for them than the person speaking.

One of the basic problems in shooting a dialogue scene is deciding which of the actors the audience should see at each point in the dialogue. Often the scene is recorded two ways. In one recording, the audience observes the person speaking, and in the other, the listener. In the cutting room, the best choice between the two scenes can then be made.

There is less of a problem in working with a light dialogue scene than where there are long speeches, or a heavy and extended interchange of dialogue between two characters. One solution may be simply to keep the camera on the speaker or speakers. On the other hand, this might prove boring to the audience, who may not want to see the speaker at all, but would rather hear him speak over some other image, much as a narrator would. In such cases the guiding factors are the content of the lines, the meaning to be conveyed with the scene, the relationships between the characters and the sense of dramatic flow.

The last, but perhaps least worrisome, problem in the sync dialogue situation is the problem of "flubs" or "fluffs," omissions, additions and mismatches in line delivery. Actors themselves are acutely aware of the mistakes they make, and can usually be depended upon to call attention to them if they have not already been noticed. But actors are less conscious of omissions and additions to the script. In this case the script supervisor calls attention to the mismatch. Occasionally an actor simply does not feel emotionally able to deliver a line as it is written in the script. He may wish to change the wording to something he feels is more comfortable, sometimes doing this spontaneously without consultation. On other occasions the actor may actually have a better ear for dialogue than the writer. He may suggest an alteration of the line because he feels it is more accurate to his characterization. In either of these situations, the suggested changes must be made openly. It can then be decided whether or not the line or lines should be changed. If the actor's change has not been a good one, it cannot be allowed to remain. If the change is beneficial, it should be used. Any deviation from the script, however minute, must be noted in the script supervisor's copy of the script, and must be cross-referred to any effects it might have upon other scenes already photographed, or to be photographed.

FIELD RECORDING

As equipment has improved, sync recording in the field, once a most difficult operation, has become more and more common. Whether the crew is shooting exteriors on a city street or in a tomato field, or interiors in some small hotel room or a bar or train station, the recording engineer is met with conditions seldom found on the sound stage. Spurious sounds, unwanted reverberations, hard reflecting surfaces and nuisances such as wind blowing into microphones are just a few. Although the director is not usually involved in the technical aspect of making a good recording in such situations, he must be cognizant of the problem and so plan his shooting to minimize the amount of unwanted sound presented to the recording engineer (fig. 8).

First, in the initial work on the script and in planning the location shooting, the amount of sync field recording to be done should be carefully considered. Camera angles less favorable to a situation that is already difficult recording should be avoided, such as medium shots with sync dialogue, full face shots with dialogue, or any set-up where the microphone, in order to escape being photographed, must be placed some distance from the actor, or where direct lip sync is necessary. If possible, the dialogue and action should be so arranged that lavalier microphones can be concealed in the actor's clothing, or wireless (radio) microphones used. In off-screen dialogue, reaction shots of the person listening rather than sync dialogue shots of the speaker are possible. Alternatively, if the budget allows, the scene may be photographed so that it can later be post-synced in the recording studio.

During actual shooting in the field, locations, angles and positions for the actors should be selected which will offer the best acoustic characteristics. Where there is a choice of location, as, for instance, between two hotel rooms, either of which would make a suitable environment, the room with the best natural acoustics should be chosen. Often there are appreciable acoustic differences between rooms which are otherwise quite similar. Drapes, stuffed furniture, rugs, screens or other baffles, or rough textured walls and ceilings can make a great difference in the quality of sound produced.

When the location has been chosen and shooting has begun, angles which allow the microphone to be placed near the actor can be used. Long, continuous dolly shots during dialogue, which could mean dependence upon several microphones with a consequent change in acoustic pattern for each microphone, can be avoided. The actor should not be placed next to hard reflecting surfaces during dialogue sequences. Windows, doors, kitchen appliances, hard surfaced walls and marble staircases are troublemakers in this respect. An under-running "room-sound" buzz track, which will minimize

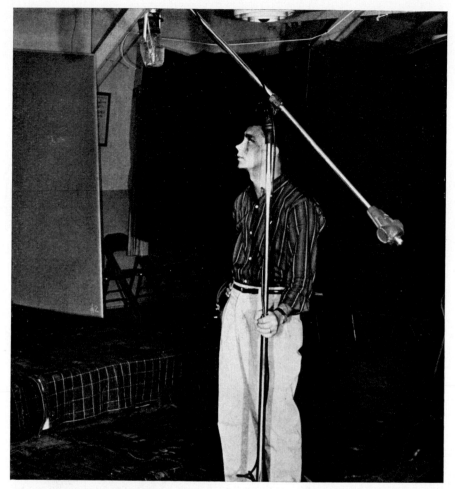

Fig. 8. Sound-absorbing blankets on the floor and hung across the air space help minimize unwanted noise in a poor acoustical situation. Microphone stands of this type often cast inconveniently located, unwanted shadows.

differences in recording quality, is recorded in sufficient quantities to cover the entire sequence to be performed in the room. This sound, placed behind the entire dialogue sequence, will not only disguise differences in recording quality but will lend a consistency to the recording impossible for the engineer to achieve on location.

In such a situation, clear line delivery is vital. Because of poor acoustics, the lines will be more difficult to understand when recorded. All of this must be done without apparent laboring which would betray the difficulties to the audience. And, of course, the dramatic quality of the scene must never be compromised so as to defeat the scene's purpose.

Post-production Recording

Either dialogue or narration may be recorded after the action has been photographed. In dialogue situations, post-recording is a relatively rare event. In narration situations, it is the usual procedure.

Dialogue Post-recording

When, for one reason or another, the dialogue for a scene is added after the picture has been photographed, the process is known as "post recording," "post syncing," or, on occasion, "dubbing." This is a time-consuming and expensive process, but there are several good reasons for resorting to it. After the shooting period is over, for instance, some fault or mismatch in the recording of certain lines may be discovered.

If the fault cannot be corrected by other means, or masked in editing, it may become necessary to call the actor back to the sound recording studios. There he can see the scenes needing to be redone, projected over and over again. Working with a microphone, he tries to repeat the lines indicated by the picture in such a way that they look as if they were recorded in sync. He must recapture the exact tempo of his original speech, the production of each word must match, particularly if the scene is a closeup. Usually he rehearses at length, and the picture, having been spliced into a loop, is played over and over again. Sound takes are then made of his voice until he finally is able to recapture very closely the timing of his original speech. Needless to say, he will find his job more difficult as the length of the speech increases. While it is comparatively simple to "dub in" a few words of dialogue, to replace whole speeches, or speeches over closeups, needs patience.

Occasionally even more complex circumstances present themselves. Whole scenes or sequences, and sometimes whole films are so poorly recorded that the entire job must be done over again. This may be because of the sound crew's deficiencies, the deficiencies of the recording equipment or location or because of the actor's performance. Usually some deterioration of the total film takes place in such cases. To save time, patience and money, various methods are used in editing to minimize the number of scenes to be "dubbed." The editor may depend heavily on long shots, where matching need not be so exact, or upon reaction shots, inserts and cutaways. Excessive use of such devices, where they are not called for dramatically, can weaken the impact of a film.

The third circumstance which makes post-recording necessary arises when the actor's voice is in some way inadequate. Post-recording is used for dubbing a dialogue track in a language other than the language in which the film was shot. If the dramatic quality of the voice is lacking, a new voice can be recorded over the image of the original actor. Carefully done, this can salvage an inadequate performance. Of course, the larger the part played by the actor, the more difficult the technique becomes. The suitability of the new voice to the old image is an important consideration in casting.

In all of these post-recording operations, the new recording must be made to blend with the old, and the lines and tonal quality must match, as well as the rhythm and feeling of the vocal expression as a whole.

NARRATION POST-RECORDING

The first, and perhaps most important step in the process of narration post-recording is in the selection of the narrator, the casting of the voice to be used. Usually there are three groups of voices from which to choose: those experienced in radio and television broadcasting, those who are stage or film actors, and non-professionals. Radio and television announcers have extensive microphone experience to offer as qualification. They are accustomed to producing reliable performances, have pleasant voices, good enunciation and use proper pronunciation. However, announcers often have dramatic limitations which offset their technical capabilities. They read narrations, which are essentially dramatic prose (and sometimes poetry), as if they were news announcements, or, even worse, commercials. Their pattern of speech tends to be fixed and they have a "vocal personality" which may be incompatible with the personality of the film. Most broadcasters lack the flexibility and experience necessary to adapt their voices to the needs of the film.

A good narrator is more actor than announcer. He must have a sense of drama, of timing, of the meanings and individual values of words. He must exercise dramatic taste in his delivery, based upon his knowledge and understanding of the film and of the words used in conjunction with it. Occasionally, he must even act, or at least react to some visual element in the film. He must be able to offer both consistency of characterization and vocal variety. Sometimes his voice is subsidiary to the picture, sometimes it leads. Sometimes it comments but always it carries great weight and import to the audience. For these reasons, selection of a narrator is an important interpretive step in shaping the quality of the film. He must possess not only a vocal quality suitable to the film, and competent microphone technique, but more important, he must be able to act and to take directions flexibly.

Only occasionally are non-professionals capable of bearing full responsibility for a film narration. Usually their microphone skills and ability to convey vocal drama are limited. But for occasional passages or special effects, a non-professional can add an element which all the professional skill in the world can fail to produce, the effect of authenticity. This is especially true in documentaries. If, for instance, the voice of a south Australian farmer is needed, it may be better to use a farmer than an actor who is skilled in mimicking such a person.

During the recording session, patience and a good ear are essentials, whether the recording is done before the film is photographed, after it is photographed and before it is cut, or after cutting. Narrations recorded before the picture has been edited are produced in the simplest and most flexible of recording situations. Here the primary factor is the best delivery of lines and attention to time limits is minimal. The narrator can be coached closely in the approach to the words, the point of view or attitude, and in the line-by-line delivery. Dealing with the narrator is very much like dealing with the actor on the set. But now the complexity of the situation is reduced because voice only is being recorded and because fewer technicians and less paraphernalia are present to distract from the production of sound. Again, attention to line delivery, consistency, meaning, errors and pacing is necessary. Again pauses are considered: although in editing it is a simple matter to lengthen a natural pause artificially, introducing a pause where none existed is usually less successful. Each word said by the narrator is important in a narration film. No word can be "thrown away" as unimportant or irrelevant. If the word is irrelevant, it does not belong in the script. The meaning of each word and phrase must be considered carefully in relation to the whole, and given thoughtful delivery. The completed film is in mind as a guide and the relative importance of the narrator's function at each moment in the film determines the manner of delivery.

Narrations recorded before editing allow the speech and picture tracks to be composed simultaneously. This is usually the best way to achieve a truly coherent, unified work. Narrations recorded after editing offer less flexibility. The picture track has been edited, sometimes in a rough, but more usually in a finished, form. In doing this, the cutter has had to imagine the quality and feeling of the narration as the various elements of the film were composed. Even skilled editors occasionally find that their "imaginings" are inaccurate when they are confronted with the tapes produced in the post-production recording session. This means that the picture track must be re-edited—needlessly repetitive work—or that the narration track timing must be made to fit the picture artificially—pauses being inserted or cut out by adding or deleting silences between the narrator's words or phrases. To a certain extent such manipulation can be successful, but the technique has its limitations, which become more noticeable the greater the compression or extension necessary.

To help in what is at best a difficult job, the narrator can be requested to perform his work within a specific time limitation. Such self-imposed timing may be guided by projecting the film during the recording session, or by setting time limits to the various sections of the narration script as they are recorded. The drawbacks to narrating to picture are obvious. The narrator must divide his attention between his script and a projected film, and he must try to control his production of sound in response to a film he has seen at most only a few times. With his energy split three ways watching a film, trying to anticipate and control time, and producing sounds, his vocal performance is likely to suffer. Even the highly skilled narrator can find this a frustrating experience. Less skilled narrators retreat into mechanical readings which have no feel for the film, and which can hardly be said to approximate the true timing needed. The situation is made even worse when an attempt is made—as, unfortunately, it often is—to run through the entire film in this way. Persons with little sense of timing and less taste may be satisfied with the results of such sessions. They are, after all, economical because no editing need be done when the recording session is complete. But aesthetically and technically, the results are usually poor.

Narration to time is little better. True, the narrator is not distracted by having to watch his script and a film simultaneously. However, he is given certain minute or second boundaries within which to produce his sounds. Often he has little knowledge of the film which he is narrating, and he feels he is working against a mechanical limitation, the time clock, rather than working with the feelings engendered by the special juxtaposition of word and image.

Where post-recording the narration for an already edited film cannot be avoided, it is often helpful to project the film several times so that the narrator can become familiar with its distinctive tempo. Discussing the meaning of the words in relation to the images, and perhaps allowing the narrator to try some portions of the narration in the projection room away from the tension of the sound recording session, can also help. After such rehearsals, the number and extent of which will vary with budget, time and the ability of the narrator to benefit from rehearsal, the recording session can be scheduled. During recording, the narrator must be kept relaxed and yet alert to the very stringent limitations within which he is working. All attempts produced during such sessions should be recorded. The best part of each take can be used for the completed film. Even if no editing after recording is possible, there is still choice of one of several takes, to be selected when the tension of the recording situation is gone.

5

The Object in Space

TIME IN ITS continuum yields event and a film is an event, a potentiality, a promise growing out of its characteristic of continual change. But it is also more than this, more than the words progression and development suggest. It is reality, as well as eventuality. Promises and potentials, after all, are really little more than possibilities. They are not real in the sense of present existence.

Reality lies in results, in the contents and nature of events; it is concrete, objective and spatial. Films have this spatial quality as well as their temporal being. They may be said to exist in space even though the actual volume they occupy is trivial. Just as the phenomenon of human persistence of vision, when coupled with a rapid succession of photographs taken over fractions of a second yields the illusion of motion, so the illusion of space, even what is interpreted as three dimensional space, is induced merely by a meaningful play of light and shadow upon a screen. In this spatial aspect, films share the two and three dimensional world of sculpture, architecture, dance, theatre and especially painting.

And yet, the differences between films and these other arts make impossible the use of traditionally regular ways of thinking which serve the other arts so well, but which do not suit this paradoxical and yet technological means of expression.

It would be simple to say that, like painting, film is a visual art. It is. You look at it, so it is visual.

But the singular, instantaneous impression which is normally implicit in the word "visual" is insufficient as a description of film. Film is a vision in motion, images in continuity. Painting, however charged with a sence of impending or potential movement, remains static. Its province is a moment, a mortal instant, frozen into immortality by the choice and skill of the painter.

Film, by definition, moves. The continually changing nature of the image, sense of action, of process, gives it life—movement not only of objects

90

within the frame, but of the frame itself and the idea. Filmic impressions other than this one of continuous flux and development occur only rarely, and then fleetingly, when an especially arresting image catches the attention and the emotions.

Beyond this fundamental difference in the nature of painting and of film, there are certain similarities. Like a painting, a completed film has permanence when work on it has ceased and it becomes a fixed object. This superficial pictorial similarity with painting, however, points to a basic dissimilarity of films with the continuously changing arts of theatre and dance, where the live performer's response to audience reaction helps realize the art. And yet, from still another standpoint, the action of a film is like that of theatre and dance; it is produced in three dimensional space (even though such action in films is presented to the audience within a two dimensional frame). Like theatre and dance, the action of a film is usually a planned, rehearsed performance, yet the performance occurs away from its audience in the relative isolation of the shooting set. And though the film depends for its life upon audience response, the audience and its emotions—at least so far as the performers are concerned—are at the moment of creation an unknown.

A tangle of aesthetic paradoxes—two dimensional spatial movement, permantly shaped performance, audience art created in the absence of an audience: these are the nature of film as art, as communication and as a designed product.

Composing the spatial aspects of filmed images, therefore, calls for some adaptation of the traditional methods of pictorial analysis. The factors of mass, line, color, tonal value and the illusion of depth, all are used in composing film images. But in film it is mass in motion, line in motion, color, tone and depth in motion. Motion and change are constant. If camera movement within a shot does not change the image, an actor's movement will. If an actor's movement does not change, if there is no physical action, change will occur between shots because of the juxtaposition of images. Even attempting to stop motion by using lengthy static shots will not succeed because the film's time is not static.

Some who have been trained in older art forms, and who wish to work in this new one, react to this change in condition by discarding everything learned in the other forms. While this method has rarely been successful for whole films, at times it has produced new understanding of the ways in which older ideas and older methods can adapt to new art forms. Ultimately these ideas must be incorporated within some framework that an audience can understand.

Much can be learned, and much insight gained into the craft of film making, by studying all serious efforts to explore, and define, the nature of the film medium.

CREATING SPATIAL DESIGN

Creating the spatial design of a film, that is, composing moving images for use in a continuity of shots, is a process which occurs during the same period in which the time design is coming into being. Indeed, the two designs cannot be created independently. Every tempo is embodied in a moving form, and every moving form has its tempo. Methods of spatial notation are available to help in the task, at least notation of selected moments in the continuum of moving images: line sketches, rendered drawings, photographs and three dimensional models. Although it is unwise to expect too much of notation—the hazards and realities of production can make exact execution impossible or undesirable—notation does enable a more complex design to be created than might be possible when the creator depends upon memory and imagination alone. The methods of notation are far from perfect. Notation can approximate, or at least suggest concretely, the characteristics of select moments of the final image, but not the image as it will exist in the film and not its movement. As with the time design, plans for movement and visualizations of the moving image remain in the imagination and memory. Not until rehearsal, which usually occurs immediately before the recording of the image, does movement become a reality.

As he creates his spatial design, the director is alert to the elements of visual design that are capable of movement and change. Colored lights, filters and paint can vary the colors of all or part of the scene, and, if desired, color can be made to change during the scene. Through blocking actor and camera movements, line and mass relationships within the frame can be manipulated. Tone can be changed by adjusting all or some of the lighting or the camera, or by selecting part of the illuminated scene to photograph. The illusion of depth can be emphasized or minimized, by the way the camera is set up and used, by use of architectural features of the set, by varying the lighting of the scene, or by blocking the action relative to the camera, and also through use of sound perspective.

Although the spatial design is created simultaneously with the time design, the two have different characteristics. The time design is always oriented toward the completion of the story. Smaller units of composition in the time design have no meaning in themselves. Their meaning, like all moments in a continuum, lies in the fact that they are going somewhere. The total experience is what counts, and the nature of that totality is not apparent until it occurs. As in a symphony, where the only tone that makes the "whole" of the symphony is the last tone, it is the last moment in a film which defines the cumulative whole of the time design.

Spatial design, on the other hand, is oriented toward the whole in a different sense. Here the whole is the instant, the immediate visual and spatial experience of the audience apart from any time dimension but related to the experiences which precede and follow. This is the meaningful unit in the spatial design. Its impact results from intensity and from its place in a flow of action, rather than from accumulation.

Visualizing

The spatial design begins with the process of visualizing, which, in film directing, is creating in the mind the images in motion that will carry the film idea. Because of the number of variables available in forming the spatial design, a few of which were suggested above, the visualizing process is complex. The script must become images and sounds, intricately interrelated. This is more than translation. It is, as was the time design, a transformation.

Beginning with the plan or idea, the same principle applies in making the spatial design as applied in the time design: the principle of no quantitative relationship between printed words or sketches and filmed images. In the script, some descriptions occupy much space. Within the film, what they describe may be conveyed in a glance. Abstractions and ideas which the writer is able to communicate economically in verbal form may be difficult to convey visually. They can be suggested visually only indirectly, by inference. Pictures, particularly photographed pictures, tend to have specific meaning. They are pictures of things. Unless distorted optically, or produced graphically, their literal meaning tends to override their symbolic significance. It is only when they are combined (juxtaposed) that they begin to take on the quality of abstraction. Concepts, abstractions and generalizations, the substance of much verbal communication, can be inferred but they cannot be seen or heard. The specific, the special, can. In a film, showing one mother with her dead child in her arms is more effective than stating that a thousand died. The image is filmically comprehendible whereas the statistic is not. Using a shot of a bulldozer pushing over dozens of bodies from a large heap into a common grave, as Resnais does in *Night and Fog*, shows unforgettably the magnitude of murder undertaken in German concentration camps. With such a shot, there is no need to say how many died. Those whose bodies we see far outnumber a rounded-off, abstract figure such as six million.

Even simple, lower level abstractions can make visualization difficult. The words, "George felt sorry for Gladys," for instance, represent a fairly low level of abstraction, but nevertheless one which, should they appear in a script, must be conveyed in the terms of images and sounds. One solution might be to have George say, "Gladys, I feel sorry for you," and if the line were delivered by an actor with some skill, the audience would hear and be affected by the words. But what if the story could not be interrupted at that moment for this kind of declaration, or what if George is not conscious of his feeling for Gladys? Then visual and spatial means would have to be used to convey the idea. In the composition of the shot or shots, in the spatial relationships established between George and Gladys, and in the movement of both the camera and the actors, the director would suggest that George felt some emotion toward Gladys, and this emotion was something like sorrow or pity. In the context of other shots, the "feeling sorry" experience would impress itself upon the audience.

This extremely simple example of what is sometimes a complex problem is simple because both George and Gladys are real objects existing as themselves within the picture. Only the words "feel sorry" are abstractions. Higher level abstractions hopefully would never appear in a shooting script because the writer would have gone at least part way in translating such ideas into specific sounds and images. Often an abstraction will appear in a script as a description of an actor's attitude or a clue to characterization or line delivery:

> CLOSEUP. Ross' reaction to the Defense Counsel. From the lieutenant's silence, Ross knows that his sentence has been confirmed.

> MEDIUM SHOT the Defense Counsel. He seems depressed and stunned and does not know what to say.

At other times, abstractions may be used as descriptions of environment:

> MEDIUM SHOT. Ross approaches the camera and sits down on a rock to rest for a moment. The afternoon sun is warm and Ross is sweating. Callahan gestures grandly toward one leg of the fork, the prettier of the two. It is lined with trees and has the appearance of a peaceful country lane. The road appears to lead to the mountain, which is in the distance and directly beyond it.

Abstract concepts such as these do not present the director with any great difficulty. Neither does any problem arise with the abstract concept which is embodied in action:

> FULL SHOT. The members of the Court Martial have gathered outside the courtroom (Blake's office). The trial is about to begin. The men are talking informally with one another—the meeting has something of the atmosphere of a social gathering. Everyone but the Colonel is there. The officers are gathered around Blake, who has just said something amusing—at least the other officers laugh. Blake glances at his watch as Sackett enters the room. When Sackett enters, all attention immediately turns to him as the officers salute.

The atmosphere of the scene is clearly suggested. But what is more important, the relationship between key members of the gathering (the character called Blake, the one called Sackett) and the others is made visible, described in terms of action, with such phrases as ". . . who has said something amusing—at least the other officers laugh" and "all attention immediately turns to him [Sackett] as the officers salute." The hierarchy of authority is established by appropriate and briefly described gestures.

But abstractions of one level or another will occur. Wherever the writer has failed to visualize his story completely, or wherever he attempts to describe non-verbal concepts with words, or to suggest other-than-verbal qualities he hopes the film will have, or where the director wishes to change the writer's images—in these cases the director must reduce ideas to action.

Synthesizing

Designing images that contain the spirit of the film idea or script is the first part of the visualizing process. Since these images are to be staged in a specific three dimensional location, creating and defining the boundaries and contents of this location and planning the relationships of actions and symbols within it becomes the next step in creating the (fig. 9) spatial design.

Fig. 9. Setting, action, significant properties and camera angle complement one another in a simple, harmonious, memorable moment. [The Bed, *James Broughton*.]

Fig. 10. Identical camera angle and actor movement, but the change in environment gives the viewer a completely different impression.

The spatial environment of the action consists of the set or location, its decor and properties, and the actor's clothing and make-up.

In elaborate production situations, the physical design work is performed either by or under the supervision of a production designer, or art director, as he is sometimes called. In less elaborate situations, the locations, costumes, and properties are planned and selected by the director. In either case, the determining factor in making and selecting them is the script idea, and the needs of the film story as interpreted by the director.

Words such as "place," "location," or "set" or "setting," often used in scripts, imply more than simply "space in which to work." Setting is environment, atmosphere and mood which acts upon the action occurring within its boundaries. Made out of elements of form, structure, color, ornamental detail, properties and lighting, this environment for action is physically static but psychologically dynamic in its relation to the action. It modifies any action occurring within it, so that the same action, performed in two different locations is in effect two different actions. Obviously the environment affects action in quantitative matters of physical size and pattern of action (fig. 10). But there is a qualitative effect also. A kiss in a church is not the same as a kiss in the train station, even though the characters involved may be the same. Audience response is conditioned by what it expects in an environment (fig. 11).

Any two environments differ from one another, even though they seem similar. Again, the differences are both qualitative and quantitative. The size and height of the room, state of repair, amount of light, and condition and variety of furniture all affect action, because their appearance and total effectiveness evoke emotional reactions in the viewer and lead to different expectations as to what kind of action might occur in such a place. Such expectation can be used to reinforce the action of the scene by staging expected action, or it can be used to contrast and surprise or to counterpoint, by staging unexpected action. The brutal beating in the antiseptic, efficiently organized prison communicates a different meaning than the same beating in a dirty, poorly kept jail. An example of this environmental effect upon audience understanding of action occurs in *Open City*. The German commander's office lies between two other rooms, one of which is a drawing room where German officers relax amidst laughter, piano playing, elegant crystal goblets, chandeliers, and lush rugs and furnishings. To the other side of his office is a small torture room where the crucial event of the film takes place with the death under torture of one of the major characters. During one of the scenes of torture (which are never actually seen by the audience, the effects of torture being heard and the type of torture suggested by the reactions of other characters), the German commander walks through his office as the sounds of torture are heard in the background, and enters the more delicate sounding atmosphere of the drawing room where soft voices, tinkling of glasses and the piano can be heard. The juxtaposition of the two environments adds a dimension of brutality characteristic of the individual, and gives some insight into the culture from which he came. None of this would probably have been evident had the action taken place in an ordinary prison.

The soldier on the front lines reaching towards the butterfly in *All Quiet on the Western Front*, the ironic Christ figure traveling by modern helicopter over Rome in *La Dolce Vita*, traveling by bed down the streets of London in *The Knack*, arguments about creature comforts in the middle of an empty ocean in *Lifeboat*, intoning a Biblical phrase as the painter tries to capture some sort of "reality" in *Odd Man Out*, the unexpected eruption of violence of the St. Valentine Day's massacre in *Some Like It Hot*—all actions seeming out of place in the environment in which they were presented, were given a strong element of irony by virtue of their relationship with the environment. Whether the action or the environment was first to be conceived by the director is immaterial. The actions gained increased effectiveness because of the surroundings in which they were set.

After the basic mode of action has been planned, determining the environment of that action and the relationship of the environment to the action accomplishes the next step in the visualizing process. The environment may be a designed and constructed set, or a carefully selected location, or just an image of a setting built up in the audience's mind through selection of details of existing locations, so photographed and cut together as to seem to be an actually existing place. It is within the physical restrictions of this selected environment that specific actions are performed which tell the story. These physical restrictions—real space with real human beings moving within it—are the beginning point. Mass, line, color, tone and depth, the

D

Fig. 11. Physical similarities between these two settings are outweighed by their differences: they differ in mood and in possibilities for action within them. [Sand Pebbles, *20th Century-Fox*.] [Goldfinger, *United Artists*.]

components of design, are manipulated within this environmental boundary. This visual and spatial design is achieved out of physical elements available to the director, the dynamic force of the actor and such mundane things as windows, chairs, shadows and spoons, each of which conveys meaning according to its relation to and effect upon the action.

TRANSMUTATION

At this stage in the development of the film from the film idea or script, visualizing has progressed to the point where the basic action has been determined and the sequence of action among the several shots has been outlined. The environment of action has been synthesized. So far, the work may have been accomplished with minimal reference to the problem of filming itself, although most practiced directors work with the camera in mind. The problem of channeling the visualized environment into the camera lens now remains, and that lens must be placed at the best point in space relative to the action (the point from which the most meaningful action will occur) and the relative movements of action and camera must be planned. Such planning involves the three elements of composition in motion, scene (set, actors, action), the camera's view of the scene, and the movement of the camera and the action relative to one another. However tenuous or vaguely noted these plans for transmutation may seem, the execution of the plan must be exceedingly exact. Changes from the planned action typically occur, but the necessity for a complete plan, a completely thought out idea, still exists. With a complete (but flexible) plan, the director has a goal, some indication, at least, of the film as he imagined it before shooting began. Without such a plan, the danger of forgetting and/or being distracted from intended effects is always present. It is one matter to act, to have thoroughly considered the consequences of various choices of action, to select one and to discard it later for another; it is quite a different matter never to have considered consequences, but merely to react to the particular condition in which one finds oneself. In the case of film making, this condition is almost always charged with human problems, technical failures and financial deficiency. Film ideas often must be realized in spite of, rather than because of, the situations in which they are produced. For these reasons, the director must anticipate problems which might arise. The plan he creates must allow for correction of any miscalculation, or for minor change in intended meaning. Variations from the previously conceived pattern can be important, but usually are minor, adjustments and corrections, and only rarely need the design be reformed part way through the project. The shooting stage is no time in which to rethink the needs of the film idea and it is a rare director who has enough time, money and human and technical resources to do this. Rather, the shooting stage is approached with a basic plan of action in mind, and perhaps partly on paper. With such a starting point, the whole of the idea will not be lost or dissipated in the exigencies of the shooting situation.

There are stylistic variations between different directors in the approach to shooting. Some directors "block," or lay out, their action first, and then fit the camera to this action. Others plan camera first, shaping the action for the camera. Others, again, plan the two simultaneously, working with a concept of "action" which includes the combined effect of action of the actors and action of the camera.

Actor and camera action is often compounded for increased emphasis; at other times no overt action, either in the scene or with the camera, is used. The factors influencing such decisions about action are intangible. A sense of the dramatic, aesthetic and personal taste, the relationship of the scene to the story, the over-all design, the need for points of emphasis, and many other variables directly or indirectly determine what the completed film will be like.

COMPOSITION IN MOTION

Visual composition for film is continually changing. Objects within the scene move in one or more of the three dimensions of space or, the camera moves in relation to the scene in one or more of the three dimensions. Often these two events occur simultaneously. And even if there is no apparent movement of camera or action, there is still the implied movement which occurs between shots—within the cuts, fades, dissolves—and the sense of change which inevitably occurs as the composition is watched by the audience in time. The active quality of the relationship between objects, events and people in time gives the composition meaning, and all the elements of the scene are potentially active—even those which in life are considered inanimate: setting, light and set dressing for instance. The properties of change—tempo, rhythm and pattern—hopefully always lead toward the film's goal.

Because of its inherently dynamic nature, film composition is so potentially expressive, so powerful, that some directors feel that other parts of their work are relatively insignificant. And yet for this they must usually depend upon another person who operates the camera while the shot is attempted. One extreme reaction to this dependence of director on the camera operator was expressed by von Sternberg:

> There are some directors, among whom I am numbered, who can photograph their own films. Personally I have often preferred to work without a photographer, and where I have worked with one, he has used light and position of camera with precise instruction from me, even when he afterwards accepted "Academy honours." I find it wastes time to instruct in something which I can equal with little effort, and therefore have com-

bined the technical function of director and cameraman to the intense disgust of the companies I have worked for who have repeatedly challenged me to stop "fooling" with the camera.

This "fooling" with the camera saves time and energy, as otherwise director and cameraman must outguess each other and waste valuable effort in synchronizing their work.[13]

Whether or not such an extreme position is justified, von Sternberg's feeling for what a director is attempting to get on to the screen and to his audience through camera work is important.

The number of variables at work in the dynamic composition of a film make it exceedingly difficult not only to devise rules which insure success, but even to make generalizations which can be accepted without question. The problem can probably best be approached by assuming that for each shot there is some "best" composition within the context of the meaning of the sequence and of the film. Guidelines can be used to reinforce flow and can be violated when it is necessary to interrupt flow. Although generalizations about the intrinsic meaning of compositional forces are usually valid, any director is free to give his own meaning to such forces, *if* he can do so successfully. In other words, "anything goes," anything, that is, that in the final version of the film achieves the audience reaction desired.

Also, in a larger sense, all film composition is intrinsically dynamic. The idea includes both the dynamics of the filmed material and the resultant series of kinesthetic responses induced in the audience by the images. In life, and in film, an event is described as dynamic if its effect is one with vigor, force, and power. Yet it is obvious that all film compositions are not equally dynamic, that, in fact, many seem to impart a feeling of stillness, quiet and momentary pause. These are described as "static," but the term is used to imply only a relative difference. A static film composition is not a lifeless or dead composition; it is not made of components at rest and is not a fixed thing. Rather, it is a situation in which the dynamic factors are for one reason or another momentarily in balance. It is more a temporary equilibrium of forces than a true rest. In the context of motion, however, it can imply peace, rest, or serenity. It can be as interesting and as effective as more active events, though in a different way.

This relationship between static and dynamic compositions accounts for much of the adaptation that is necessary in considering and using basic compositional elements. The idea pervades all thinking about use of line, mass, color, tone and depth in creating composition in motion.

LINE

In one aspect of statics and dynamics, the important consideration is the relationship between the line of movement in the action and the characteristic line of the background. Such movement can be contrary to or accord

Fig. 12. Horizontal composition from a relatively low camera angle so that sky and earth occupy approximately equal portions of the frame. [Sinful Davey, *United Artists.*]

with the basic line of the background material. Action which accords with the basic line (such as horses galloping over a desert) tends to be less dynamic than action against it (a rocket taking off from a desert) because the relationship is simpler and more direct.

In general, it is the predominating line relationship between action and scene which determines the static or dynamic effect. For example: the basic line of the background material may be horizontal, as an eye-level shot taken in the desert, field or ocean may be. Such shots, particularly if there is emphasis on the sky (a clear sky occupying a relatively large portion of the frame), tend to give a feeling of space and peace because of the stability of the basic horizontal line (figs 12, 13). The hero in *The Asphalt Jungle* finds his final moments of peace in the horizontal open grassland of Kentucky. Many of the long shots in *Giant* emphasized a predominantly spacious and stable feeling to life at the ranch, a feeling which was contrasted at other points in the story with close, more dynamic compositions revealing the inner turmoil of the characters. Movement across the frame, in the same horizontal direction, does not disturb this feeling. A horizontal movement of the camera (panning)

Fig. 13. Horizontal composition accentuated with silhouette lighting and modified by faint clouds and the block of figures moving on to the beach from the water. [The Russians are Coming, The Russians are Coming, *United Artists.*]

could intensify the effect. If movement should take place in a vertical direction, however, with the action moving from the top to the bottom of the frame, or bottom to top, a different effect would result. An element which could be used to reinforce or to contrast would have been introduced. A tilt could produce, for instance, an effect of massive solemnity or quietude, or, in another situation, the exact opposite, irony or surprise.

Vertical composition, in films as in architecture, gives the spectator a feeling of uplift, sometimes of vigor and strength, of solidity, and, if symmetrical, of stability. Vertical movement within the frame, a man climbing a tall stairway, a cat climbing a tree or a woman descending a stairway, can be reinforced by the composition, and the total effect may be one of dignity, sometimes nobility, of statuesqueness, of hope. Again, tilting may either accentuate or de-emphasize this feeling. Moving up the stairs and toward the unknown but promising future with Fellini's characters in *La Dolce Vita* and *Juliet of the Spirits* is reinforced by upward movements of the camera, or shots taken from successively higher points along the stairs. Movement across the basically vertical composition, particularly if the line of the object moving is itself horizontal, would produce a somewhat staccato effect. An automobile moving in front of a row of trees, such as in the final scenes of *The Asphalt Jungle*, gives the viewer the feeling that it is moving faster than when it moves past a field, because the speed of its motion can be measured with reference to the trees.

These two kinds of composition, the vertical and the horizontal, especially in their purer forms, are on the static end of the compositional scale. Diagonal and circular compositions, on the other hand, give dynamic effects, particularly when movement is diagonally across rather than diagonally with the background, or counter-rotational to a circular background.

These generalizations are not to be taken as "rules." The ways in which we, as an audience, respond to such compositions are in part the product of our observation of nature, and in part the result of association of ideas. Nature seems placid and powerful when it is characterized by horizontal or vertical lines. The calm ocean, the desolate desert or beach, vast fields or highlands often seem to mean peace and quiet. Stands of trees, tall buildings, a series of posts in a fence, all seem to offer stability and strength. Put them on the diagonal, defy gravity, and the dynamic or the unstable is introduced. The potential for movement, for change, for action is increased because of this instability, and our interest in the outcome is what helps give us the dynamic feeling. The churning, conflicting, diagonal movements of choppy water give this effect. The tree leaning before the fall, the fence about to fall give this effect. Thus the dynamic might be looked upon as the static unseated.

The extremes of static and dynamic composition, if they are used at all, occur rarely in any film, and then only for brief moments. The element of time is at work. The peace and calm of a horizontal composition can, if it is held long, make the audience restless with its monotony and its foreboding. The firm, stable, uplifting quality of vertical composition, unless varied, will depress rather than uplift because emotions can always sink from, as well as rise with, such composition. Diagonal movements, if sustained or particularly violent, can be confusing and upsetting. Excessive confusion results in loss of audience attention because the mind will not continue to focus upon what it cannot comprehend. The extremes in composition should be reserved for selected moments of particular emphasis and accentuation and moments of culmination. Elsewhere, variety and change, exploring and expanding the territory between the extremes, is usually more successful.

Mass

The second element which varies composition is that of mass in motion. Since the objects with which the director deals are almost always three dimensional he is continually confronted with effects, both predictable and accidental, of mass in motion. With film techniques the mass or apparent size of objects and their relationship to others can be changed at any time such change is desirable. This power is unique to the art. A closeup can make a small object appear massive on the screen because it magnifies its size in relation to the frame and to the objects around it. Even more distortion is possible when a small object is positioned near a wide angle lens. Foreground objects appear massive while those in the background very noticeably diminish in size with distance. Thus distortion of size relationships within the frame, as well as between shots, is possible. If the camera position is changed, then this distortion can be changed, and the small object can assume another scale in relation to its background and to the other objects in the scene. An object that was small in an earlier scene can assume great importance and can dominate the frame, while the formerly massive object can be made insignificant. With either the object or the camera in motion during the shot, the distortion can change before the viewers' eyes. This can produce powerful emotional response.

So flexible is the motion picture camera and lens system that, for almost all purposes, there are no limits to the distortion of mass that is possible. A beetle can appear massive in one shot, overpowering a large building shown in long shot in the next. In *Giant* an extreme long shot of a rider on a bucking horse is followed by a cut to an extreme close shot of the rider's heel digging into the horse's flank. The effect is violent and startling, principally because of the large size difference (and thus action difference) in the two shots. The horse is insignificant in extreme long shot. In close shot it becomes a violently moving mass of flesh.

Effects of mass are not only dependent upon the size of objects within the frame, but upon the characteristics of the scenic material as well. Scenic mass, like object mass, changes whenever the camera changes position relative to it. Once the camera has dollied past a massive pillar, for instance, it can no longer be seen and ceases to be important in the composition. Another scenic element may take its place, and still another as the camera continues to move.

This is one of the principal differences between filmic and theatrical composition, where scenic elements remain throughout the play. Pillars are always the same size in relation to human figures, and they cannot change size before the audience's view.

The same scenic elements are used in film, but they are not fixed elements, either in size, spatial relationship, or even color, line, or tone, because one or more or all of these characteristics can be changed, and can continue to change throughout the scene or throughout the film, if this fulfills the needs of the script.

In film, mass is not fixed. It is something to be manipulated from moment to moment as a means of emphasis, accentuation and communication of relationships.

COLOR

The emotional effects of color are well known. All human beings form associations with colors, and while the associations are not all identical, some associations tend to cluster around certain colors within any one culture. In Western society for instance, red tends to be associated with life, blood, vigor, love, violence; blue with coolness, placidity, valor, honesty, strength. Yellow is associated with sunshine, gaiety and cowardice; green with growing things, life, fertility and purple with nobility and sacrifice.

While most of these associations are vague and amorphous, and none of them could be proved to exist in any absolute sense, relative associations probably do exist and work upon audience feelings. If an audience were to see what appeared to be a virtuous young lady in the story dressed in a bright orange and red dress, for instance, it would probably tend either to be suspicious of her, or to believe that there was more to her character. If she were dressed in pale blue or white, no conflict would exist in the audience's conception of her as a character and its visual image of her. Fellini uses a progressively brighter and more daring color scheme to give visual testimony to the spiritual growth of his heroine in *Juliet of the Spirits*. In the early portions of the film she tends to appear in white, whereas by the end of the film she has appeared in a vivid red dress and is moving toward a lush green landscape.

In such ways color can come to have a kind of symbolic activity in film. If color symbolism can be established within the context of the film, the director need not depend upon generalizations concerning color symbolism. But the element of color is seldom used to full advantage. Most of the objects within the scene are designed and colored by the production designer (with or without the directors' help) and have a color similar to their color in life. Even here control over color could be exercised by modifying the color of light which falls on them. This way, colored areas or colored objects can be manipulated differentially. The color of an object can even be changed during a shot by changing the color of light falling on it.

A whole scene can be given a certain color cast by filtering lights or camera lenses, or, later when the film is prepared for printing in the laboratory, by varying the printing light or filter pack.

When the power of color suggestion and color symbolism is taken into account, it is remarkable that comparatively little care has been given to color as an expressive device in films. Of the more recent attempts to use color consciously and expressively, *The Red Desert* and *Juliet of the Spirits* are notable. In *The Red Desert*, Antonioni resorts to artificial coloring of objects in the scene, whereas in *Juliet of the Spirits*, Fellini uses white not only for his heroine but as the predominating background. The settings, the costumes and the lighting reinforce the impression of whiteness. Into these are introduced various shades and intensities of color according to the specific character or the specific feeling of the scene. By providing himself with, in effect, a white backdrop, much as a painter is provided with a uniformly colored canvas as he begins to paint, Fellini has given himself the opportunity of calling attention to any color which is introduced into his otherwise monochromatic scheme.

Color has such power, and such a small change is necessary for distortion, that extreme care and taste must be used when modifying color for effect. For films more concerned with "realism" only minor changes in color are usually desirable. But color distortion is not something to be avoided just because there is danger of misusing it. Using it thoughtfully can result in a communication of feeling obtainable in no other way.

TONAL VALUE

The amount and distribution of light in relation to shadow and darkness, the relative tonal value of a scene, is a primary visual means of setting mood (figs 14, 15). Like other compositional factors, tone changes both between and within shots, particularly with camera movement toward or away from the scene. As the actor moves through the setting, the lights can be so fixed that he walks through areas of shadow and bright light. Tonal values are easy to manipulate when using black and white film, as lights can be dimmed, individually if required. Certain kinds of studio floor lamp are equipped with built-in rheostats which allow changes in light output. Other means of controlling light intensity are moving the lamp towards or away from the object being lit, or placing scrims or other filtering devices in the light beam.

Light intensity can be controlled and changed while the scene is being photographed, much as the lighting of a stage play can change from moment to moment to reflect the mood of the characters or to create an atmosphere for action. If necessary, the instruments themselves can be moved while the scene is being played.

The relative tonal values of the whole scene, or any part of it, or the relationships between one part of the scene and others can be planned and changed at will. In addition to simple intensity, there is the quality of light, its relative hardness (meaning light which casts a sharply defined shadow) or softness (often diffused or reflected light, the shadow from which is blurred or soft-edged) which can be used as an expressive element, especially with black and white raw stock.

Tonal value is often used to set the mood for a scene, sometimes a whole film. In *The Knack*, white walls, white ceiling and the white floor of an empty room, lit with sun shining in large windows, gives a sense of gaiety, almost of lightheadedness. Predominantly somber tones, many shades of grey, some black, but almost no white, are used in *Throne of Blood*, based on the Macbeth story in a setting of medieval Japan.

Fig. 14. Flat lighting and low contrast with a simple, uncluttered, diagonal composition accentuate the actor's struggle. Emphasis of earth instead of sky adds to the
effect. [Bed Sitting Room, *United Artists.*]

When using color film, tonal values are not so easily manipulated. The
lamps cannot be dimmed here because they change in color temperature as
well as intensity. This would upset the true rendering of color in the scene.
However, light reducing devices such as scrims can still be used to dim
individual lights and actor and camera placement can effectively modify
tonal distribution in the scene as a whole. Though the initial values of the
scene will in large part carry throughout (since the attention is largely
distracted by the presence of color), loss of the additional manipulation of
tone is probably not as great a limitation as would at first appear.

Depth

A film is of course two dimensional, even if the appearance or semblance
of three dimensions is achieved through special optical or stereoscopic
systems. Most directors elect to create some illusion of depth, probably
because their audiences live in a three dimensional world. Unless all human
actors and all ordinary objects are excluded from the scene, movement is in
a three dimensional space. It would be difficult, and would yield quite an

Fig. 15. Hard, sharp lighting and high contrast. A more complex diagonal composition seen through a vertical pattern from a low angle. The character moves diagonally within the frame. [Laughter in the Dark, *United Artists.*]

unnatural effect (though possibly interesting) to attempt to make real objects and human actors seem to move only over a two dimensional area.

Then too, most audiences are accustomed to seeing the semblance of reality and prefer to have their stories portrayed in three dimensional fashion. Film directors, therefore, in an attempt to increase the sense of credibility in their efforts, make use of the capability they have for portraying space and spatial relationships. They work in the opposite direction from two dimensionality, to accentuate the impression of three dimensional portrayal wherever possible.

There are several ways this can be done, over and above any optical effects which might be used to simulate the third dimension. The set can be designed so that it contains much space within in. High ceilings, deep corridors, stairways, windows looking out over exterior scenes and large rooms all tend to accentuate space. The cavernous interiors of the mansion in *Citizen Kane* were purposely accentuated to give the feeling of lush but overpowering emptiness. If necessary, and if no human actors are to appear in that part of the scene, portions of the set can be designed with forced perspective, increasing further the illusion of space. Using foreground objects or

Fig. 16. Foreground material not only accentuates depth but in this case adds
a circular "frame" to the composition. Compare with (Fig. 12). [Sinful Davey,
United Artists.]

shooting through windows or doorways emphasizes that the action is taking
place in depth. This object-in-the-foreground technique is often overdone,
and is particularly inappropriate when the object has no story significance.
But, for the occasional dramatic effect, shooting through openings or including objects in the foreground calls attention to the difference in size between
foreground and background objects, and thus emphasizes the space between.

Camera movement through a space adds still more to the effect because
the relative size of objects changes with camera movement much as it would
if a human being were walking through the set. Light which falls on the
action from the side and/or the back of the scene increases the effect of three
dimensionality, because highlights are thrown on receding surfaces.

Directing actor movement toward and away from the camera's view
further emphasizes the three dimensional illusion. Action vertically up and
down or back and forth does not contribute to three dimensionality, since
these are the two dimensions of the frame.

Use of sound perspective, variation in volume, quality and "presence",
further enhances the illusion of space. Low volume from an object in the

frame gives the impression that the object is either very small or far away—if the audience knows the object's true size, then interpretation will favor distance, and hence depth. A change in sound quality, in addition to sound volume, can increase the illusion.

Line, mass, color, tone, and depth, when used in the film composition, must all be conceived not only in terms of motion, but as a timed, two dimensionally photographed image. It is easy to forget, in the exigencies and distractions of the shooting situation, that the photographed image, not the real set or the real actors, is the means of visual communication with the audience. The world of production reaches an audience only as it can be portrayed through a camera lens, and then only in fragments. What an audience does not see, it cannot know, even if it lies vivid in the director's memory.

Spatial and temporal relationships obvious in life must be created anew by filmic means, with any change and distortion necessary to the meaning of the story. Real space and real time—in fact, real line, mass, color, tone or depth—have no meaning intrinsically. They assume meaning only as they are used to convey the idea of the film.

6

Internal Composition

FILM COMPOSITION ACTUALLY consists of two interrelated and inter-dependent aspects: internal composition, that is, composition within the frame, and external composition, the composition arising because each shot occurs in the context of other shots.

EVOLUTION IN CONTINUITY

As in other matters relating to film technique, long term stylistic differences have emerged, not only among individual directors, but with time. Speaking very broadly, the use of internal composition as the primary story-telling device tended to precede use of external composition. D. W. Griffith was using external composition early in the history of film, but in spite of his ability to use film techniques in this creative and dramatic way, other directors continued to accentuate the use of internal composition. They successfully used the camera in the two basic ways developed even earlier by Méliès and the Lumières: to achieve what seemed to be magical effects and to record action. Both of these methods characterized the work of many directors even far into the 1920s. In Chaplin's *The Gold Rush*, for instance, most of the action is staged in front of the camera, with the camera acting as observer of, never participant in, the action. There is very little use of a moving camera, although there are occasional follow shots where the camera moves slightly to keep a character in the frame. Not only was the camera relatively static, and the method of staging the actors in front of it simpler, but both camera and actors were used in a more elementary fashion. There was nothing inherent in the so-called silent film which demanded such an elementary approach—Eisenstein proved this when he created his elaborate silent montages. In the case of Chaplin's films, however, there was little need for external means of story-telling, since all the points to be made in the story happened within the shots themselves. Atmosphere, mood, tempo, story development, character development, were all presented to the camera. Lapses or changes in time and space, essential dialogue and gaps in continuity

112

were literally spelled out with title cards. External time had no need to exist. Time compression, rather than taking place between shots, could occur within the shot. In *The Gold Rush*, for instance, internal time compression takes place when Chaplin takes a drink, and then becomes intoxicated almost instantly. Again, in *Easy Street*, after sitting on a hypodermic needle, he reacts almost instantly to the shot of drugs. The techniques used in these films were appropriate to the ideas within them, to drawing attention to the internal incongruities of human beings rather than to the incongruities which exist in their relationships with one another. More "film technique" would have clouded, and could have destroyed, the characterization through action. Not only Chaplin's films and similar comedies, but more serious silent films— Dreyer's *The Passion of Joan of Arc*, for instance—emphasized the internal, rather than the external character of the action, giving it a concentration and intensity that, in the absence of sound, would have been difficult to obtain by other means.

More recent film styles have made extensive use of external methods of film making, with an emphasis upon the spatial and temporal relationships of shots, rather than upon their internal content. But regardless of which style of story telling tends to predominate, images are today never composed in film with regard only for their internal elements. No shot, no matter how important nor how carefully or beautifully executed, would ever be conceived except as part of a sequence (unless the shot *is* the film, as is the case with some of Warhol's films). Thus, the internal composition of any one shot is affected by the internal composition of the surrounding shots, as well as by the time factor. For the sake of clarity, elements of internal and external composition are treated separately in the following discussion. But in production no such distinction is made. Images are created for both their intrinsic and for their relative value, for their interrelated and interdependent qualities.

CAMERA ANGLE

Internal composition is achieved largely by choice of the camera angle which provides the most advantageous point of view at that moment in the film (figs 17, 18). To describe the intended shot to other members of the production team the director specifies the size of shot, the vertical position of shot, camera or subject movement, lenses and other special pictorial considerations which affect the content and nature of the final image.

The variables which affect the choice of camera angle are many. In a sense, each shot or situation has its own "best" angle, one place from which the action can be most effectively realized. Nevertheless, some of the factors affecting this choice can be mentioned, although these are by no means all such factors as exist.

Of course, physical restriction is the overriding limitation upon camera

Fig. 17. The extreme of stable, angular and still composition, achieved largely through choice of camera angle. Sharp focus, straight on camera angle and longer focal length lens increase effectiveness of the shot.

angle. Any shooting situation must be assessed in terms of this limitation before the camera angle is chosen, although if there is talent and skill among the operators, and appropriate equipment available, it is quite a broad limitation. In most situations (an exception would be where a wall cannot be moved), the camera can be considered able to move anywhere in relation to its subject, with any amount of speed, in any direction. When the situation to be photographed has been determined, and the physical limitations implicit in its setting have been assessed, then there is freedom to exercise judgment and taste in the matter of choosing camera angle.

Among the first factors affecting such choice is the location within the setting of the primary subject of the shot, and the relationship between subject, setting and story. Again the final shot of *Juliet of the Spirits* can be used as an example. Fellini places Juliet, dressed in a bright red dress, in an extreme long shot, where she moves away from a house (frame left) toward frame right which is filled with a tall and dense group of very green trees. His camera is at eye level. It moves slightly left to right with Juliet, thus excluding the house from the frame during the shot and emphasizing the trees. In the context of the story, the reasons for the choice of such an angle are clear. It

Fig. 18. Extreme of dynamic composition achieved through choice of camera angle with unstable, circular and moving subject-matter. The feeling of motion is enhanced not only by the high angle but also by the out of focus effect and the choice of a wide angle lens.

is the end of the story (long shot) and Fellini's character has found some sense of identity, an identity which, for Juliet, includes a recognition of her ability and desire for passion, for gaiety and for life. Hence the gentle move toward the lush greenery, supported by the camera's subtle but sympathetic move with her. A closeup would have made the change too violent.

To this first variable in the relationship between character, or subject, and setting is added the factor of continuity, which always underlies choice of camera angle. This continuity, of course, is affected by intercuts and inserts. The visual appearance of the preceding and following shots must be kept in mind, to make sure that the flow of action over a cut, or other transitional device, will be continuous in the mind of the audience.

COMMENT WITH CAMERA ANGLE

The interpretive power of certain camera angles, the "comments" that all angles, to a greater or lesser extent, make upon the scene being photographed, is another consideration. The subjective–objective relationship of the camera relates participant or observor to the scene and is a part of the relationship between subject, setting and story. In *A Place in the Sun,* the hero receives a call on a pay telephone in the hall of his rooming house. A typical angle to use in this scene would have shown the character fairly close and facing the camera so that the audience would be able to see his expression during the conversation—which is to bring him discomforting news. But the director reveals other elements at work in the scene by choosing to show the young man's back as he stands humbled before the telephone, taken in a long shot through a doorway from a point half way across his room. Instead of seeing facial expressions, the audience instead feels like an unwanted observor waiting in the room. It experiences the tense isolation of the long shot, the loneliness of the young man's back, the confused, hesitant shyness of his mumbled responses—all more effective than any facial expression could be.

SUSPENSE AND SURPRISE

Suspense and the gradual revealing of information, as well as spatial relationships, determine whether the scene should be photographed in long shot or closeup, from a low angle or a high angle or with a fixed or a moving camera. Part of the suspense of any situation in a film arises from this power to select only that portion of the subject which is to be emphasized at the moment, and to exclude from consideration other portions which are either unimportant, or which should be momentarily concealed. A shot in *Sunset Boulevard* is a famous example. Disregarding the usual method of story exposition, which would include a series of long shots, moving toward closer shots, and finally coming to rest on the subject to establish the scene, the director uses one medium shot of a dead man floating face down in a swimming pool taken from the bottom of the pool. It is startling and sensational, just as the murder was, the audience later learns. This shot immediately establishes the most important element in the scene while arousing audience curiosity.

TIMING SHOTS

Time enters into the choice of camera angle. If in the final film the shot is likely to be very short in duration, an extreme long shot generally will not be taken in by the audience in the same detail as a closer shot. An extremely close shot, on the other hand, if held on the screen only for an instant, may confuse the audience unless it has had some opportunity to adjust itself and see the shot in relation to the whole scene. Internal timing as well as external timing must be considered. The speed of a moving camera, the extremity of the angle, the amount of relative motion in the shot (motion of the subject in relation to the frame), static or dynamic qualities of the composition, and optical distortions of the lenses all affect the sense of timing as it appears in the final scene, and thus affect the choice of angle.

Mood, atmosphere and the psychological feeling of the characters all play a part in the choice, as well as the sense of form. This includes the desire for visual variety, the sense of audience interest, use of suspense, the need for clarification, the pattern of movement and progression in time, and psychological, as well as physical continuity.

The final consideration in internal composition is the moving camera. Often the camera is used to follow a mobile subject. The moving camera can change audience attention from one object in the frame to another, redirect its interest to something within the scene or allow material out of range of the first setup to be included in the shot. Any movement directly toward something leads attention to it, and movement in concert concentrates the audience attention on that movement. The director may wish to relate two objects. Panning from one to another will establish a firm relationship between the two. If the director does not wish to move too far away from the action, but wants more of it to be seen by the audience than would be contained in the initial camera setup, he might pan, tilt, or dolly. By moving the camera instead of cutting, he allows the audience to see more of the detail of the scene, and he maintains a close relationship between objects or actions.

Still another factor, although one which might be questioned, is the wish to relieve monotony of stationary shots. This, of course, assumes that stationary shots are by nature monotonous. It is true that they can be, if that is the intent, or if the director has failed to give them life and vitality. But to move the camera simply to be moving is the least acceptable reason for doing so. A camera angle grows out of, and is not superimposed upon, the scene. Buñuel.

> I've a horror of films *de cadrages*. I detest unusual angles. I sometimes work out a marvelously clever shot with my cameraman. Everything is all beautifully prepared, and we just burst out laughing and scrap the whole thing to shoot quite straightforwardly with no camera effects.[14]

The "Right" Angle

No director checks down a list of variables as he exercises the judgments and makes the evaluations necessary to choose what he feels will be the "right" angle for that shot. The experienced director working on the set approaches his subject in a personal, rather than a mechanical way. Anthony Mann comments:

> Wasn't it Lubitsch who said there are a thousand ways to point a camera but really only one? You can't find it in every shot, that's for sure. If you

can find it fifty per cent of the time you're very lucky; but if you do find it then the scene immediately plays. If it doesn't play, it's not only the writing, because the writing can easily be changed, but it's the set up of the cameras, their juxtaposition to the actors. This becomes an individual thing. It's a measure of your personality.[15]

It is to his sense of "story" that the director has recourse in choosing angle, more than to any verbalized or intellectualized plan. He wishes to make others see with his eyes. Through his experience and his over-all sense of form, he creates visions for others. Explaining how he works out camera positions, Preminger remarks:

I don't really do this according to any principle, or design. It is a thing that forms visually in my mind. It has usually to do, when I look back on it, with the essence of a scene. I never, for any reason, favor a star or a woman like some people do—because they think it is better for the audience. I try to use the camera to make the point of the scene; that is about the only principle I can tell you, so it always works out differently.[16]

At times the director will wish his audience to see the scene intimately and sympathetically; at other times an objective approach might provide the very sense of irony or counterpoint that achieves the effect desired. Preminger continues,

I believe that the ideal picture is a picture where you don't notice the director, where you never are aware that the director did anything deliberately—naturally he has to do everything deliberately. That is direction. But if I could ever manage to do a picture that is directed so simply that you would never be aware of a cut or a camera movement, that, I think, would be the real success of direction.[17]

The director may approach his action boldly or subtly, according to the quality of the action. He may be discreet or obvious, blunt or evasive. While there may be one "perfect" camera angle, seldom are there two angles which say exactly the same thing. If he is not completely certain that his choice is correct, or if he wishes to allow opportunity in the editing process to vary and manipulate the scene, then the director may decide on two, or perhaps three, angles from which to shoot part or all of the action. This decision may develop into a combination of carefully planned and directed, precise camera work with a rather spontaneous, serendipitous approach, such as Peter Brook describes in referring to his use of two cameramen on the film, *Lord of the Flies*:

If this particular story were to be caught on celluloid in the time and conditions available, I realised that I must put every penny we had into an unlimited supply of film stock. This meant that I could stop the gaps of time and money and children and everything else running out by keeping on shooting, speaking through shots, going back without cutting the camera. And at the same time there was a second cameraman, Gerry Feil, a man who worked for *Life* and was used to the routine of the morning story conference, who knew exactly what we were doing on the picture, down to the intention of every shot, but who worked with as much freedom as a newsreel cameraman. Through the official cameraman I would set up, say, a tracking shot; and without trying to go in for conscious compositions, all those futile bits of vanities that you will regret in the end, I would still be working to a precise pattern. This was, in other words, controlled shooting. At the same time this second cameraman would be scouting around, taking a set up which had been brought into existence by the director but trying to find other aspects of it which would fit. And the really interesting thing is that about a third of the picture, I suppose, comes from his material. You'd have said on the spot, while you were filming, that the fellow who's stuck away behind a tree, shooting from the back, couldn't possibly have got the really expressive moment. Then in the rushes you see that some particular hunch of the shoulders he's caught with his camera may be expressive enough; and in cutting you realise that the situation preceding the shot makes it so clear that the jerk of the shoulder is all you need at that moment.[18]

In this way, Brook was able to gain the advantages of good fortune and spontaneity without losing the absolutely necessary precision in development of the total film and achievement of the effect of the total story which he was telling.

A director, then, considers these things in setting up a shot: story motivation, logical physical placement of the characters, psychological motivation of the characters, the relative dynamics or effectiveness of one angle over another, continuity, the visual effect desired, the emotional effect desired, the editing plan and use of cutaways and intercuts, his sense of the form and structure of the story and the film, his feeling about how much of the picture should be revealed at any moment, his desire to change and vary the area of audience interest, the decision to use an objective or a subjective camera, the amount of time the shot will probably occupy in the scene, and the desire to establish or change the relationships of objects in space. This general list could be extended to include factors unique to the particular situation, but above all, the director must use his "dramatic sense" and "filmic sense." These are the things he must search for and cultivate: a sense of story and a sense of meaning.

Size of Shot

The terms describing size which are generally used in discussing or in calling for a particular shot are long shot, medium shot and closeup. This idea of "size" is a relative, not an absolute, unit of measure. The script might ask for, or a discussion of a shot might be in terms of, a "long shot," for example, a long shot of a person. In this case the size of the human figure establishes the unit of reference, and the term long shot would here mean a screen image in which the human figure would be small relative to the total compositional area, i.e. the subject would seem to be at some distance. On the other hand, a long shot of a desert might include an area twenty or thirty miles wide. Since the size designation of a shot is always relative to the subject of the shot, this same long shot of the desert could be otherwise described as a closeup of the earth.

Physical distance from the camera to the subject is not necessarily what is meant by the terms long shot, medium shot and closeup. Various combinations of camera distance and lens will give these effects. For example, a camera located at some distance from its subject could take a closeup with a long focal length lens. Conversely, a wide angle lens could give a long shot of an area fairly close to the camera.

EXTREME LONG SHOT

First in order of the "largest" to the "smallest" shots usually referred to in film is the extreme long shot. The effect given is of a subject at a great distance from the audience. Like the other terms, it is relative, since the camera-to-subject distance might vary from an inch to a hundred miles or more, depending upon the actual size of the subject and the lens being used. The cameraman taking an extreme long shot of a mite would find his camera perhaps one inch from his subject. If his subject were the earth on the other hand, he might find himself in a space ship. However achieved, in the extreme long shot the subject occupies a small part of the entire frame— exactly how small is a matter which varies from shot to shot, and from director to director.

The effect of an extreme long shot is to give a sense of the relatively insignificant size of the subject in relation to its surroundings. Often the importance of the subject is subordinate to its setting, which may, by comparison, seem grand or awesome. The extreme long shot establishes distant spatial relationships as well. Often it is somewhat static, since even the most violent movement of the subject is only distantly perceptible, and would proscribe only a small arc in a large frame. Peace, remoteness, the power of space or magnitude, scope—these terms describe the effects usually obtained from use of the extreme long shot.

LONG SHOT

There is no sharp dividing line in the progression of "sizes" of shots. As the extreme long shot subject comes closer, it becomes the long shot.

The subject is still small in the frame, but not so small as before. Thus the balance of interest between the subject and its surroundings changes, and the subject assumes greater importance, although not necessarily the major point of interest for the audience. Long shots are often used in the beginnings of sequences to show over-all spatial relationships. They are still sufficiently broad to show the whole area, and yet the audience is able to discern much more detail than in the extreme long shot. Subject movement is more noticeable than in the extreme long shot.

Often the long shot is used to "get away" from the subject—to disentangle the audience's emotions, to give a more objective view of the action, or to relate the action to its surroundings. The long shot, like all other shots, is affected by the shots around it; thus the long shot can have different meanings according to its placement in relation to other shots. Going from a long shot to a closer one gives the feeling of movement toward something, concentrating attention and interest on it. Going from close to long shot generalizes attention and directs it to the relationship between the subject and its surroundings.

Medium Shot

In the medium shot, the audience's potential interest is about equally divided between the subject and its setting. More detail, more concentrated attention and greater involvement, are characteristics of the medium as compared with the long shot. Though the audience can perceive more detail the larger spatial relationships of the long or of the extreme long shots are lost.

Often the medium shot forms a bridge between the extreme long shot, or long shot, and the closeup—since cutting directly from long shot to closeup can give an abrupt effect which might be undesirable.

Occasionally the medium shot is described as the "normal" shot, the view most people take of the objects around them. Actually, the human eye is in constant motion, and the "size" of what it sees is related to its focus of attention. As it ranges over its subject the eye, without changing the distance between itself and the subject, can "see" long shot, medium shot, or closeup because focus of attention shifts in the mind from the whole object to parts of it. When the eye, or mind, is interested in the object and its relationship to the things around it, it will "see" in long shot. (Actually the object of attention probably appears more as a closeup, but the awareness of peripheral vision includes a large compositional area.) When the eye, or mind, becomes interested in a detail, it will "see" something like a close shot, with a smaller compositional area. The medium shot, then, would be used when the attention is directed less intensely to the subject, and when showing the larger spatial relationships of the long shot would serve no immediate purpose.

CLOSEUP

With the closeup, the audience can see detail, feel involvement or experience subjective responses, and consider the subject independently of its
surroundings, as a separate entity. All but the slowest or most subtle movement is accentuated in the close shot. Even more, the whole subject of attention now is a detail of a larger subject. An emotional charge, whether it is an
emotion of love or violence or pity or hate, is implicit in viewing a closeup.
Nothing else matters but what is happening to that subject at that moment.

The effect is intensified in the extreme close shot, in which the audience
sees its most intimate view of the subject. All sense of time and spatial
relationship is lost. Sensuous audience impact is at its greatest.

VERTICAL POSITION OF SHOT

The vertical angle of a shot, as well as its size, is often included in a shot
description. Angle, in this case, refers to the height of the camera relative to
its subject. If no angle is specified, it can be assumed that a "medium angle"
shot is meant. However, this term is never used because it is a norm, some-

Fig. 19. The low angle blocks out distracting elements in the composition and
gives a feeling of potential movement and power.

Fig. 20. A low angle not only emphasizes the opening mouth, giving a sense of potential movement, but excludes unwanted background—the statue is set in the midst of other statues, shrubs, trees and plantings. Without outside reference, it is impossible to determine scale.

thing which is assumed to be desired unless excluded by the terms "high" or "low." With a normal angle the camera looks more or less directly at its subject across the intervening space. If a low angle is specified, the camera looks up at its subject; for a high angle, the camera looks down. In some situations, the adjective "extreme" might be attached to a shot description, as in extreme high or extreme low angle. How far is up, and how far is down? Here again, the terms are only relative.

Low Angle Shots

A low angle shot could be approximated to the view that a person gets when he looks up the side of a building as he stands a few feet from it, when he looks up at something falling on him, when he is lying on the ground looking up at the branches of a tree, or, if he is a small boy, the view he gets when he looks up at the figure of a man standing near him. This low angle view was used effectively in *Great Expectations*, where the boy, who thinks he is alone in the graveyard, suddenly discovers he is not when the camera

Fig. 21. Actor placement, low camera angle, and horizontal composition combine
to produce a simple but effective shot. [The Bed, *James Broughton*.]

takes a low angle shot of the menacing figure of a man standing over him.
Perspective, particularly of near objects, is distorted. There can be a sense of
being overpowered, subjugated (witness the straight up shot in *Rashomon*
when the "rape" occurs), dominated, in danger of being crushed, an insecure
feeling on the part of the person viewing the scene because the subject has
gained a power it did not have before. The effect varies, of course, with the
extremity of the angle. A low angle may be used not only to call attention to
some specific spatial relationship between camera and subject, but to exclude
unwanted or unnecessary background behind the subject—to frame him
against the sky or a ceiling, or a part of the set above him which should, for
the purposes of that shot, be visually related to him.

HIGH ANGLE SHOTS

Viewed from a high angle, the same objects which seemed so important
in the low angle can lose their power and dominance. Now the viewer is
dominant. Looking down into a valley from a high mountain, watching the
broad landscape from the window of a plane, looking down toward the street

from a window high on the side of a building, looking down at a small boy —these experiences are quite different from those shot from a lower position. With interiors the elevation of the high angle shot is, except in fantasy situations, limited by the real or imagined ceiling of the room in which the action takes place. Because the camera cannot physically separate itself from the subject to any great extent, this kind of shot tends to focus attention on some aspect of the interaction between the characters involved in the scene. An example is in Buñuel's *Belle de Jour*. The heroine's first experience in a brothel is shown with a high angle shot in which her fellow workers, along with a customer and the madam, are arranged rather awkwardly around a room. The previous lower angles gave the impression of little more tension than an ordinary cocktail party. When the camera moves to the high angle, however, the awkwardness of the heroine's feelings, her uncertainties and her sense of artificiality, tend to be emphasized.

In exterior scenes the almost limitless high angle can often not only show larger spatial relationships between various characters in the film, or emphasize the loneliness of a single character, but relate the character or characters to the surrounding territory. Whether made from a conventional studio crane or a helicopter or low flying airplane, the high angle exterior shot can provoke a sense of unity and identity between characters as a group, rather than as individuals, and their environment. The impression given is that the character or characters are either more imprisoned or more at one with their surroundings. The low angle exterior shot is of course of a much more limited nature than the high angle exterior. In effect, the high angle shot has no top, while the low angle shot is limited by the earth's surface. Thus generally there is no greater difference than five feet between a normal angle and a low angle shot (unless the subject itself is elevated), while that between a normal angle and a high angle exterior shot may be several hundreds of feet, or even more.

In *M*, Lang repeatedly uses high angle shots for varying effects. A conventional use of the high angle occurs when the man who is talking to the little girl is approached by a much larger man who accuses him of being a child molester. There is a series of interaction shots between the two men, the accuser being seen from the abnormally low angle perspective of the accused, the accused man seen from the high angle perspective of the accuser. Lang again uses a high angle shot when the paper bag, an important clue to the fate of the little girl, is found. In the scene, the high angle shot not only allows Lang to do away with the necessity of having a large set in the background (since the camera sees mostly the ground), but it gives a sense of the over-all activity of the police in searching for clues to the child's disappearance. As the narration picks out the person in the scene who is finding the clue, the audience can observe the total activity in the area. Shots of an underworld gathering are likewise taken from a high angle, paralleling them to the related high angles showing a number of police raids.

Fig. 22. A high angle gives the city environment a dominating effect over the human figures, which seem small and insignificant by comparison. The semi-vertical composition directs attention down to the bottom of the frame. [Stolen Kisses, *United Artists*.]

OBJECTIVE-SUBJECTIVE ANGLES

Choosing the angle of a shot sometimes involves an additional decision which need not be made in choosing the size of a shot. The size of a shot determines, at least in part, the camera-to-subject relationship; it is implied in the shot designation. This relationship is *not* implied in the vertical angle designation. Whether the angle is low, medium or high, the shot description should suggest camera attitude toward the subject.

An objective camera puts the audience in the position of an unseen but interested observer who is in an ideal position to witness the action. A subjective camera puts the audience within the scene in the place of a character. Often the subjective camera is indicated in the script as a "POV" or "point of view" shot, where the camera takes the point of view of a character or object in the scene. With a subjective camera, the audience is no longer spectator to the action, but part of it. The actors within the scene are aware of the camera and react to it as they would to another character. The camera is limited to whatever viewing position the character could take. Camera-as-camera has been used as a particular form of subjective camera: the camera may not be identified specifically with any character in the action, but may frankly be a camera which is present when the action is being played—without the fiction that it is a "character" or an "audience." In *The Connection*, the characters in the film refer to the camera directly, not as another character, but as something else (whether their reference is to the camera or to its operator is not clear). In one scene, the paraphernalia associated with filming, lights and cables, are even allowed to appear in the final film, seemingly to give evidence that the characters of the film knew they were being filmed.

Generally in making a film, the camera is used both subjectively and objectively. The subjective camera is often used for special effects or moments of emphasis, or when it is desirable to involve the audience in the action. In *The Quiet One*, many of the shots showing the slum life of the disturbed child are taken straight-on from the child's eye level, thus giving a sense of seeing that portion of the world the child sees. Even when the child is included in such shots, a semi-subjective effect is obtained.

When the change is made from a subjective to an objective camera, or vice versa, some motivating device usually eases the transition between the two shots that have differing frames of reference. One way of making this transition is to take a shot of the person with whom the camera will be identified, and then take that person's point of view of the action in the next shot. Another way is to include a shot of an inanimate object to which the subjective camera is directed. The audience does not readily identify with an inanimate object, and thus looking at the object can become a means of softening the transition between these two uses of the camera.

For the shots described so far, the subject has been considered as generally facing towards the camera with the camera shooting towards the subject. If, however, the subject is in the foreground of the picture, and for the most part turned away from the camera, the result gives the audience a different impression. The effect of having the subject in the foreground of a shot and facing the action (when the camera shoots past the subject), is to give the camera a subjective power, allowing the audience to see the scene as the subject sees it, without the camera actually taking the place of the subject. Audience attention is now divided between the person in the foreground watching the scene, and the scene activity in the background, which the audience views directly. To see a low angle shot of a tall man gives one feeling; to see a low angle shot of a tall man, from over the shoulder (or overshoulder) or a small boy gives another. The audience sees the tall man as if it were the small boy seeing the man. Whatever emotions the subject has will be shared by the audience more intimately than might otherwise be the case.

The overshoulder shot can be, and most often is, used from the medium or normal angle. While audience involvement is not as great as with the low and high angle, there is still an increase in subjective feeling. This increase in feeling is enhanced when the characters are in conversation or are moving relative to one another, and the background character refers his speech or action to the foreground character. Once this relationship is established, effectiveness can be increased even further by going a step beyond and replacing the foreground character with the camera (subjective camera), so that speech and action are referred directly to the audience. Care and taste must be employed with this kind of subjectivity, as the audience can tire when it feels put "on the spot." It can become anxious, restless or even make a sudden mental change to a completely objective viewpoint. In the latter case, a serious scene might suddenly appear comic, or a comic scene dull.

One variation of the overshoulder shot has the actor facing the camera instead of the scene. If the actor is aware of the scene behind him, this variation tends to give the feeling that the actor is alienated from some element in the scene. It establishes a psychological disparity, or isolates that actor from other characters in the scene. This shot gives a feeling of counter-involvement and sometimes of conflicting involvement. The actor has turned his back on the scene both physically and psychologically. The result is conflicting involvement because the audience still wants to identify with the actor, and yet also be involved with the scene beyond. The audience must make a decision between the two; the conflicts inherent in its decision-making can be used to establish or intensify feelings of psychological conflict between characters in the story.

If the actor is not aware of the scene behind him, then an entirely different effect is obtained as far as the audience is concerned. The alienation and isolation effect still exists, but now it is accidental or incidental, and not purposeful from the character's standpoint. Since the audience can see what is happening beyond the actor, it assumes an almost supernatural point of view, a feeling of omniscience, because it knows what is going to happen when the actor does not. Identification with the actor continues, but now the audience sees the entire scene with both subjectivity and objectivity.

Another way to use the camera subjectively involves camera movement. The most familiar example of this is the man standing on a mountain and looking over the landscape. The initial camera setup is made as an overshoulder shot; the actor turns his head as he looks over the broad expanse before him. Then the camera moves in imitation of the actor's eyes, or head —across the scene, sometimes to the extent of panning off the character onto the landscape itself. With such a setup, the audience gets the impression that it has replaced the actor, or, at the least, that it is standing next to him and looking at the scene in exactly the same way as he does. For the next few shots, the audience tends to retain its subjectivity, until such time as the actor is again included in the frame, whereupon the audience will resume an objective view of the action.

Increased use of a subjective camera is characteristic of some film makers, particularly those whose films center on a character's perception of reality. In this use, the camera more often takes the view of one or two of the characters within the scene than it does the view of an onlooker. Often it is a fantasy or memory view, rather than a direct observation of reality.

The element of subjectivity–objectivity is an elusive one. Usually the effect is not noticed until, through some error or special effect, the audience becomes conscious that the camera is always looking at the action from some particular point of view—as a disinterested or interested observor, as a participant in the action or as a character in the action. Although films have been made with all subjective or all objective points of view (*Lady in the Lake* experimented with an all-subjective experience), usually some combination of the two is used.

CAMERA MOVEMENT

When camera movement enters into the matter of internal composition, it becomes effective not only because of the movement itself and its results, but because of the continually changing viewpoints of the action. Shots containing camera movement tend toward the dynamic because of this. Depending upon the combination used, the effects can intensify, amplify or weaken what had been achieved when size, angle and subjectivity factors had been determined. In shooting, camera movement has the power to change all of those aspects of camera potential previously mentioned.

Camera movement may be simple, in one dimension, or compound, combining two or more of the dimensions. A tilt is a simple camera movement in which the camera is moved or pivoted in a vertical plane. During the tilt, the angle is changed from high or medium or low to some other angle. As with any camera movement, the effect of the tilt depends not only upon the successive views the camera sees, but the relative speed of the camera as it moves through its viewing arc. It depends as well on whether the tilt is in an upward or downward direction, and it varies with the subject and the audience's attitude toward that subject.

POTENTIAL OF THE TILT

A slow tilt can give the audience the feeling that it is carefully examining the subject of the tilt, particularly if the camera is being used subjectively or semi-subjectively. Not only the feeling of examination, but expectation results from this use of a tilt. Once the camera starts to move, the audience senses that there is more to the scene than it can immediately see: curiosity, suspense and expectation are increased. When the tilt is obviously nearing its end, expectation turns into a feeling of culmination, as if something were going to be accomplished. The tilts up to the mountain to be assaulted by advancing troops in the war documentary *The Battle of San Pietro* seemed to predict that eventually the mountain would be captured. The audience

E

experiences a feeling of accentuation or increase—increase in power perhaps, an increase in fear, but always the feeling of leading to something. Toward the end of *Planet of the Apes*, the camera tilts slowly up what seems, at its base, to be a jumble of wave washed rocks. But as the camera continues to move up, it becomes clear that the rocks are remnants of a great carved statue, the identity of which is revealed in the goal of the tilt, the final image which includes the upraised arm of the Statue of Liberty. The final bit of effectiveness derives from the importance which is attached to the view upon which the camera finally comes to rest. This final framing gains significance because it appears to be what the tilt was looking for.

Often the upward tilt gives a sense of increasing the area of scene to be viewed, as if the audience were going from a smaller to a larger view of the subject. There may be an expansion if the composition opens out on the top of the tilt, or a compression, entrapment, if it closes over. Most of the effectiveness of this kind of tilt is derived from the fact of movement followed by stillness. The movement is interpreted as anticipatory, with the still scene at the end as the objective.

Still other effects are made possible by tilting, stopping and then continuing the tilt. With this kind of camera action, audience subjectivity tends to increase. The audience has the feeling of being a participant in the scene, rather than an impartial observor. If the script called for a shot of a bombed out building, for example, one way the director might achieve this effect would be to use a slow tilt, start at the base of the building which might look comparatively normal, continue the tilt up until the first signs of damage appeared and then stop the camera to allow the audience to see the damage. The tilt could then continue slowly up the building until the camera was looking through the shell of the building to the sky above. This kind of movement, stopping, and then further movement has a cumulative effect upon the audience. The stopping points are added up, one by one, and the final view of the scene contains not only its own, but the accumulated significance of all that was seen before. A similar, but not identical effect, could have been obtained with an extremely slow but steady tilt up the building—the speed being inversely related to the sense of expectation—and would still have allowed the audience to catch images as the camera moved.

Tilting, stopping and tilting can be used for comic effect. Taking a girl as the subject, if the tilt began with her feet and travelled up her legs to her knees and then stopped, then continued to tilt to her torso, and then stopped, then continued to her face before its final stop, the camera would have "looked over" its subject much as an appreciative young man might. The slow, lingering quality of the tilt would be humorous now (since the subject is different), where it was increasingly tragic when used with the the bombed-out building.

A fast tilt up gives the audience a clear view only of the final stopping scene. Thus, much of the cumulative effect of the tilt is lost, but it is replaced by the effect of vigor and drive resulting from the speed. The fast tilt has punch, surprise, suddenness, a kind of startling effect which is absent in the slow tilt. The material viewed within the duration of the tilt is unimportant, because it cannot be clearly seen. What is important is the final moment. It is, in fact, more important than if no tilt had preceded it. The effect of a fast tilt is akin to that experienced in life when the eyes are quickly moved up or down to look at something. The drive of the movement coupled with the fixed quality of the final view gives the action power.

Whereas upward movement is associated symbolically with increase or uplifting if the shot is objective, or with a feeling of loss of power if it is subjective, a downward movement is associated with decrease, depression, pessimism in an objective shot, and gain of power in a subjective one. Just as speed and stopping accentuated the upward feeling, so speed and stopping accentuate the downward feeling. Slow tilting down gives a sinking, slowing, introspective, close feeling. Fast tilting down makes this sudden and sharp. Stopping allows the same kind of examination as in the upward tilt. The continuing composition along the arc of the tilt alters the impression also. To tilt down to an increasingly closed, crowded or boxed-in composition gives a feeling of compression or restriction. To tilt down to an open, free composition gives a feeling of broad peacefulness.

POTENTIAL OF PAN SHOTS

As with the tilt, the effects of the pan vary with direction, speed and stopping, and subject matter.

Direction of the pan, whether the pan shot moves from left to right or right to left generally has little significance for the audience. However, one theory is that most people in the Western world, when they first glance at a sheet of paper (or at any rectangular, flat object) tend to glance toward the left side of the object first, rather than to any other point. They theoretically tend also to glance toward the upper part of the rectangle rather than the lower part. The supposed reason for this is that the ordinary printed page begins in the upper left-hand corner in Western linguistic groups, and that is where the viewer has been conditioned to start his search for information. When he looks at a picture, this strongly implanted response continues to operate momentarily, even though the information this rectangle contains may be somewhere else in the frame. If this theory has any substance, panning from left to right, or from right to left, may have a significance which is distinguishable from the subject of the pan.

A movement of the camera from left to right is therefore said to have more of a feeling of flow and continuity, more easiness and more sense of relaxation. Left to right pans are repeatedly used, for instance, in *Song of Ceylon*, together with left to right actor movement, to obtain a sense of tranquillity and unity. It is particularly true in the religious life section of this documentary, where there is an unusually effective use of camera movement, actor movement and optical effect to achieve a strong rhythmical experience.

Movement in the opposite direction, right to left, is, according to this theory, more disturbing, more inherently threatening, more foreboding, even if the movement itself is smooth and slow. It would be a mistake to believe that these are, without exception, mutually exclusive effects. There are many relaxed pans which move from right to left. But still the tendency remains, and if another effect is desired, countermotion by the actors, or other compositional factors, must be used to achieve it.

Changing the rate of camera movement in a pan affects the shot just as such changes affect the tilt shot. Slow speed allows intermediate effects, and can work toward a final, cumulative effect. Higher speed gives added emphasis to the resting spot. Stopping, just as in the tilt shot, increases the sense of audience involvement.

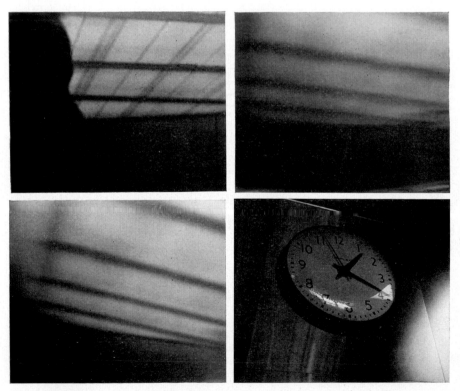

Fig. 23. Swish pans can be used to focus attention and increase tension in the sequence synthetically. The effect is achieved simply by panning the camera quickly off the subject to give a blurred image.

SWISH PAN

A special kind of fast pan is occasionally used—the swish pan, which is accomplished simply by panning the camera so quickly off the subject that the result is a blurred image. In the editing room this blur at the end of the shot is juxtaposed to the next shot with a cut (fig. 23). The audience gets the impression that the camera has "swished" away from one subject and is quickly focused on another. The cut itself is imperceptible. *A Time Out of War* opens with a series of peaceful, bucolic shots, slow pans and tilts and static shots of a river, of water flowing and birds flying. This calm is interrupted by the simultaneous sound of a shot and a swish pan, abruptly beginning the story. The effect is obtained by starting a tilt up from water running, then swishing abruptly away (10 frames), cutting to 4 frames of clear leader, and then cutting to the next shot which has on the head of it an abrupt (7 frame) swish toward its subject. This turns out to be a close shot of a soldier who has just fired his rifle. As a transitional device, or for shock effect, the swish pan can be effective, if carefully done.

POTENTIAL OF DOLLY SHOTS

The dolly, truck, crane or boom shot all produce essentially similar effects, although of different magnitudes. The dolly enables the cameraman to move short distances toward or away from his subject (and even completely around it, such as the 360° dolly around the gossiping girls in *The Group*). A dolly arm can also move the camera in limited arcs up and down and sideways. A truck extends the range of possible movement. The crane and boom go further, allowing the camera to make extensive excursions freely in all directions, including the vertical.

Dollying involves movement towards or away from, or around the scene. It may be a long movement or a short one. As in other moving shots, the direction of movement, speed and stopping, as well as the subject matter, combine to produce the final effect.

Movement toward the subject, depending upon the speed, gives the effect of walking or running toward it. Thus there is the feeling of approach, of expectation, of progression or movement toward the future. If the subject is stationary, there is added to this the changing effect of the size of shot. As the subject increases in size within the frame, all of the impressions associated with different sizes of shot come into play, but without risk of destroying the spatial relationships inherent in cutting to a closer shot from a distant one.

The same principles apply to movement away from the subject, which could be likened to backing away from the scene. The feeling of retreat, finality, regression or rest increases as the subject becomes smaller in the frame. Speed effects operate here as with other moving shots. A slow dolly away gives the effect of letting go of the subject, letting it pass away into the distance and of gradual disinvolvement, the reverse of a slow dolly in. Dollying away quickly gives a much more startling effect of recoil. Suddenly the scene becomes larger, more complex, with more detail and new spatial relationships. The quickness of the movement can be like the recoil of an animal from something which is distasteful or potentially harmful to it. Dollying quickly toward the subject reverses these and adds the sense of haste. It is vigorous, dynamic, positive. In the fast dolly in there is decisiveness and certainty as opposed to vagueness. The subject quickly becomes focused, specific, particularized as audience attention is directed forcefully to a specific area of the larger image.

Moving a camera from one portion of the scene to another, instead of cutting, can be a way of revealing information to the audience about the larger scene without risking disorientation with a cut. In addition, audience participation in a scene that is revealed before them continuously through time can produce an additional emotional effect.

An example in *Belle de Jour* illustrates how flexible and expressive the moving shot can be when it is sensitively related to the action being portrayed. In the taxi where the heroine and her friend are discussing the possible existence of houses of prostitution in Paris, the two women are seen in a medium shot riding in the back of a taxi. Throughout the conversation, which begins as they discuss a mutual friend who supposedly is working in one of these brothels on a part time basis, the camera continues in the relatively close two shot. At a point in the conversation where the two young women ask one another whether such houses do in fact exist, the camera suddenly pulls back as the taxi driver assures them that yes, they do exist. Having forgotten that of course there *is* a taxi driver, the viewer's reaction is one of surprise and amusement, a dimension that is added to the scene by means of camera movement alone. Still another example from the same film of the revealing effect of a moving camera occurs when the camera follows a young woman walking down the street and dollies and pans with her as she approaches a doorway. She opens the door and goes in. As the door closes behind her, the camera tilts up to show the house number above the door, a number that the audience has previously been informed is the number of a house of prostitution. Thus, after a brief period of curiosity and suspense, audience expectation is fulfilled.

In several places in *Viridiana*, Buñuel uses a fast dolly in to suggest the inner states of mind of the characters in the film. Early in *Viridiana*, the uncle approaches Viridiana's bed while she, terrified, pulls the covers under her chin. As the off-screen uncle approaches, there is a short, quick dolly in toward Viridiana, expressing some of her feeling of apprehension and terror at his approach. The movement is used again toward the end of the film, when the son first comes upon the debris of the beggars' feast. As in the previous shot, he is in medium shot and the camera makes a short, quick dolly in at the end of the shot to express his shock and dismay at the scene before him. Elsewhere Buñuel uses a slower dolly out to suggest, but not show, the completion of an action. When the son pulls the maid toward him in the attic of the house, he pulls her out of the camera's view as the camera dollies out past the odds and ends in the attic, as if searching for a place to lie down, moving slowly and uncertainly to imply an end to the shot that is never seen. In an identical way the slow dolly out is used as the last shot in the film. Viridiana is shown playing cards with the son and the maid as the camera dollies slowly out of the room and over the table where the beggars had their feast, again implying an end to the action that is never seen.

SCOPE OF TRUCKING SHOTS

The trucking shot, while it is very similar to the dolly, usually includes a large area and a more extensive movement of the camera. It has no limit. The effect is, in fact, similar to the effect an observor gets when he looks out the rear or side window of a moving automobile toward the traffic moving with him. What is more important is the differing relationship of the subject to the camera. Where the dolly shot often moves either with or against its subject, the trucking shot almost always moves with the subject. The subject does not usually change size within the frame since the camera-to-subject relationship remains more or less constant. Thus it gives a feeling of companionship not usually present in other moving shots. A trucking shot, often found in Westerns with shots of galloping horses, was used also with horses in the film version of Shakespeare's *Henry V*. In the battle scene, the camera makes a long and exciting trucking shot with the horse-mounted soldiers, starting out with relatively slow trots and gradually increasing tempo until they are at full gallop.

CRANE AND BOOM

Crane and boom shots may include a vertical movement in relation to the subject as well as movement toward or away from the subject. When the camera takes a full frame shot of a man standing in the middle of the street (a notable example is in *High Noon*), and then moves back and upward, away from the man, the shot was probably made on a crane. Had the same shot been made on a larger boom, the camera could have moved upward to a height equivalent to the second or third story of a building. This ability to rise or sink in relation to its subject, with or without a change of high or low medium angle, varies with the equipment being operated.

Some dollies have an hydraulically operated arm which permits limited movement up and down, usually from a low point of about two and a half or three feet to a maximum height of about six feet. Crane and boom arms, because of their greater length, offer greater height variations, some being able to rise as much as twenty or thirty feet. Whereas in tilting the camera pivots vertically about a point, in craning the entire camera body moves up and down. In doing so, it can maintain a head on, but rising or falling, view of its subject. Or it can tilt up or down while craning. In addition, the crane arm can be swung horizontally in a 360° circle in either direction. During this movement the camera mounted on it can pivot horizontally, or pan, in either the same or the opposite direction. Any of these movements can be combined.

COMPOUND CAMERA MOVEMENT

In fact, any of the effects achieved with simple camera movements (tilt, pan, dolly, truck, crane) can be and often are combined. Such compound camera movements increase the range and subtlety of the camera as a means of expression. Compound movements can be used sequentially within a shot: a pan, followed by a tilt, as described in a Buñuel example above. Or they can be used simultaneously, panning and tilting at the same time, or tilting up while dollying out. It is well to remember that not only are the movements compounded, but the effects achieved with them are compounded also. This compounding can take the form of reinforcement or of dissipation of effect, depending upon the combinations chosen. The complexity, as well as the nature and degree, of camera movement must be tailored to fit the individual needs of the shots being produced.

How compound camera movement can lend a flowing continuity to action, without monotony and without sacrifice of tension, is illustrated in Buñuel's *Viridiana*, notably in two places. The first is in the scene where Viridiana returns to the farm from the bus stop. The second in her conversation with the Mother Superior, when she decides not to return to the convent. The first example has almost no dialogue whereas the second is a heavy dialogue sequence.

In the first example, Viridiana (always moving from frame right to frame left) is shown waiting for the bus that will return her to the convent. As she is about to board the bus, the police tell her she cannot leave and that something has happened. The group turns to go. There is a cut to a car moving in medium long shot, not far from the house (intervening time has been deleted). Moving from left to right, it rolls to a stop as figures enter the left of the frame close to the camera. The shot continues as they move slightly toward the car and the camera moves slightly left to right. Still without a cut, several men get out of the car in long shot and move toward the camera, framed on the one side by the figures, leaving the right side of the frame open and thus indicating the direction the men will take. The men approach the camera, and the camera again moves slightly to the right as the figures approach and the men come into a medium shot. The men continue toward the camera and to the right and the camera continues to move to the right, thus almost seeming to draw them in that direction. As they continue, they draw close enough for the audience to see their facial expressions. Since leaving the car, their attention has been focused off the right hand side of the frame, which has been left open and indefinite. For a brief moment, the camera tilts slightly to emphasize their expressions and then swings suddenly away from them, toward the right, past the figures in the background, and finally across an empty space to a pair of feet hanging off the ground. The camera comes to rest on the feet and holds there to the end of the shot. The next shot is a static one, a medium shot of Viridiana, her head resting on the frame of the car door. She looks to the right of the frame, then lowers her head. The next cut is a close shot of the rope round the uncle's neck, the handles of the rope at the bottom of the frame, almost unnoticeable. Slowly the camera tilts past the head, up to the other end of the rope tied around the branch of the tree, the handles showing in close shot. Now the camera holds on the handles with a short fade out that ends the sequence. This sequence is tied to the next with a short fade in; a low angle shot looking up through trees. The camera moves right to left past the rope-like strings of trees in the foreground and tilts down to a medium long shot of the child jumping the rope as in the first scenes of the film.

In the second example from the same film, Viridiana tells the Mother Superior of her decision not to return to the convent. After several introductory shots, the camera focuses on a head and shoulder shot of the Mother Superior at the left of the frame. The right of the frame is empty. As she speaks, she moves to the right and the camera pans with her to a two shot of the Mother Superior on the left and Viridiana on the right. A picture on the wall behind them is framed almost as a third character. The Mother Superior tells Viridiana to make a confession. Viridiana replies that she does not intend to return to the convent. Now the camera begins to dolly around the two figures, behind the back of the Mother Superior, as she asks Viridiana if there is some impediment, something standing in the way of her return. As she asks this, the camera has swung around to the back of her head which, with its black habit, almost fills the frame, concealing Viridiana's face completely. Then, Viridiana's face appears in overshoulder shot on the Mother Superior's left as the camera continues to move. Viridiana is now on the left, the Mother Superior on the right, her back to the camera, her black habit still dominating the frame. Between them is now framed a window to the outside (replacing the picture) as Viridiana replies that she feels that she can carry on her work in other ways, speaking almost to the camera over the shoulder of the Mother Superior. Now the camera moves again as the Mother Superior moves toward frame right and turns to Viridiana, forming a two shot, now over Viridiana's shoulder. As the Mother Superior turns toward Viridiana, both of their faces can be seen. Now the white front of the Mother Superior's habit predominates visually. As the dialogue continues and the Mother Superior questions Viridiana's pride, she moves toward Viridiana again, and towards the camera, which now looks over her shoulder toward Viridiana. The camera is just next to the Mother Superior's head as Viridiana looks up for the first time and it becomes evident that her resolve to stay is firm. The Mother Superior turns to go toward the right of the frame, the camera following. She turns once more in medium long shot to deliver another line, turns again to go toward the door, right, and arrives at the door. Once more she turns back toward Viridiana, who is now off frame left. Viridiana enters the frame, the Mother Superior forgives her and turns once more to go out frame right. As she leaves, Viridiana moves right toward the door and closes it.

This sensitive intertwining of character movement, camera movement, dialogue, gesture and use of setting externalizes the inner meaning of the dialogue and suggests not only the emotions within the characters, but the forces acting outside of them which are influencing their behavior. With a relatively simple blocking of camera, action and dialogue, Buñuel has achieved close shots, medium shots, medium long shots, overshoulder shots of several kinds, one shots, two shots, and has subtly let tension build and subside, to fluctuate, with a skillful orchestration of movement combined with static moments at points of emphasis.

Ophuls achieves a similarly extended effect in the opening scenes of *Le Plaisir*, which carries its main character from a moving carriage up a flight of stairs into a room filled with partying people, through the room with a variety of encounters with different characters and on up another stairway.

Camera movements such as these affect not only spatial relationships between camera and subject and between objects in the scene, but temporal relationships as well, since there can be no movement except in time. Thus in planning camera movement, allowance must be made both for the time that is consumed in making the movements and for the modification of time sense which results from one or more of these movements. The speed of the camera movement itself changes audience perception of time lapse, either increasing or diminishing it, even if there is no change from angle to angle, and no movement within the scene. Moving the camera is one way to build time into a scene, the kind of time which is difficult to change in editing. Cutting in and out of moving shots is not easy, and, unless carefully done, seldom successful. Still shots on the other hand, that is shots in which the camera does not move, can be manipulated with ease during editing. They can be left full length, cut short, other shots can be cut into them, or, of course, they can be discarded. Except for discarding the shot, the same kind of flexibility does not exist with the moving shot.

The number and length of moving shots used in a film, and their proportion to static shots, affects the overall sense of time and can be an expression of the director's style and attitude toward his subject. The continually flowing shots used by Ophuls and often Buñuel, for instance, makes the still or non-moving shots in their films even more noticeable than they would ordinarily be. With an overriding background of a moving camera, the insertion of a relatively sudden, staccato, unmoving shot tends to focus greater attention on its contents.

Conversely, in a film where staccato cutting between relatively still shots is the principal style, as in much of Lester's work, the flow of a long moving shot calls attention to that shot. Such effects of contrast between moving and still shots can be accentuated with the length of time the moving or unmoving shots are left before the audience.

HAND HELD CAMERA

Most of the movements described—tilt, pan, dolly and truck—can be obtained in different forms with a hand held camera. The difference is in the less steady hand held camera movement, and the smooth appearance of the mounted camera movement.

Shoulder pods and body braces are available to help the operator support the camera, and enable him to make tilts or pans while leaving him free to walk toward, away from or with his subject. In a limited and more awkward movement, he can sometimes get the effect of craning by sinking to his knees, rising, or climbing stairs while the camera is running. When used to good effect—as in the opening sequence in *A Hard Day's Night*, where an appropriate feeling of freedom and informality was obtained as the Beatles, followed by their fans, rush to catch a train, or in *Primary*, where more impromptu, less premeditated action could be recorded because time-consuming camera setups did not have to be made—the hand held camera extends the range and possibility of film expression.

It is less successful when used to achieve an ersatz "documentary" effect, the theory being that unpremeditated actions are by definition more "truthful" actions. Within limits shots made with a hand held camera tend to have subjective qualities.

OPTICAL MODIFICATIONS

Selective use of camera lenses can also help to bring out the meaning in the story. Lenses not only have differing magnifying powers, they have a characteristic much more important to the composing of meaningful images, that of spatial alteration.

When beginning to work in films, the film maker often selects a lens only for its magnifying power, while its more important interpretive properties are yet unknown to and used by him. Two effects can be obtained from lenses, diverging from a so-called "neutral" or "natural" portrayal which supposedly approximates the viewing experience of the unaided eye (with a 35 mm camera, this neutral effect is obtained with a 50 mm lens; in 16 mm work, a 25 mm lens is the equivalent). Moving from this neutral situation, in one direction is a flattening effect produced by the longer focal length lenses, and, in the other, a depth-accentuating effect produced by shorter focal length lenses.

LONG LENS COMPRESSION AND FOCUS

The long focal length lens, or telephoto as it is sometimes called, can seem to bring distant objects close, eliminating the need for moving the camera toward the subject—which at best might be inconvenient, and at worst, impossible. But because of their construction, long focal length lenses not only magnify, they tend to record objects at varying distances from the lens as if all such objects were at the same or nearly the same distance from the lens. The sense of depth, of space and of many planes is gone, and the longer the focal length of the lens, the greater this effect. For example, a shot meant to portray a high speed collision between two automobiles is set up from a safe distance. One of the automobiles is to move away from the camera and the other toward the camera. The film maker uses a long focal length lens with the expectation that bringing the subject closer to the camera than would otherwise be possible will increase the shock of collision in the audience's mind. But quite the reverse happens. Because the apparent distance between the two cars is reduced by the long focal length lens, their movement on the screen is minimized. The cars approach one another over what appears to be a confined space, colliding without the preparatory sense of tension and build-up necessary for full effect. The collision itself visually lacks the essential thing in a collision, the violent reduction of space between two objects over a short period of time. The violence is lacking both because of the spatial distortion, and the effect of such distortion on the perception of time. The audience looks upon the collision as an incident— the shocking, terrible moment is lost. If the shot were a prolonged one, the ultimate effect might even be comic.

Of course, if it is intended that the audience should remain unimpressed by the impact, or be unaffected emotionally—viewing the action objectively —then the scene might be successful.

The space reducing or flattening effect characteristic of long focal length lenses can be used consciously other ways. It can appreciably distort the "fact" of reality. Photographing a fleet of scattered ships on the horizon at sea, for instance, might be done with a long focal length lens, selected purposely to minimize the distance between the various vessels. With the distance between them reduced, the fleet looks more powerful, more massive, more unified. Lacking any other scenic element which might betray the planal distortion, the long focal length lens in effect amasses the ships. Space distortion with a long focal length lens makes the hero's desperate race toward the church seem endlessly ineffective in *The Graduate*. Tremendous physical effort is obviously being expended and yet the young man does not seem to move any closer to the camera. In Enrico's *An Occurrence at Owl*

Creek Bridge a similar effect is obtained as the hero, photographed with a long focal length lens as he runs toward the camera, makes a fruitless effort to achieve an unobtainable end.

In closer work, the restricted depth of field characteristic of the long focal length lens must be taken into account. At times this can also be used for effect, particularly when part of the scene must be thrown out of focus, or when it is desirable to change the focus during the scene, so that the audience sees only selected parts of the image clearly.

The normal eye looks only at what is in focus. Any part of an image that is out of focus will get no more than a passing glance as the eye searches for the point of clearest focus in an image. Thus eye movement can be accurately controlled within the frame. As the long focal length lens has a characteristically shallow depth of field, it may at times be advantageous to move the camera far back from the subject purposely, use the long lens, get a medium or even a long shot, and have only certain portions of the frame (one plane) remain in focus. Such differential use of focus is more difficult on exteriors because of the light available, although neutral density filters could be used to cut down this light to achieve out-of-focus effects even here. But on interiors, out-of-focus effects are quite simple to achieve.

Wide Angle Depth and Focus

The short focal length lens, or wide angle lens as it is called, has opposite characteristics to the long lens. The short lens tends to accentuate distances between objects, and it has greater depth of field. Had it been possible to get close enough to the impending automobile collision to photograph it with a wide angle lens, the visual effect from the moving image on the screen would have been even more powerful than the visual effect in life. Because the two automobiles would have appeared to be at a greater distance from one another at first, and to have collided within the same relative time segment, the viewer would assume they were travelling at much greater speed. The fleet on the open sea, photographed with a wide angle lens, would barely seem a fleet at all. More likely it would appear as a sprinkling of ships widely scattered and disorganized.

The psychological distortions which occur with high and low camera angles can be increased if a short focal length lens is used. Apparent distance between viewer and subject is accentuated, as is the difference in size between the foreground and background of the shot.

Again, in closer work, the distortion would become even more noticeable, together with an increase in depth. A human face, photographed close to a wide angle lens, would appear to have a very prominent nose, since the distance between the tip of the nose and the principal plane of the face would be apparently increased. A hand striking out towards a wide angle lens would carry a violence it might not have in life, as it would seem to travel speedily through considerable space in order to reach the lens. When it neared the lens, it would seem to grow larger, much too large for the arm that carried it, because the wide angle lens accentuates the apparent size of near objects and diminishes that of far objects.

Out-of-focus shots are more difficult to achieve with wide angle lenses because these lenses have great inherent depth of field. But any lens, the wide angle included, when used close to its subject and with an open diaphragm, can be made to go out-of-focus. The title shot of *To Kill a Mockingbird* effectively puts everything out of focus except the trinkets which, during the story, are found in the tree. The camera focuses on an extreme close shot of the trinkets lying in relative darkness on a table, and then trucks slowly past them.

In *The Fox*, the heroine, seen over the hero's shoulder in an especially intense dialogue sequence, is allowed, at the end of the interchange, to walk away from the hero and out of focus as she moves into the distance. Her retreating figure becomes blurred with the white, snowy background, and the hero, part of whose head and shoulder are still clearly outlined, seems far more isolated and distant from her than had she remained in focus. In this case, the hard and soft focus tends to accentuate also the un-yielding masculinity of his part in the action, and her uncertain, confused femininity.

STANDARD LENS

The normal focal length lens is so named because it seems to "see" more like the human eye than the other extremes of focal length. It supposedly magnifies about the same as the normal eye, has similar depth perception, and has the rough equivalent of the depth of field of a normal eye. Unless one of the extreme focal length lenses is specified in making a camera set up, the cameraman assumes that a normal lens is desired, just as he can assume a medium vertical angle, unless directed otherwise. The normal lens is the lens of least distortion, the lens most likely to interpret action as it appears to occur in life. Out-of-focus effects are still possible, however, because of the differences between camera lenses and the human eye in the matter of focus.

ZOOM LENSES

With the improvement of its optical systems, the variable focal length, or zoom, lens, has taken a place in professional work, where it has an exact and limited use much as any other lens.

To the less disciplined photographer, the zoom seems at first to have great powers, because it appears to enable him to achieve all the advantages of a dolly shot without the bother of changing focus, or the expense or trouble of securing proper equipment. However, used like this, the zoom is no more than an ersatz dolly.

There is an extremely important difference between the two methods of enlarging or diminishing the audience's view of the subject. With the dolly shot, the effect of perspective changes continuously throughout, just as it would in life if the viewer were actually approaching or retreating from or moving in relation to the subject. With the zoom shot, however, perspective remains constant, as the lens is actually only increasing magnification. The "movement" has no equivalent in reality. With a dolly, the camera moves through space toward its subject. With a zoom, the subject seems to move toward the camera by enlarging itself, thrusting itself upon a stationary observer. In a context where a semblance of external reality is unnecessary, or where the distinctively enhancing effect of magnification within a shot is advantageous, the zoom can be both useful and expressive. Such a zoom was used in *The Graduate*, where it served partially as an ersatz dolly but also as a magnifying device in going from close to long shot, pushing the hero out of isolation and into a large area shot in the midst of a college campus.

On rare occasions, a special distortion lens may be needed to give a surreal quality to the images photographed. One such lens is the so-called "fish-eye" lens, which gives an image with all the optical distortion that would occur in shooting an image reflected in a shiny, hemispherical surface (fig. 24). Split, or multiple image lenses can multiply the number of times the image occurs within any one frame, much like a kaleidoscope (fig. 25). Other lenses artificially elongate or widen images, much like trick mirrors. Images produced by distortion lenses have an effect, which, depending upon the particular situation, can be comic, disturbing, fantastic, terrifying, or, if poorly used, simply "gimmicky."

FILMING SPEED MODIFICATIONS

Still further technical means can be used to reveal meaning in the action: movement itself can be slowed down or speeded up artificially. High camera speeds (page 39), yielding slowed motion, are sometimes used in dream sequences, for surreal effects, in chases, or to give an unreal quality which ordinary movement does not have. In Enrico's *An Occurrence at Owl Creek Bridge*, the entire "fantasy" sequence, which is most of the film, is set within a framework of slow motion, which is used both to give an unreal quality to the action and to externalize internal emotional states. In the escape scene, the slow motion is almost imperceptibly introduced when the main character sinks beneath the waters of the river. Soon it becomes evident that it is more than the water which is slowing the action for, as the man rises to the surface, both his action and the actions and words of his executioneers have been slowed. Gradually the action assumes a more normal

Fig. 24. Looking down from the top of the main mast to the deck below through a fish-eye lens gives the audience a 360° view. [*Courtesy 20th Century-Fox.*]

tempo, except for the scenes which cut back to the wife. Here the slowing of the motion, together with a purposeful repetitiveness in the cutting, lends an agonizing sense of anticipation never-to-be-fulfilled to the shots of the man striving (taken with the long focal length lens mentioned earlier, so that he seems to run but not move through space) which are intercut with the timeless, dreamy, slow motion shots of his wife, holding out her arms to him. The entire sequence, and the film, is resolved in a shot taken at near-normal speed (the characters slow their actions instead of the camera being slowed) where the two finally meet, and the wife affectionately places her hands on her husband's neck.

Slow motion was one of Cocteau's favourite devices to alter time and space conceptions. In *Orpheus* the hero passes beyond the magic mirror into the other world of the future–past where he is to be judged. His journey takes place in a scene of tortuous slow motion where his movements seem impeded by wind and other-world resistance to his presence. A similar impression of other-worldness is obtained in *Beauty and the Beast* where Beauty moves in slow motion down a long corridor, toward an unknown fate.

Even when such far-from-normal effects are inappropriate to the needs of

Fig. 25. Multiple image for special effect achieved in this case with a special prismatic lens. [Dr. Doolittle, *2oth Century-Fox.*]

a scene, slow motion shots of a more limited nature are useful. Waves, railroad trains, a falling tree or any object moving toward the camera, if photographed at a speed greater than twenty-four frames per second, seems ponderous and powerful. The apparent weight of an object is increased with an increase in camera speed. If the object is moving away from the camera, it seems to lumber, to break away with difficulty. Movement across the frame becomes suspenseful, slow and laborious.

Decreasing camera speed below the twenty-four frame projection rate has the opposite effect. Object weight is decreased, movement through space made faster, action speeded up. The once ponderous wave now simply plops over, the railroad train seems to fly along the track toward the camera, the tree, now seemingly less weighty, crashes down quickly. Movement across the frame, as well as toward and away from the camera, is accomplished more quickly—a phenomenon familiar to all lovers of silent comedies (which move in a jerky and comic way because they were photographed at about sixteen frames per second and are now projected at twenty-four).

Although it is an effect achieved in the laboratory long after the shooting period, a freeze frame—the selection from a continuum of motion of a single frame to be duplicated by an optical printer for some specified length of time—is usually anticipated in the planning stage of the film: if not the actual frame or length, at least its location in the film. A freeze frame violently calls attention to itself—suddenly the flow of motion stops, attention is riveted upon one selected frame which continues in time, one moment in the continuum of time which is "frozen" for preservation. When the image begins to move again, the effect is almost one of bringing life back to the dead, or of rebirth. Not only does that subject attain importance, but the audience half unconsciously begins to expect, at least for a time, other "frozen moments." It looks upon the action with newly sensitized vision and, if strongly affected, may even create its own imaginary freeze frames in the action that follows.

SPECIAL CAMERA ATTITUDES

Rocking, spinning, swinging or shaking the camera enables an audience to accept images subjectively, rather than objectively. Such devices are relatively frequent in *The Titan*, the Michaelangelo documentary, where camera movement was used to bring life to inanimate objects (no human actors are seen) and to increase audience involvement. A gentle rocking, when combined with other visual and sound cues, can suggest to the audience that the footage was taken on a ship at sea. In another use, the rocking movement can seem to portray the whirling, subjective view of a hangover. A spinning camera could suggest severe psychotic imbalance, or simple dizziness, or, if performed so fast that the images were blurred, the suggestion could be that of making a vigorous transition from one scene to the next. If necessary, a camera can swing from tree to tree, or between a sinking ship and a rescue vessel, or it can dangle from the end of a line lowered from a helicopter, or off the edge of a cliff. The camera can shake or shudder at an explosion or an earthquake, or it can tremble delicately in nervousness or fear.

While the camera is almost always mounted level—so that the horizon makes a level line across the frame—this too is a matter of choice and not of necessity. Again the effects tend toward the subjective. Choosing an example at random from the innumerable effects that could be achieved, a slightly off-level or tilted camera might be used, as it was in *Un Carnet de Bal*, to portray the slightly imbalanced nature of the protagonist. A more extreme off-level shot could simulate a sinking ship, or a descent into madness. Indeed, the camera might take a sideways view of life or an upside-down view (as it did humorously in many silent comedies or more seriously in surrealistic films), if these views fulfill the intention of the script.

Film Material

Not only lenses and cameras can serve as interpretive tools, but the film material itself. The characteristic qualities of a particular type of emulsion can be used to affect the meaning of the film. The same story, photographed in black and white and then in color, would have a different impact. Two different aesthetic and visual experiences would result from the change, even if no other changes were made in the film's composition. Selection from among the various color stocks or among the various black and white stocks further affects the film experience for an audience.

At times it may become necessary or desirable to have both color and black and white footage, or tinted footage, in the same film. Often this is used in documentary films where historic footage available only in black and white is partially matched with more recent footage shot in color. Even producers of feature films have on occasion used this technique, although its full capabilities for affecting the emotions have seldom been explored. Negative images are sometimes incorporated for effect into the film, intermixed with the positive images the audience sees more often.

Dynamic Frame

Some use has been made of the ability to manipulate the shape of the frame. Griffith in 1916 experimented with various shapes, changing them according to the demands of the individual scene. He used circular images, tall and thin, and wide images as means of dramatic expression. But, since his time, standardization of motion picture equipment, while necessary for quality control, has brought with it a fixed attitude toward the shape of the frame. Most films are still produced totally in one or another of the standard aspect ratios. Even though the formal frame usually remains constant within any one film, however, the informal frame—that frame provided by composing pictorial elements within the frame—can be varied throughout the film.

Subject Movement

In addition to the physical elements of the scene, size of shot, camera position, camera movement, camera speed, lens, focus, and raw stock, there is a final variable in spatial composition. This is the variable of subject movement.

While the subject of a film does not have to be a human actor—it may be an automobile, a mathematical concept, the digestive system or almost anything else—it is still valuable to think of the subject as being an actor. Whether the actor is human, animal, mechanical or conceptual makes little difference so far as its function in the film is concerned.

The term "actor"—meaning something which moves or acts—can be retained in film usage in its literal sense even with inanimate objects such as a chair, a window, or machines, and with concepts, because these things can be given the appearance of motion (without anthropomorphism) through use of film animation techniques. As far as spatial composition is concerned, anything that bears upon the story actively can be considered an "actor." For example, a hand or set property, if it had significance in the story, could in effect become a character. Something akin to this happens with the falcon statuette used in *The Maltese Falcon*, the panther symbol used in *The Pink Panther*, and the murderer's knife in *M*. The object can be emphasized with closeups, lighting or the manner in which it is regarded by human actors. Similarly natural events such as a rainstorm (as in *The Rains Came*) or an earthquake (*Green Dolphin Street*), by their effect on human beings or simply by their action, can play such an important part in the story that they too can be considered "actors." Concepts, inanimate objects, natural events, animals (Rin-Tin-Tin, Lassie and Rhubard, not to mention the animals in *Born Free* and *Dr. Doolittle*)—all act on the story in such significant ways that they can be considered and handled as a human actor would be.

Planning the physical movement of the actor must be done with the camera angle and camera movement in mind. Actor movements may contrast with or reinforce camera movements. With any actor movement, there is the choice of an unmoving or stationary camera, or a camera movement which in some way reinforces or contrasts with actor movement. Each choice yields different results. An unmoving camera places the total weight of attention on the movement within the frame, or, if there is no movement, on the composition within the frame and upon contrasts between scenes. The moment the camera begins to move, the attention has a dual center—the actor movement and the camera movement.

The possible combinations of actor and camera movement are infinite. Here are two common examples:

When the actor *moves away* from a retreating camera, a strong reinforcement takes place not only because the distance between the observer and the actor increases much more rapidly than it otherwise would, but because the change of perspective places the actor in an ever-enlarging compositional area. If an actor *approaches* the camera while the camera is moving toward the actor, the result will still be reinforcing, but with an opposite effect, a sense of vigor and force.

If in an extreme long shot the actor were to move toward the right side of the frame while the camera was panning (even slightly) toward the left, the actor would leave the frame much sooner than if the camera were stationary. This same accentuating effect takes place wherever the camera movement opposes, or is in a direction opposite from, the actor movement. Whenever the camera does take this opposing view, the observer tends to identify himself less with the actor in the scene and to think of himself simply as an observer of the action.

The opposite occurs when the camera movement is in conjunction with actor movement. Here the observer tends to identify himself with the actor, or to become otherwise more involved in the scene. A kind of reinforcement takes place that is different from contrasting movement. No longer are actor movements accentuated. They are now minimized, sometimes almost neutralized if the camera moves at the same speed as the actor. If the camera rises as the actor stands up, the actor is still the focal point of attention in the center of the frame. His action is reinforced simply because attention has not been diverted from it, and because the audience feels as if it had stood up too.

In these cases of movement in concert, the environmental background of the action is momentarily minimized. When the camera accompanies an actor strolling down the street, it is allowing attention to remain focused on the actor himself. When the camera moves with the man approaching the door, and even dollies in fast as his hand reaches toward the knob, the observer might almost feel as if he had approached the door and taken the knob in his hand. The movement almost substitutes for the tactile experience of opening the door.

From increased objectivity, to impartiality or neutrality, to increased subjectivity—subject and camera movement, or the lack of it, can affect the audience's relative emotional involvement or disinvolvement in a scene. When made more than a means of avoiding cutting or to relieve monotony, movement can heighten dramatic effectiveness. The use of these effects, of course, is governed entirely by the story and this is the key to any possible manipulation. Whatever is done *must* be done to tell the story. How well it is done can be determined only by the affect upon the audience. Here alone can the degree of success be assessed.

7

External Composition

THE SEQUENCE OF production in a film is usually that sequence which makes most economical use of the equipment, space, time and talent necessary to the production. Since economics, not art, is the deciding factor, the production sequence rarely bears any relationship to the sequence of events as they are to occur in the completed film. This is possible because of the nature of the film medium and the production method itself. Sound and action tracks remain separate until the end, so there is no reason why they must be produced simultaneously or in logical sequence. It is unnecessary from a technical standpoint for the shots to be collected in any particular order, as the cutting process allows any desired sequence to be made out of the material. Also, the mobility of both sound and picture recording equipment makes a shooting sequence based on logical, causal or sequential bases immaterial.

Immaterial economically perhaps, and technically—but, speaking aesthetically, this film production method presents what sometimes seems an insurmountable barrier to success. Materials gathered in such apparent randomness, scattered over time and space, with no allowance for their final temporal, spatial and audial relationships can, if not extremely carefully designed and produced by persons of experience and skill, betray the nature of the situation in which they were produced. This situation, revealed, is anathema to dramatic effect.

A film has meaning only in the sequential arrangement of the scenes in the completed film. Any other sequence, the production sequence, for instance, is meaningless. The individual shot takes on meaning as it relates to other shots in terms of the order of images and the sense of flow between such images. The total meaning of the film is carried by this mechanism of arrangement, timing and flow. Image is the result not of internal shot composition alone: it results from the arrangement and timing of the shots together with the sense of flow achieved between the shots, a result of their internal composition being created with reference to the external factors. Thus the most meaningful filmic element, the interrelatedness of and flow

150

between images, is of no consequence to the production system. This fact presents the film maker with a dilemma unique to his art.

In no other dramatic medium is the attainment of spatial flow achieved under such difficult conditions. The director of stage presentations, for instance, finds his production sequence is the same as his performance sequence. Generally speaking, scenes or acts are rehearsed in the same order as they are to be performed. If any fractionalization does occur, it is with relatively large units of action, usually whole scenes or even acts.

The director of live television works totally within the performance sequence. Sequence for him must never vary since the whole purpose of rehearsal is to help actors and technicians learn all the cues necessary to string events together in the sequence in which they will finally occur.

The film director, by contrast, though he always keeps the total sense of order and the total film in mind, actually works during production with disconnected and disordered fragments. In every moment of his work, the disorder seems ready to take over. If this did occur in the final film, the fragments would not fit together and make sense. Every time the camera and sound recording mechanisms come to a stop, there is the possibility of a flaw in continuity.

But fractionalization, much as it is a disadvantage or a danger to flow, also has an advantage. For within the process of creating order out of fragments there is the power to create new order and meaning and to impose new continuities upon the images and sounds of the film.

This is possible because the human mind will, when presented with events (or images) in sequence, attempt to detect some meaning in the sequence itself, and will, in fact, impute a cause–effect relationship to such series of events or images, even when none exists. Capitalizing upon this phenomenon, the director can bring dimensions to a film far more complete and more complex than the most basic and the simplest sequential approach —the chronological one.

CONTINUITY

Early in the development of film making, directors discovered that stories occurring simultaneously and in different locations could, if properly cut together, be understood by the audience as happening in parallel, even though they were actually seen sequentially. The "gaps" in time and space of unseen material—what was left out—would, it was discovered, be automatically bridged by the audience so long as the gaps were not great enough to prohibit the "leap" over the "void." Soon film became capable of showing both the past and future times and of moving freely among many locations in space.

Audiences became accustomed to cutting conventions which separated

and identified the intended time and/or place of the event they were experiencing through the film. Early in the history of film, the iris-out, iris-in;
fade-out, fade-in; focus-out, focus-in; the wipe; the dissolve; and other
optical effects, as well as the later use of sound, warned the audience of an
imminent change in time and/or space. For a number of years, so long as
fictional stories adhered to a linear (essentially chronological) narrative
style, major shifts in time and/or space were so indicated. (Documentaries
had, from the first, usually based their continuity on elements other than
chronology; conceptual or functional continuities were more common than
time sequence.)

There was nothing inherent in either the film production or the film
viewing process, however, that made the chronological approach more
desirable or more acceptable than other, more abstract approaches. Eisenstein was one of the earliest and most vocal film makers who held that the
essential nature of juxtaposition was $1 + 1 = 3$, not 2. In other words, the
audience, in finding the relationship between shot A and shot B, was itself
adding to the film. If this addition could be logically and reliably "pro-
grammed," the audience itself could supply and participate in the story-
telling process.

Freedom from a slavish use of chronological continuity meant freedom
to move between differing time/space situations, and hence to suggest that
the "present" reality of the film (shots are actually always seen in the present,
even though they portray some other real or imaginery time/space situation)
and of characters within the film, was actually a mosaic of fragments from
many time/space experiences. These fragments occurred not in any ordinarily
expected rational order, but were more randomly brought into view by the
emotional or psychological continuity of events. To make the story flow more
easily, and to suggest that other times and other places were relevant only
as they affected the now and the here, directors began to cut between shots
and scenes widely separated in time and space. Since separation and identification of other time/space situations was no longer necessary, the conventions used for these functions were, in this style of film, discarded in favor of
the more simple and direct method of using the cut.

In one of the earliest and most effective of such uses in fictional film,
The Captain's Paradise, the two stories—the domestic and foreign affairs of
the captain—were bridged by means of matched cuts rather than dissolves.
The cuts, which often occurred on a noticeable action, such as Guinness
swatting his mistress, gave a crispness to the narrative technique which
added to its comic effect. Fellini in *Juliet of the Spirits* cuts freely between
present and fantasy, so that present and fantasy become intermixed to such
an extent that the contents of "reality" seems to consist of an almost equal
measure of each. "Reality," in such films, tends to be the state of the character's psyche at any particular moment in time.

Extreme economy of action is one by-product of the continuing exploration of the bases of continuity. In chronological styles of film making, often it seemed necessary to adhere closely to a theatrical manner of presentation, giving a rather complete rendition of a scene from beginning to end, with minimal deletion of parts of the action. Thus the total number of time/space sequences which could be included in any one film was relatively limited. With increasing dependence upon audience sophistication—ability to bridge larger and larger gaps—only enough need be told to establish a scene.

The film maker, using a small amount of highly selected detail, has compressed the function of establishment into an extremely economical and brief time period. Since the continuity of such films tends to lie more in relationships between the scenes than in the internal contents of the scenes themselves, the director is free to use a much wider variety of scene, a greater number of scenes, in different times and different places, and to concentrate the action upon the psychological, rather than the physical, flow of the story. As the film's form does not become fixed until the final stages of production, any image can be juxtaposed with any image, any sound with any sound, and any image with any sound. So long as the juxtapositions carry meaning to the audience, any juxtaposition can be used.

Mechanics of Spatial and Temporal Flow

Spatial and temporal flow are endangered in two places. First wherever a cut or other method of transition from one shot to another is made, and second, wherever sound is added to picture. In other words, flow lies in the process of juxtaposition itself.

Randomly gathered shots, which could destroy the impression of an uninterrupted flow of film material, are kept consistent from shot to shot through a combination of activities in a process called "matching." This calls not only for consistency in larger matters such as speech and direction of action and similarity in physical environment, but for attention to the consistency of extremely small detail, such as placements of pocket handkerchiefs, lengths of cigarettes, hair style, and the countless other matters of physical detail which can and do actively distract audience attention from the film as idea and toward the film as process. "It *is* easy to lose time on this business of matching shots," Jean Renoir comments,

> even when you're just trying to match physical continuity. You take a close-up, and then comes the medium shot which is to follow it in the montage, and which is filmed the next day, and everyone on the set is asking "Was he like this; wasn't his voice sharper; no, not at all, it was less sharp . . . I promise you it was exactly like this . . . I had my elbow bent just this way . . ." And then the cinema finally becomes a job for the continuity girl, and then a job of composition and inspiration. For myself, I'd really rather call a truce to all these problems and shoot a scene in one go.[19]

In matching, a script clerk is often employed to make notes of action, property and set details. Stills are taken of the set or location and the lighting setup, and notes made of light readings and other camera information so that any shot can be duplicated if necessary. This same information provides an aid to maintaining tempo and timing, and psychological and visual continuity. But at best these devices provide only for a superficial physical similarity between shots. It remains for the director to provide for the dramatic flow necessary to a successful film sequence. To achieve this means thinking in terms of past, future and present simultaneously; in working on any particular shot the sense of what will precede it in the film must be retained, and the sense of what will follow it. Work completed and work to be done are both kept in mind. No shot is directed for itself alone. Every shot is constructed as a link in a total chain of scenes, in a total flow of action.

TEMPORAL LINKS

Audience memory must be taken into account in this process, together with an estimate of its sense of what is happening beyond and outside of the material it sees within the frame. An audience will not only bring memories of previous actions to mind as it views the present action, but it will bring interests in characters and objects generated in previous scenes. Buñuel repeatedly capitalizes upon audience memory and association. In *Viridiana*, it is so much a part of the film that it would be nearly impossible to describe all of the many uses he makes of it. Again and again he returns to objects, properties, camera angles and movements, sounds and motifs, each time imbuing them with new meaning. A few of the more prominent are: repeated cutting or moving from shots of feet to heads; handles of the jumprope being used first by the child, then by the uncle (who hangs up the jumprope and later hangs himself with it), then by the beggar for a belt, and finally in the rape scene, where Viridiana is shown tugging at the handles; the uncle's pity for the bee trapped in the water, and his son's pity for the mistreated dog; Viridiana's first experience with worldliness as she puts her hand on the cow's udder, her last in the film as the son places his hand over hers; the uncle's tragic wearing of the corset in the early part of the film, the beggar "comically" wearing it during the feast; the beggars' first meal under Viridiana's patronage, and their last feast; the maid's child is joined by a crying baby and finally there is the expected child of one of the beggars. The initial dolly shot of the Uncle with Viridiana is repeated later with the son and Viridiana. Buñuel uses similar motifs for contrast: the hard bed of Viridiana's religious life and the soft beds of her seduction; the full length mirror into which she first looks and the broken scrap of a hand mirror which she uses in the end. The total effect of the heavy use of this technique is to give the viewer a sense of saturation, a feeling that the major theme of the story—as life itself—is a continuously repeating thing and that, though change does occur, man moves around slowly in a never-ending cycle of his own human problems. This feeling is strongly evoked by the final shots of Buñuel's *The Exterminating Angel,* where he suggests that the entire action of the film is to begin again.

Thus in making a shot it is necessary not only to keep the immediate surroundings of the shot in mind—the shot preceding and following—not only the flow of action within a particular sequence, but all the relevant audience impressions of characters, objects and events, which might be far from the immediate scene, as far, in some cases, as an audience association which spans several films.

Fellini uses large open exteriors symbolically for his final sequences in *La Dolce Vita, 8½* and *Juliet of the Spirits.* Cocteau not only uses recurring motifs, but relates them between films, as with *Orpheus* and *Testament of Orpheus.* Each shot in the design of a film must be a part of the larger totality —the whole film—as well as part of a sequence, part of a scene and part of a particular series of shots.

Visual Reiteration

The consistency of purpose evident within the separate pieces of the film is what creates the expectation of purpose in the audience. This feeling of progression or satisfied expectation can give the audience a sense of completeness and unity in the work. There may be moments, however, when this progression should be interrupted, when a return for emphasis or effect will be advantageous. The flow of continuity may be purposely diverted in order to make some point in the story. The interruption becomes a point of emphasis. The audience now becomes conscious of a progression which may have been felt only subconsciously before.

Lester's insistent cuts back to extremely brief flashes of a previously experienced event in *Petulia* only take on meaning cumulatively. Repeated use instructs the audience in their purpose. The insistency of their interruption emphasizes their importance to the meaning of the story. If a previous action is approximately repeated, the audience can experience a sense of return, and such returns, by serving as units of measure, can contribute strongly to the sense of progression. Or if not progression, then to the circularity of experience, as illustrated in *La Ronde,* where the entire film takes the form of a round, the ends of the circle being tied to the beginning by means of the meeting of the two characters. Sometimes exact repetition is used—at least, the action is repeated exactly, although, hopefully, the effect on the audience is a different one than that evoked by the previous action, since it has experienced intervening action. Exact repetition of a camera angle and a gesture is used to measure the beginning and end of the final judgment scene in *M.* M is first shown as he confronts the underworld for the first time. He is identified by the blind man in a shot in which the blind man's hand enters frame right and is placed upon M's shoulder. At the end of the scene, during which M has pleaded for his life and his accusers have attempted to condemn him and ultimately begin to advance upon him, there is another, identically framed shot of M in which a hand, entering frame right, is placed upon his shoulder. This time it is the hand of the police.

Various kinds of repetition and return are, in fact, one of the major story-telling devices used in film, where they serve to interrelate parts of the story, to provide a measure of progress, to make analogy, and to add to the effectiveness of a scene by adding to the number of meanings it carries. Such uses allow the story to take place in a simultaneous and not wholly sequential manner.

Ophuls uses repetition of camera movement and camera angles to relate parts of the story and to provide an emotional measure of the action. In *Letter from an Unknown Woman*, as an example, the camera follows the heroine in her first exploration of the musician's apartment, past doorways and down halls, giving a sense of the complexity and depth of the place. The child's curiosity is satisfied at much the same rate as that of the audience, as it, in a sense, discovers the apartment with her. Later, when the heroine is confined for the birth of her child by the musician, the camera follows a nun who walks through halls and around walls to reach the heroine, just as she did as a child in her lover's apartment.

Sometimes duplicated camera angle or camera movement is extended to include a duplicated sequence of actions or to combine two previous scenes into a new scene which carries the memories of both of the two previous actions. In an early part of the film just mentioned, the heroine is shown running away from her parents as they prepare to depart from Vienna by train. The girl returns to the apartment from which the family has just moved and to the nearby apartment of her lover. Later in the film she is shown saying goodbye to her lover as he departs by train. Still later, after she has borne her lover's child, unknown to him, she sends the child away in a shot which duplicates the shot in which her lover left. This is followed by a shot recalling the flight from her parents as she again returns home from the train, just as she did as a child, and makes the same trip through her lover's apartment, the camera taking the same angle, the same movement, the sequence of shots recalling her previous experiences.

AUDIAL REITERATION

Recurrence and repetition is not limited to visual elements: a recurring sound motif may be used much the same way as a reminder and as a device to tie together various parts of a film. In Buñuel's *Belle de Jour*, the sound of ringing bells is used in the opening scene where the horses pull the carriage

carrying Belle and her husband. Again, as she drives out to the stately mansion with the Duke to participate in a sexual session with him, the horses
wear bells. With each of her lovers in the brothel, bells become part of the
scene. Again, at the end of the film, the horses are seen pulling the now empty
carriage down the lane and bells ring for the final time.

Occasionally, as in *Belle de Jour*, a coda-like effect of return is used at the
end of a film, where the last scenes recall or duplicate first actions, and attention is drawn to the fact that the audience's perception of and feeling about
the action has changed because of what has been experienced in between.

SPATIAL CONTINUITY

The temporal and spatial components of film flow are interdependent.
Neither component can achieve its maximum effectiveness individually.
Interruption or loss of cohesion in the spatial design not only disrupts the
flow of action and the visual sensation of spatial sequence, it can disturb the
flow of time and feeling of rhythm. Fortunately, there are spatial mechanical
equivalents of cutaways, cover shots and overlapping action which provide
footage necessary to create visual as well as time, flow. These spatial devices
include maintaining consistent frame relationships and screen direction,
using establishing and reestablishing shots, matching composition, connections between shots, inserts, changes of angle, clean entrances and exits,
overlapping and coverage.

To maintain a sense of visual flow when constructing an apparently continuous action out of many strips of film, it is necessary to maintain consistent
frame relationships. That is, actors and objects must maintain a consistent
relationship to the audience's only real point of reference—the frame of the
picture.

With film it is quite possible for the audience to lose its sense of the spatial
relationships of the actors or objects within the scene if the visual relationships of actors or objects to the frame are allowed to vary without apparent
motivation. In the absence of any purposeful attempt to disturb or confuse
the audience, the consistency of this visual and spatial relationship must
obtain even though the viewing point of the action—the camera angle—
changes.

FRAME SEGMENT AND LINE OF ACTION

Two factors are at work in establishing, maintaining and changing frame
relationships smoothly, without reverse angles. The first is frame segment,
which may be described as the portion of the frame occupied by the character
or object of interest, and roughly identified as right, center or left, with the
center being a neutral or transitional segment. Frame segment may be

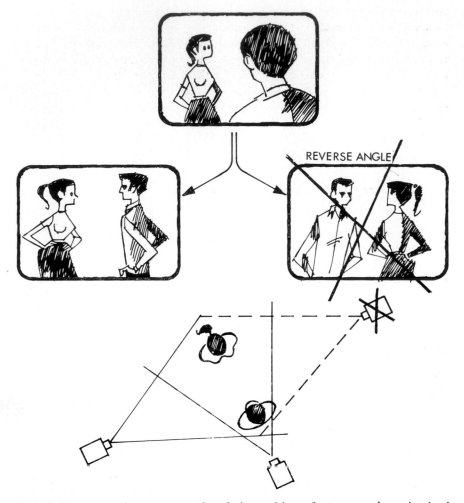

Fig. 26. When changing camera angle, relative positions of actors must be maintained without confusing the audience. Moving outside the "hemisphere of action" in one cut reverses their positions; working within it maintains them.

changed from right to left, or vice versa, by use of an intervening neutral shot, or by camera or actor movement within the shot, i.e., changing relationships without a cut.

The second factor at work in frame relationships is the line of action. This is an imaginary line that could be drawn as an axis through the center of the action. If only one character appears in the frame, the line is drawn through the character toward the implied action. If two or more characters appear, lines of action are drawn between all characters.

With one character, consistent frame relationship is a function both of frame segment and line of action. The line of action, in practice, is one side

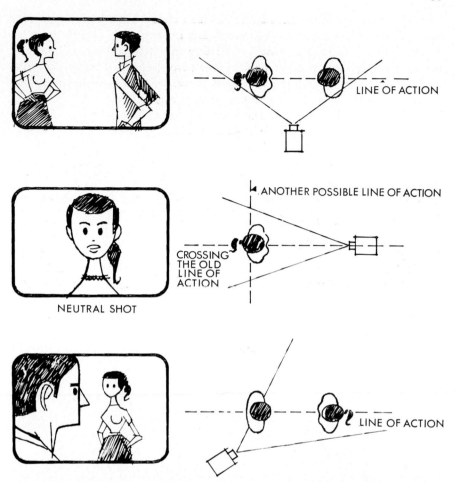

Fig. 27. The camera can cross the line of action by including an intermediate neutral shot which establishes another possible line of action and allows a changeover from one side to the other without loss of sense in the frame relationship between shots.

of a hemisphere of action (hence the term commonly used, the 180° line). A succeeding shot taken anywhere within the arc of this hemisphere will be visually and spatially consistent with the previous shots. Essentially the same principle applies when two characters appear. The line of action is the line drawn through the two characters. Like the single character line of action, it is a 180° line, forming a hemispherical segment. As long as the camera is located at some point on the arc of the curve of the hemisphere, a reverse angle will not occur between two shots. Unless the actors themselves move and change relationships within a shot, or unless a moving camera changes the relationships within a shot—thus establishing new hemispheres of action —spatial relationships will remain constant.

The diameter of the implied hemisphere ends where the frame crosses the 180° line. To maintain consistent frame segment, the camera must be aimed towards the pivot point on the line of action. The hemisphere is actually formed as a rotation around this pivot point. To move to a new line of action, an intervening neutral shot can be used—the neutral point being the point where the two lines of action would cross.

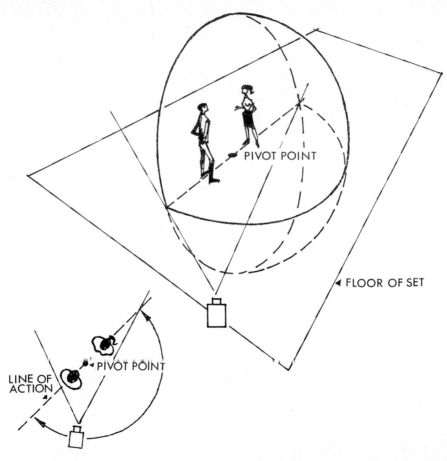

Fig. 28. The hemisphere of action, within which the camera angle may be changed, is taken from a pivot point on the line of action between the two characters.

The shooting segment (the area within which the camera can be used and still maintain consistent frame relationships) becomes increasingly limited when three characters appear within the frame. Drawing the line of action between each of the characters forms wedge shaped sections of a hemisphere. Further limitation occurs when more characters are added to the scene. Extending any of the lines of action will give the boundaries of

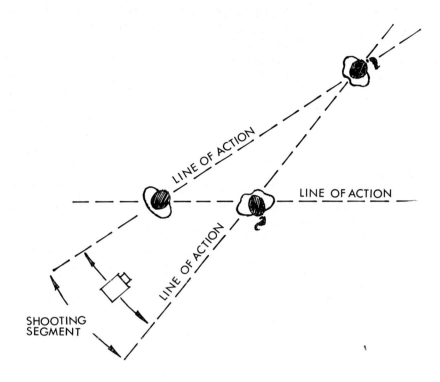

Fig. 29. With three or more characters, the shooting segment may become considerably reduced. In effect, there are three lines of action and crossing any of these lines will alter the actor's relationship to the frame.

the shooting segment, and indicate what portion of the initial hemisphere is now usable. Any action begun in any one segment and continued there will remain visually and spatially consistent.

The shapes of the blocking patterns which result from diagramming the lines of action have no particular significance so far as visual and spatial composition is concerned, although the number of characters in the frame does, of course, affect the perceived complexity of the shot and does limit the freedom of choice available among shots. The relative prominence of any of the actors is more a function of frame area occupied and action performed than it is a position in a geometrical pattern.

The matter of spatial consistency extends over any sequence of shots which shows a continuous action and which is unbroken by inserts or cutaways of sufficient interest to allow the audience to disregard spatial inconsistency.

The initial shooting segment is the first camera–character relationship

F

which the audience sees. Consistent frame relationships are achieved if the camera, during a change of camera angle, is placed within the initial shooting segment. To shoot an entire action within this initial shooting segment could of course, become monotonous. It might be used to convey a feeling of boxed in, restricted space. Whenever it seems the desirable and effective thing to do, the initial shooting segment can be changed by camera or actor movement, or a neutral angle. A neutral angle occurs whenever the camera is placed *on* the line of action. The camera may be moved across the previously established line of action by means of a neutral shot or by movement of the characters. In practice, new lines of action are being continually formed as the film moves on.

The factor which determines where in the scene the line of action lies is audience attention and interest. In a scene which includes actors, audience attention usually, but not always, centers upon the actor himself. But inanimate objects can also assume importance and attract attention, as well as prominent architectural features in the environment. On such occasions, the line of action may exist between an actor and an object, or even between two objects.

Some generalized observations can be made concerning this system for maintaining consistent frame relationships. Each of the combinations—two, three, four, or more characters—contains the limitations of the lower number. The more characters, or focuses of attention, the more limited the choice of shots. An implied object or character, even if invisible to the audience, if it is of sufficient interest, can affect the location of the pivot point and thus the camera angles possible. Any object or actor which attracts attention becomes a dominating element in composition—whether or not this was the original intention in creating the composition. Massiveness, color, movement and brightness in an object—and distinctive sound attributed to an object—are all elements capable of attracting visual attention, even when an object seemingly has no other significance in the composition. At times, such visual factors may threaten to conflict with, and perhaps dominate, the principal line of action. They must always be taken into account when determining the line of action. When an actor is alone in the frame it is particularly important to consider other prominent visual elements, especially when the actor relates himself to them.

Maintaining strictly consistent spatial relationships between objects or actors creates in the audience an expectation that such consistent use of frame segments will continue. Such expectation can be used to give meaning to partially empty frames (the audience will psychologically fill the frame with the expected object or actor). Also it can create and relieve feelings of suspense within the audience, and surprise the audience on the occasion when the expectation is purposefully not fulfilled—or is perhaps temporarily reversed. Space can be as well used by keeping it empty as by filling it with some story element.

Screen Direction

Expectation is also a part of the next factor affecting spatial flow: that of screen direction. Just as frame segments can, in the audience's mind, come to be unconsciously associated with certain objects or actors, or even certain ideas, so a continually consistent movement of an object or actor in relation to the frame can set up audience association. Even where no such association is the aim, maintaining consistent screen direction within any one sequence, or within a film, helps to create a sense of spatial credibility for the audience. The principle of screen direction means, simply, that between any two shots which portray a continuous action, the actor or object of principal interest should move in a consistent direction relative to the frame.

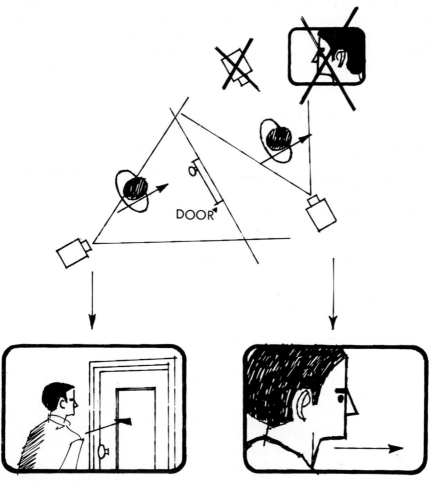

Fig. 30. Between any two shots which portray a continuous action, the actor or object of principal interest should move in a consistent direction relative to the frame.

If he is shown moving from left to right in one shot, he should be shown moving from left to right in the next shot—otherwise it will seem as if he surrepititously turned around and is returning to his point of departure.

The same principle obtains when two actors or groups of actors are to be shown moving consistently relative to one another. A chase offers the clearest example: If a group of Indians is shown moving from left to right in one shot, and if this shot is followed by a group of cowboys moving from left to right, the audience assumes that the cowboys are chasing the Indians. If, in the next shot, the Indians were shown moving from right to left, the audience could assume that they had turned upon the cowboys and that a battle might ensue. But perhaps this was not the intent of the sequence. Perhaps all that has happened is that the principle of screen direction has been violated by crossing the same 180° line which caused a reverse angle when two actors were involved.

A change in screen direction must be done purposely, just as a change in frame segment. An audience should ordinarily be allowed to assume consistency of direction unless the actor is shown to the audience turning around or unless the camera moves in relation to the actor during the shot to establish a new screen direction. Confusion, suspicion and conflict can arise, accompanied by loss of attention and interest, unless such spatial relationships remain clear, or unless the reason for not using them consistently is clear. Beyond this, consistent screen direction can be used for its psychological and aesthetic effects, just as frame segments can.

An audience can be led to create symbolic significance for motions in one or another direction. It can quickly learn to identify one side of the screen as being the source of cowboys (hence, perhaps, justice, rescue, persecution— whatever they represent), while the other side of the screen is identified as the source or haven of Indians (hence savagery, the persecuted, defenders of their homeland and their freedom, revolution—whatever *they* represent). This symbolic identification can be useful throughout the chase period and even beyond, because it provides an area of audience understanding and a way for the audience to locate an emotion in space. Implied or expected screen direction and implied or expected frame segments, and, on occasion, implied or expected camera movement, are among the most useful and economical film tools. Through them meaning can be achieved without actually occupying screen time or screen space.

ESTABLISHING SHOTS

Since a completed film is nothing more than a series of relatively disconnected strips of film, which become apparently connected only by the contents of each strip, it is easy for the audience to lose its sense of orientation, its spatial sense, particularly in a long series of closeups where overall spatial relationships tend to be forgotten. This may or may not be the intention of the scene. If it is hoped that the audience will remember the larger or more distant relationships which they do not see, the hope will be unfulfilled beyond a certain number of shots, particularly when the intervening action is emotionally charged, suspenseful or violent. The audience becomes quickly involved in the detail of action, and, unless periodically reminded, forgets what relationships this detail has to the larger pattern.

The reminder that is used is called an establishing shot, a shot which shows the spatial relationships between objects, usually on a relatively large scale. Thus the establishing shot is often a long shot of some kind, a shot the audience keeps in mind in the scenes which follow and which the audience uses as a reference for purposes of identification. Whether or not, and when, an establishing shot should be used varies with directorial style and taste.

Because the film director usually wants to "set up" his audience for the action which follows, he often starts his scene with an establishing shot. Then, periodically throughout the scene, he plans re-establishing shots, as reminders to the audience. On other occasions, however, a director takes just the opposite point of view and starts the scene with a series of closeups and gradually works back to the long establishing shot. This can have the effect of increasing curiosity, focusing interest on the specific action and creating suspense—if it is used well. But unless he wishes to completely disassociate his details of action from a larger scene, the director sooner or later uses a longer establishing shot. If the director is careless in omitting establishing shots from his coverage of a scene, he may seriously limit not only the process of achieving continuity in editing, but limit as well the kinds of emotional value which might be given the scene.

MATCHING COMPOSITION

As important as frame relationships in establishing and maintaining spatial continuity is the matter of matching composition. As the human eye looks at the picture within the rectangular frame, it moves over that frame until it finds a point of maximum interest on which to fix attention. Usually the point of interest is an object in focus, a moving object, a near object, and/or an object which receives converging lines—because these are all things which attract the eye. Presented with a static shot, the eye moves immediately to that part of the shot which is in focus and which moves. If nothing moves, the eye will tend to look first toward the brightest part of the shot, then usually at the warmest color or largest object, particularly if it is close. Then it will look at the object where lines converge. Thus, even in a static shot, the eye is in constant motion.

This natural eye movement is used in editing to make a smoothly flowing visual continuity, and to induce emotional reactions as a result of eye movement. Given the proper material, the editor can lead the eye between one shot and the next, making the transitions between them as smooth or as abrupt as the action requires. While the director's primary concern is with the movements of his audience's eyes within the shot, he must at the same time be aware of the editing problem, and, as with time and spatial relationships, must supply materials with which visual continuity can be achieved.

Whatever the transitional device to be used between shots—cut, dissolve and even fades—the matter of matching composition must be considered. The term, matching composition, means that, toward the end of one strip of film and in the beginning of the next strip (the part of the film in which the transitional device is used), a smooth cut, or smooth dissolve, will be possible only if there is some point on each strip where the general flow of movement matches (if there is movement within the scene) or where the eye is focused upon or interested in the same part of the frame (whether or not there is movement).

If at the end of shot A the eye is looking toward the upper right hand corner of the frame, and this is placed next to shot B, which, from its beginning, makes it necessary for the eye to look at the lower left hand corner of the frame, the eye will, immediately after the cut from A to B, make a violent, diagonal sweep across the frame to the new point of attention. If the director had hoped for a continuously flowing scene, the expectation would not be realized. It would have been realized if he had so planned shot B that its initial point of attention were in the upper right hand corner of the frame; then, immediately after the cut from A to B, the eye would remain in the same part of the frame—it would not be required to make that violent sweep. Wherever the eye is led after the initial point of attention will vary with the intent and content of the shot. Toward the end of the shot, however, the director would have to begin thinking of shot C if he wanted to maintain a smooth flow of action "across" the cut, as it were.

Disruption, violence, conflict, confusion or disorientation can result from forcing the eye to "pop around" the frame from shot to shot. If these feelings are desirable, then the shots should be composed without such matching composition, working away from a flowing continuity and toward a staccato effect. Battle scenes, scenes of violent emotional conflict, natural disasters, and scenes of physical violence are some instances in which this may be used. By planning shots which force the eye to move violently over the frame, a sense of violence can be added to the images, even where little or none exists within the images themselves. It is sometimes possible, through such attention to eye movement, and often using it in combination with violent camera movement, to create a feeling of violence in shots which of themselves contain no violent action. Of course, the limits of eye fatigue must not be exceeded; and when the device calls attention to itself, then it begins to fail.

BRIDGING SHOTS

Smooth continuity results from the relative composition of the connecting shots, as well as the relative movement of the eye within the shots and the flow of action within the scene. Bridging shots, sometimes referred to as transitional shots, intended primarily as connections between two shots, scenes, or sequences within the film, usually continue the flow of action, and advance it if possible. Bridging shots might be necessary to pass time or to show change or progression in space. Such shots can either sustain the temporal and spatial relationships of the scenes or sequences they bridge, or they can be the means by which tempo and space can be changed. Powerful effects can be achieved by giving as much care to the preparation of bridging shots as to the action scenes themselves.

One kind of bridging shot is the insert, which is useful in several ways: it allows the audience a close look at specific items of importance to the action, it provides something to cut to in the event of an editing dilemma, and it is a means of controlling spatial and temporal continuity. When an actor in the story focuses his attention upon something which is too small or too obscure in the frame to be readily recognized by the audience—the page of a book, the key in the lock, a ring on a finger—then an insert can be used to satisfy the audience's curiosity about the object. An insert can also be used to focus attention upon an object in the scene which will play a part in the action about to occur, whether or not the actors themselves are aware of it. An insert is an attention-focusing device, but, since it still remains in the flow of continuity, it should be as carefully timed and composed as any major shot in the film.

The importance of change of angle between shots was mentioned in connection with temporal continuity. This change is equally important for maintaining spatial continuity. Unless the subject changes from shot to shot, then the angle usually changes. Without change of one or the other, a disruption in spatial continuity occurs because of the change in the subject's relationship to the frame. Changing the camera angle masks this difference. On rare occasions, however, the director may purposefully fail to change angle. He may, for instance, go from a long shot, to a medium shot, to a close shot of the subject, all the shots being taken from the same angle. To be successful, the compositions in each must be matched carefully, so that the eye does not become confused. Such a sequence of shots tends to give its subject a sense of formality and importance it might not otherwise have.

ENTRANCES AND EXITS

One of the most important cushions provided so that spatial continuity can be achieved in editing is the use of clean entrances and exits. The word

8

Ideas in Physical Form

THE IDEA

THE FILM BEGINS with the story or idea, usually embodied in a script. This may or may not closely delineate the film in a completed state. About one of his films, Hitchcock said, "When a screenplay is finished, my picture is finished."[20] For Anthony Mann, the script is, with other materials, merely a starting point:

> . . . on this one (*The Heroes of Telemark*), we had the book, *Skis Against the Atom*, and another book, *But For These Men*, and got a war film from Colonel Wilson. Out of these materials we started formulating a story, then we went to Norway, and everything for the story was there. I saw the visual possibilities. I would say that I went to Rjukan and looked at the whole place and picked locations because of the pictorialness of it. You keep elaborating and collaborating and eventually the place brings ideas to you that aren't in the scenario. Films above everything else are pictures and you ground them pictorially. I don't believe in talk, not for films. That's for the theatre. Here you see it   [21]

The script can be the blueprint and the reference, providing guidance throughout production. To be most useful, the script should be complete but not too restrictive. Like any good plan, it should leave room for the interpretation and change necessary in bringing a film into reality. Such interpretation should ordinarily be based upon some script element and not upon a factor which, though of personal interest to the interpreter, may be irrelevant and destructive to the story.

The director's job is to define the implicit values of the script, whether it was written by himself or another. He must examine the story for basic structural pattern and detail.

As soon as the director starts work he finds himself entangled in a problem that will be with him until he finishes his last shot—how to transfer this conception into another medium. It is inevitable that, during this, some modification must occur.

170

A script is simply an intermediate step between a film idea and the film itself. It has value only as a means of communication between the writer and director. Such communication between two human beings is complex in itself. When the two parties are both creative personalities, each of whom is an intensely energetic, subjective, individualistic being, the difficulties are much greater.

Perfect communication or agreement, if it exists at all, is rare. Between a writer and a director it sometimes seems impossible.

Nevertheless, it is to the director that responsibility for understanding goes. He has to turn the script into a film, whether or not he thinks the script is clear, or has any personal feeling for or against the idea of the script. Inadvertently or purposefully, directors at times appear to seize upon certain ideas in the script and give them an emphasis and importance out of all proportion to the intention of a writer who stated, or at least thought he stated, a somewhat different set of ideas. Innocently or intentionally, the director may begin to impose ideas on the material of the script. Those working with him in production will fall prey to the same kind of activity. But the director has more room to err and change than others. Unless he understands the script's intentions, and in practice honestly attempts to pursue the same goals, the director can, even at this early point, begin to violate the plan. This is a choice he must make before he begins his work.

If he aims to follow the script literally, as he understands it, he may still find portions of the plan that must be changed. For reasons of budget, availability of men and materials, and feasibility of ideas, modifications to the plan begin to re-shape the director's idea. Whether the result is still like the original vision—though it may have changed some aspects of its physical form—depends upon the director's judgment. He must know what he can and cannot change, and what will retain or enhance, degrade or divert the original idea.

Script Readings

As the design for the film is developed, the director reads and re-reads the script many times. The first reading is an attempt to experience the initial impression an audience will have of the completed film. In this early stage parts of the plan may begin to form. Some scenes will come without effort. The director may be unable to shake them off, and he should not try. Nor should he try, at this stage, to force his imagination to picture those scenes which do not come without effort. The reading should be comparatively fast, though attentive to details that can give clues to the script's intent. Probably the director should not yet attempt to make notes because this can interrupt his sense of the story's unity. Essentially, he is trying not only to experience a new action, but to experience it with an intensity which will later allow accurate recall of that first experience. As in life, there is only one first time and thus this first script reading has special significance.

During the next few readings, the director begins to visualize more systematically the ideas inherent in the words. He makes marginal notes of images or details of action or sound which come to his mind. As he slowly reduces the ideas to action, he tries to retain his sense of the basic structure of the work and to fit his images into this structure. The script begins to have a temporal quality for him, a rhythm and tempo that he can relate to the structure.

Characters start to form as real human beings and he begins to think about casting. At the same time, details of set construction and ideas about the atmosphere of the set and its lighting emerge from the study.

As he visualizes the characters' actions, he may at the same time visualize the place in which these could occur, and imagine how the spatial characteristics of the set—its open places, its solid forms, its entrances and exits—would give his planned action limitation and form. Ideas about sound effects, and perhaps even musical themes, invade his thinking, together with some conception of where in the action such things as cuts, dissolves, fades and other optical effects might occur. He makes plot plans of contemplated camera movements in relation to a still or moving subject, and sketches of camera angles with lighting notes.

All this time the dramatic form is kept in mind. Exposition is planned to subtly join the current of action, developing story values with understanding and insight, working toward a climax or climaxes with a sense of purpose and achievement, and providing a denouement appropriate to the preceding action. The director is not slavish to the elements of dramaturgy, however. His guide is his sense of what affects an audience, whether or not it happens to conform to any dramatic rules.

At times the director works from a script or idea of his own. In this situation the problem of communication is solved. The words on paper only serve as reminders of his conceptions rather than first hand carriers of meaning. Therefore the idea need no longer struggle through a verbal intermediary but goes directly from imagination to film. While in a sense this eliminates a major directing task, it increases his responsibility for critical examination.

When the writer–director is one person, the sense of unity and coherence is intensified, but so is the danger of excess and disproportion. It is comparatively easy to detect flaws—but only in the work of others.

STYLE

Regardless of the source of the film idea however, matters of style, symbol, and structure are involved in putting it on film. Style is easy to identify (though hard to define) because it is personality projected into the work. It is an impression, not a trademark, something that emerges from the way in which a director works and typically solves problems. It is not something superimposed on the story. Bernard Weinraub reports Richard Lester reacting this way when asked about style:

> "I don't set out to impose a style on a film at all," he went on, with just a trace of annoyance, "I work totally instinctively. If I want to get across a mood of exuberance or claustrophobia or freedom I do it in the best way I can."[22]

Though the director's work may spring from that of another, it is he who gives body and life to the script idea, who explains and interprets it and adds to it his own characteristic ways of feeling and understanding. He uses the raw materials of his own emotions, his experience, his perceptions and imagination, passed through the men and machines which are his tools. It is in such characteristic patterns of expression, based upon individual experience, that the director's style lies.

Style in any absolute sense does not exist, but is the product of interaction between personality and work. Of this characteristic quality, Carl Dreyer remarks:

> I would define style as the form in which artistic inspiration expresses itself. We recognise the style of an artist in certain features characteristic of him personally, which reflect his nature and his outlook.
>
> The style of a film that is a work of art results from many different components, such as the effect of rhythm and composition, the mutual tension of color surfaces, the interaction of light and shadow, the gliding rhythm of the camera. All of these things, combined with the director's conception of his material as something that can be expressed in terms of creative film, decide his style. If he confines himself to the soulless impersonal photography of what his eyes can perceive, he has no style. If he uses his mind to transfer what his eyes can see into a vision, if he builds up his film in accordance with this vision, disregarding the reality that inspired it, then his work will bear the sacred stamp of inspiration. Then his film has a style.[23]

To arbitrarily impose "style" on a script idea is to court disunity and degradation of the idea. Style is not something a director strives to attain; indeed, he cannot escape it. Dreyer:

> The characteristics of a good style, itself simple and precise too, must be that it enters into such intimate contact with the material that it forms a synthesis. If it is too pushing, if it tries to attract attention, it is no longer style but mannerism.[24]

The only way the director can honestly escape his own style is to change himself. An attempt to mimic the style of others will stifle his imagination, impose needless boundaries on expression and allow irrelevancies to intrude.

SYMBOL

Because the primary purpose is to communicate meaning to the audience, and because symbols are highly condensed and potentially efficient ways to convey meaning, many directors try to achieve particularly communicative symbolic effects. Dreyer again clearly states his views:

> To make the form more evident, more striking, simplification must cleanse the director's inspiration of all elements that do not support his central idea. It must transform the idea into a symbol. With symbolism we are well on our way to abstraction, for symbolism works through suggestion.[25]

But to be successful, symbols, like style, must emerge from the materials handled, rather than being imposed upon them. Symbolic objects, events or relationships are not introduced into the scene. Attention is drawn to elements within the scene which, through the treatment given them, take on meaning in addition to their literal significance. Thus they become symbolic.

Use of symbolism is a familiar element in experimental films, which often tend to lean heavily upon this method of relating information. Many experimental films seem to consist largely of the "in" language which some of the more esoteric forms of symbolism become. Thus they are understood only by those who know the language.

Other experimental films depend upon ready associations made by most filmgoers. These can speak in a more fluent, if less subtle (or obscure) way.

Symbolism plays a part even in the apparently more prosaic approaches in documentary films. In telling a particularized story of an event or object, the documentary implies that the story is to be generalized as a comment about all such objects or events. Almost all filmgoers are familiar with the symbols which have become clichés: calendars turning over or moving hands of clocks to symbolize the passage of time; heroes and heroines walking off into a sunset which symbolizes the future; the black clothing of the villain and pale clothing of the good guys.

Audiences are less conscious, though more affected, by less obvious uses of symbolism. Examples are: the broken mirror of *A Streetcar Named Desire* expressing the shattered mind of the heroine; the rosebud of *Citizen Kane* expressing a longing for the simpler days of childhood; the checkered regularity of the floor of the Spanish Court in *Don Quixote*, not only rigid and fixed but resembling a giant game of chess on which the actors seemed merely chess-pieces; the pale haired virtuous wife of *High Noon*, and the black haired "other" woman; the flash of sunlight through the trees in *Rashomon*, signaling the moment of rape—the list could be endless. When such elements emerge as a part of the natural background of the scene and are plucked out of the surroundings for a momentary attention which focuses powerfully upon the

underlying meaning of the scene, they become highly successful and memorable parts of the film. Since effective symbolic expression involves immediate
association and insight, the symbol must be clear and simple. The obscure or
complicated symbol may exist apart from the audience's level of consciousness, or, worse, may call attention to its physical rather than its symbolic self,
and thus away from the story. Dreyer remarks that,

> The director can give his rooms a soul through simplification, by removing
> all that is superfluous, by making a few significant articles and objects
> psychological witnesses of the inmate's personality.[26]

If he is sensitive to his surroundings, the director can find an abundance of
potentially symbolic material in almost any scene.

Once he has decided to endow an object or event with symbolic meaning—or, more accurately, to draw attention to the symbolic potential of an
object or event—the director finds that he is able to manipulate the symbol
much as he manipulates characters. In effect, symbols as used in films
become characters in the story. Like characters, they must have consistency,
a continuity of usage. As the director develops their possibilities, symbols can
accommodate greater meaning on more levels, so becoming more efficient
and useful.

An entire situation, place, person or action may be characterized by a
few symbols. In *Forgotten Village*, for instance, in the scene where the wife is
undergoing labor, her arms, following native custom, have been strapped to a
cross-like affair while the witch-doctor midwife helps her to deliver her child.
The camera shows the mother in the foreground with her arms outstretched,
and shoots towards a wall in the background where a crucifix exactly mimics
the position of the mother. Thus not only information about the religious life
of the peasants is given, but the dramatic moment is heightened through the
symbolic implication of the crucifix. Story themes are thus enriched and
embroidered with overtones of meaning. Selected with care and an eye to
economy and compression, the symbol can characterize the whole, recon-
structing previous experiences or feelings and enhancing meaning of the
present scene.

By simple repetition of the symbolic device, the significant part of a
scene can be recapitulated without taking the time or space to recreate the
scene itself.

Some objects come with ready-made associations. If new associations are
desired, they must be created clearly. The difficulty in establishing a new set
of associations may be rewarded by the sense of irony that results, since the
audience tends to see simultaneously the new and the old meanings in the
symbol. If the two meanings contrast, the audience can experience a twist of
irony.

Once these strong associations have been successfully established, the stimulus to the associations must be used consistently. Audience feeling toward symbols cannot change unless old associations are destroyed and new ones built. Once their character has been established, symbols are never silent. They speak to the audience whenever they are present. Thus the director must be on guard lest he inadvertently include or imply an object or event in a scene when he does not intend any special meaning. When the symbol is not needed in the scene, or when it is no longer necessary to the story, it should be excluded from the action lest it clutter the action with irrelevant associations.

Finally, the director must be aware that audiences may create symbols on their own. Whenever something is brought to the attention of the spectator, he assumes it has meaning. If it does not, or if the meaning is unclear, the spectator supplies his own interpretation, which may or may not do service to the story.

In visualization, the director tries to reproduce or stimulate visual impressions through physical likeness, but the likenesses themselves have no other purpose. The aim is to make the spectator live within the image, not merely to be a witness to it. This psychological participation in the action enhances an audience's understanding of it. The audience not only sees appearances, but experiences more or less vicariously the total action of the film.

In order to stimulate these effects while planning and shooting, the director, looking at the objects in the frame and the action, must realize how he and others feel emotionally about the objects they see. He must think of their possible connotations and any significance or emphasis they bear. It is only through such direct attention that purpose can be separated from chance.

STRUCTURE

Again the task is to detect what is implicit in the film idea and to use it to effectively tell the story. Structure, like style and symbol, is something inherent in any meaningful story. It may need to be strengthened or crystallized, or sublimated and made more subtle. But in any case, structure, or form, is the skeleton of an idea.

Usually a story has a single idea from which all aspects of elaboration and enrichment radiate. Finding this basic idea is the first task during the early script readings. Once it is found, the key steps in its development can be located.

In most cases these steps are a few moments of significance or decision within the flow of events which propel the action to movement, driving the story to its outcome. However many the points of elaboration, all lead forward to the one goal to be achieved. While obstacles placed in the way of the action can provide suspense and reveal hidden story elements, these compli-cations should not be confused with the meaning of the story itself. They are the accoutrements of plot, and ways to bring the story into the terms of action.

They convey meaning only indirectly through the action they bring about.

In the process of developing structure, there is an ever present concern with continuity. But there is also a need for variety in order to stimulate and sustain interest, for change to lend a sense of motion to the story, for suspense and curiosity and revealing character. Above all, there is a need to be clear, to save audience energy for the story rather than dissipate it in confusing, distracting, albeit alluring, speculative sidetrips. Presumably the film idea has a goal.

To lead the audience on irrelevant, energy-consuming trails is to run the risk of not reaching the goal at all.

Structure, or form, is implicit in any action or event which is not random, which is performed with purpose. It exists in any action or object which was planned, however cursory the planning might have been. In this sense, structure *is* purpose, and its simplicity or complexity is suggested by the purpose itself. Actions or events which have single purposes are, rela-tively speaking, simple in structure. The action of putting one foot in front of the other is simple in purpose and structure. But walking is slightly more complex; walking in a certain direction, within a certain period of time, with feelings and expectations about the trip there, as well as what arrival at the destination will mean—all these increase the structural complication, be-cause the purposes are more numerous and complex. To design an object upon which a human being can sit is a comparatively simple purpose, and the result, if that is the only purpose, will be rather simple structurally. Anything that supports the weight of the human body will do and that is the only criterion.

However, if additional purposes of safety, comfort, beauty, personal expression and ruggedness enter into the problem, then the resulting design becomes sophisticated, more variables have been considered, more factors shaped to obtain specific ends. The concept will be more complex, even though the final product seems a simple and direct solution.

Length

Length affects structure also. While it is possible that a long film with a simple purpose may have a comparatively simple structure, it will not ordinarily be so simple as a shorter film with the same purpose. Time itself, like massiveness in architecture, presupposes that the purposes are larger and more complicated and that the structure to support them will have to be designed accordingly. Since a film involves manipulation of audience

attention in time, its structure is usually complex over-all, although its framework might be straightforward. The film maker must capture his audience's
full attention moment-by-moment. The structure must be sufficiently
interesting and meaningful to accomplish this, while at the same time it
heads towards the larger purpose of the film as a whole. Each detail of
planned action must have this dual quality of a "being" and a "becoming"—
of being something at the moment, and a part of something which is coming
into being, is becoming.

SHAPE

In developing story structure, the problem of shape arises—that rise to
a climax which is basic to most stories. The climax is often a moment of
revelation, a meeting point of story elements, and a time at which the purpose of the story impresses itself upon the spectator.

Everything before the climax leads to it. The exposition locates the
spectator in time and space, establishes the mood, and sets the tone or
atmosphere of possibility about the action to follow. During the development
the spectator feels a sense of direction and purpose, leading towards something,
causing suspense and expectation and interrupted periodically by frustration
and partial satisfaction, leading to new expectation, and then a growing
tension when the climax nears. All this culminates in the realization that is
the climax itself.

After the climax, or revelation, the accumulated tensions may be given
the opportunity to subside and as the action leaves the spectator he again
orients himself to the outside world. Even such relatively abstract films as the
experimental *Metanomen*, which is essentially a visual experience with no
dialogue and no narration, carries this form of exposition, rising tension,
speed and complication, to final culmination. This sense of forceful movement ahead, the impending culmination and ultimate satisfaction, is what
gives a film basic interest.

Embellishments and variations enhancing the moment must always still
move the story forward.

Changes in techniques, methods, and styles of filmic expression have
made their impression on structure as well. The concepts of story-telling
which came from the nineteenth century—crises, complication, climax and
denouement—have, in the opinion of many film makers working since
the early 1960s, led audiences to a conception of a kind of life which has
never existed. Life experience, it was recognized, is disordered, irregularly
and randomly punctuated with moments of high and low. This was accepted
as a viable form of story telling: films no longer need show life as a continuous
flow from past through present to future, but as an event occurring within
the mind.

Events themselves need not be so well defined nor have so rigid a pattern as most of the earlier story films had implied. Films could more closely parallel life. The parts of classic structure which seemed most to fall into disuse were the beginning and the end. Expositions no longer had to be clearly rooted in time and space and loose ends need not be wrapped up so that audiences could leave the theatre with the feeling that the story was finished. Films began to appear which stopped, even though the story did not end.

But while many of these films give the impression of a slice from life, actually some more closely follow the classic idea of structure than would at first appear to be the case. In Lester's *Petulia*, for instance, although the hero and the heroine are not, in the end, united, over-all story form follows a familiar pattern of complication–crisis–climax. Exposition is ignored in a narrative sense, but is still present, though it is given to the audience in what appears to be random, unexplained fragments, the interpretation of which is largely the responsibility of the audience. By all "logical" systems, the images are completely out of context. But dramatically they are *in* context in that they are in the minds of the characters. The images present themselves to the viewer much as ideas and thoughts present themselves to the individual in life—with little regard to their place in a time continuum, but with great relevancy to the consciousness and motivations of the characters. Even the Pennebaker–Leacock documentaries, seemingly random fragments from life, loosely follow a classic dramatic pattern. In selecting the critical segments of people's lives, the film makers recognize the power of climax and the events leading to it as a dramatically compelling form.

Pre-production Planning

The amount of time available for pre-production planning may vary from a few hours (for the replacement director or the hastily mounted production) to several months. A few hours, of course, is hardly adequate. Without preparation, success is less certain, even when experience and skill can be counted on. In such a situation, formulae for shooting are often used: these may not be the most appropriate way to achieve the purpose of the film.

Whatever the available time—whether a lengthy period before shooting or bits of time during the actual shooting process—a plan or theme for the film must be formed, a central idea upon which the solutions to problems can be based.

Environment and Action

The action of the story begins to form during pre-production planning; during the process of visualizing the script action is given pace and location, a sense of mood and atmosphere begins to emerge. The environment for action takes shape and has visual unity with the particular events of the story and an over-all consistency with the principal, performed action. The selection, definition and use of space and sound together create environment. The time design superimposed upon and ultimately incorporated within it creates feeling for the environment, selectively gives value to events contained with it and, hopefully, provokes selective audience response to the stimuli presented.

This over-all image and sound impression carries a large portion of a film's meaning on a level apart from and sometimes in counterpoint with an interpretation of the actual events taking place in the film. Such purely visual and audial effectiveness can dominate audience consciousness, evoking strong and immediate response. But it can also create a deeper and more lasting impression, even more profound than the impression given by the events portrayed. Thus for example an audience may respond to a romanticized war film with nationalistic ego-satisfaction, involvement in the exciting and heroic adventure, and sympathy with specific attitudes toward the use of force.

These secondary responses, a result not of the events but of the environment, may also make the most lasting impression. Long after the story is forgotten, the image of war as glory is retained.

Another film, made with the same story, could, by the nature of the secondary environment created, instill a sense of rage and disgust at man's stupidity. In this process leading from immediate to lasting response, the specific story events usually occupy some sort of middle ground—rational, conscious, easily verbalized and explained—surrounded by what may be a more irrational, subconscious, but more lastingly recalled environment which has been created apart from the film idea. How effectively the meaning of the film events become a part of the audience's thought process, its subconscious memory and experience of things, depends largely upon the appropriateness or fit of the environment to the event.

VISUAL NOTES

The film idea will suggest an appropriate environment as the initial generalized reaction to a script is slowly replaced by an ultimate, particularized shaping of each scene, each shot, each movement, each sound. Often it is useful, during this process, to make simple line sketches of the composition of key scenes. These are a basis for selecting locations or building sets, as well as defining the extent and nature of action and sound possible within them (fig. 31).

Later on, the sketches may become a storyboard, a set of perspective sketches of the complete film showing the set and its dressing, make-up, properties and costume, lighting, camera angle, camera movement, perhaps also actor movement. With or without a storyboard, there is usually a series

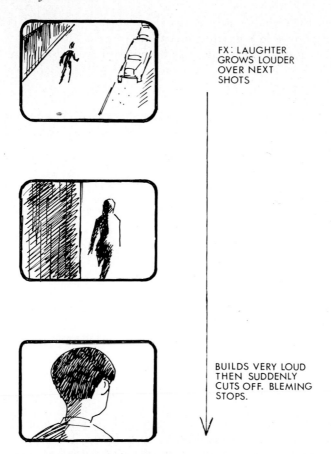

FX: LAUGHTER
GROWS LOUDER
OVER NEXT
SHOTS

BUILDS VERY LOUD
THEN SUDDENLY
CUTS OFF. BLEMING
STOPS.

Fig. 31. Even minimal sketching gives an impression of action and camera angle. At times part, or even all, of a script will consist of nothing more than a series of such sketches.

of floor-plan sketches on which are indicated actor and camera movements in relation to one another. Notes describing sounds, music and words usually accompany or are keyed to these sketches.

By the time this stage of preparation is complete, the director's script contains many notes, plus "thumbnail" sketches and floor plans at critical points. Where a particularly difficult spatial problem arises, a three dimensional scale model of the set may be constructed, complete with miniature lights and scale statuettes representing the actors.

Through a viewfinder, such models take on a close approximation of what is to be photographed.

But storyboards and models are not always available, or worth the time and energy to make them. Where a complex visual idea must be shown to production technicians, such devices are useful. But their inflexibility (compared with a free ranging imagination) makes them less useful for visualization. A practiced memory and a minimal skill in sketching have the

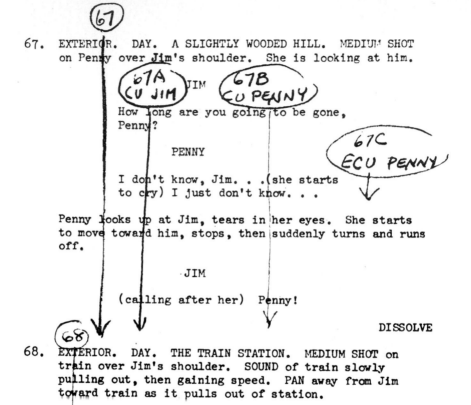

Fig. 32. A working script. Sketches coupled with notations indicating length and coverage of shots helps the director not only to visualize specifically and in detail, but to remember his original intention during shooting.

virtues of being both readily available and flexible. Describing his preparation for shooting, Donald Siegel says:

> I have the advantage of being able to envisage cinematically what I intend to do. Now if I don't know what the set looks like, forget it—there's no point in any planning. If I don't know what the location looks like, there's no point. But if I do know, I can sit in front of the typewriter with the script in front of me and have total recall of the set and where the doors are, I might have—not a sketch because they would be much too expensive —but a plan layout, or, if at all possible, I would have seen the set the day

before, so that I would know where all the furniture was, the placing of
it, and then I would lay it out as I think it would be cut . . . Let us presume
for the moment that I've laid it out satisfactorily as an editor. Now
because of lack of time in shooting, I lay it out in terms of shooting con-

PENNY TURNS AND RUNS
AWAY—SLIGHT TILT DOWN

DISSOLVE

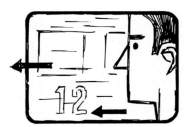

PAN OFF JIM'S FACE WITH
TRAIN

Fig. 33. Simple line sketches with short explanatory notes quickly convey information
about subject or camera movement, angles and effects.

tinuity, which does not mean that it will interfere with the type of shot
that I'm going to make, but that I'll complete shooting in one direction
before I turn around and shoot the other way, which saves an enormous
amount of time in moves and in lighting.[27]

Fig. 34. Production sketch for a pan shot, indicating setting, lighting and action across the whole field of camera movement.

During this design process a plan of action for shooting will develop: the results of this plan will become evident during the editing of the film. Just as sketches and floorplans are graphic evidence of spatial design, so the shooting plan is evidence of the time design. In making this plan, continuous scenes are consolidated for shooting purposes, even though they are to be interrupted by intercuts in editing. Generalized notations of action are made specific, locations of cuts estimated, overlapping indicated and coverage from different angles is noted. Making the shooting plan is the last opportunity, before the shooting period itself, for anticipating problems in production and providing for their solution without weakening the film.

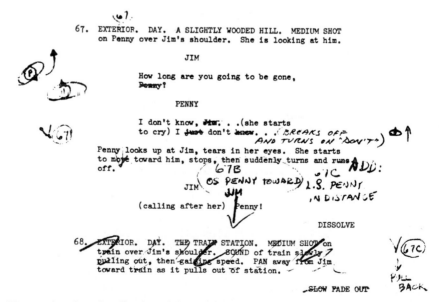

67. EXTERIOR. DAY. A SLIGHTLY WOODED HILL. MEDIUM SHOT on Penny over Jim's shoulder. She is looking at him.

JIM

How long are you going to be gone, Penny?

PENNY

I don't know, Jim. . .(she starts to cry) I just don't know. . .

Penny looks up at Jim, tears in her eyes. She starts to move toward him, stops, then suddenly turns and runs off.

JIM

(calling after her) Penny!

DISSOLVE

68. EXTERIOR. DAY. THE TRAIN STATION. MEDIUM SHOT on train over Jim's shoulder. SOUND of train slowly pulling out, then gaining speed. PAN away from Jim toward train as it pulls out of station.

SLOW FADE OUT

Fig.35. Another visualization of the script in Fig. 33. Some directors prefer floor plan layouts to storyboard type sketches. The director adapts the script to his visualization: adding shots, deleting shots, changing dialogue and locations of cuts.

Fig. 36. Production sketch for an interior shot, showing properties, lighting, costume and details of arrangement. Such sketches are usually related to some written explanatory matter.

THE EDITING PLAN

The decision to consolidate scenes, or to break them down into their individual shot components, reflects the demands of the shooting, as well as the nature of the time design.

There are two basic approaches to shooting: Either shooting all the major sequences as master scenes, or building each sequence detail by detail, shot by shot, allowing minimal overlap and duplication.

MASTER SHOT METHOD

In the master shot approach to the directing process, continuous actions are recorded in longer segments of shooting, often as one master scene, which sometimes becomes quite lengthy. Inserts, cutaways and cover shots of various kinds are then collected to provide variety of viewpoint and rhythm in the final film. In this technique, the parts of action are usually photographed from many points of view, while the whole action is covered from one or two vantage points, often in a loose medium shot.

Fig. 37. Production sketch for an exterior shot on which the camera elevation, manned perspective and any important features of the scene itself are visualized.

Shooting master shots with appropriate covering material has both advantages and disadvantages. Stylistic and environmental consistency is easier to maintain. Insufficient coverage is avoided in that the system provides much duplication, and therefore flexibility during editing. Lack of preciseness before shooting is less noticeable in the final product. Limitations in the performance of actors and shooting crew are minimized in dialogue scenes, or with inexperienced actors or non-professionals. The master shot approach, if properly planned and carried out, can allow the postponement of final editing decisions until final performances have been secured.

Too often, however, the master shot approach is used as a lazy-man's way of insuring an editable scene. The technique, while secure, can become mechanical, inflexible and unresponsive to the internal dramatic needs of the scene. Using it exclusively encourages vague concepts and an over-attention to technical editing considerations, rather than aesthetic ones. Master shot shooting is a simple, trouble-free way of achieving minimally acceptable results.

While it is helpful to the director faced with an unpredictable or un-planned shooting situation, it can become a crutch to directors who have time to spend, and who would better use that time, imagination and energy in conceiving a story.

SHOT-BY-SHOT METHOD

The alternative is a shot-by-shot approach. In this, each shot is planned precisely, and each photographed exactly as it will appear in the final film, allowing, of course, for the overlapping and coverage necessary to join the shots together in continuity. The advantages of the method are that it forces thinking in concrete terms. Final tempo, editing style and visual composition must be anticipated long before shooting begins. There is no room in the shot-by-shot approach for hazy visualizations. Forget one link in the chain of shots, or make one link which will not attach to the next, and the scene is marred. The final, edited film, as it is seen and heard in the imagination, is, in effect, the shooting plan.

Against this, the shot-by-shot approach provides less flexibility in the editing stage unless there are sufficient alternative takes. Possibilities of error in anticipating performances and editing tempo are greater. The director will probably not resort to the technique until he has gained some confidence in his ability to make his imaginings and his images match. Dialogue sequences of any length are seldom given this treatment because of the unknown factor of performance and the technical difficulty in matching sound level and quality from shot to shot. The sense of environment suffers at times for lack of consistency or dominating effect.

Most often, both techniques are used in designing and planning a film. The decision to use one or the other is determined by the kind of shooting set-up, anticipated technical problems, the nature of the script idea and its action, personal style and the vision of the finished film.

PLANNING UNSCRIPTED FILMS

The planning process involved in shooting an unscripted film such as *Primary* is quite different than that for the scripted film. Planning and experience are just as important, but they appear in a different form. Abandoning the formal pre-production methods and consultations, the team members examine the film idea for any potential they can see in their own areas of interest. They learn about the subject matter of their film, about the personalities who will be involved, about the locations in which they will work, and attempt, in somewhat the same manner as with the director using the natural event as an actor, to predict likely possibilities of action. A loose framework or motif might be decided upon, such as the moving feet in

ACTION	SOUND
74. EXT. CITY. MONTAGE. Steel wrecking balls knocking down walls of buildings.	NARRATION: A city. . . always changing. . .
75. CU hand throws beer can into gutter of street.	always the same. . .
76. MS GARBAGE DUMP, huge hills of trash being moved by bulldozer.	the same each day. . .
77. LS crowded city street, power lines overhead, walks littered with debris.	the same each year for a million human beings.
78. CUT MONTAGE sequence starting slowly and then accelerating. City shots emphasizing crowded feeling. Build to peak with sound. Then CUT	(FX: noise of streetcars, horns honking, cars, harsh city sounds.)
79. EXT. DAY. EXTREME LONG SHOT from top of hill across valley. Shoot with sun backlit. DISSOLVE	(FX: continue over this shot.)
80. EXT. DAY. LONG SHOT the beach. Waves push up on beach and withdraw (shoot slightly slow motion).	(FX: build to peak, then SEGUE to music.)

Fig. 38. The two-column script is often used for non-synchronous dialogue sequences in films, or for entire non-dialogue films. The physical layout of action in relation to sound often provides a clue to intended meaning, action-sound relationships and tempo, and can serve as a guide in cutting.

Primary, to tie together various sequences that would otherwise be difficult to relate. This pre-event planning process is then carried over to the period when the material is being collected, and the resultant material is being assembled. This style of production depends heavily upon the experience and skill of those involved, and requires a large amount of footage to provide as much flexibility in editing as possible. The process does not work so well where the director, as photographer, keeps no editing plan in mind, or if the director, as editor, has too little material available, and insufficient skill to take advantage of what he does have.

Probably the most notable example of this technique is Leni Riefenstahl's *Triumph of the Will*, wherein several dozen cameramen were placed

ACTION	SOUND
34. EXT. DAY, DAWN. AIRPORT. High angle from top of tower. Field is empty. Ted enters frame and walks slowly toward hanger, right.	FX: aircraft approaching slowly.
35. MS low angle Ted's feet moving on pavement. Goes off right.	
36. MLS Ted approaching hanger.	FX: begin slow fade in tele- type machine mixed with radio
37. INSERT CU: hand opening door.	messages.
38. MS, OS Ted. He slowly pushes door open, but does not go in.	
39. MS the runway as the plane lands. CUT at the moment it touches down.	FX: aircraft landing.
40. MONTAGE: aircraft wheels touching down.	FX: bring up teletype and radio loud and carry over CUT.

Fig. 39. The two-column form of script is extremely flexible, but can become frag-
mentary in production. Such a script is often handled with a shot-by-shot approach.

about the Nürnberg stadium under directions to gather certain kinds of
footage. Out of the tremendous amount of footage available thereafter, Miss
Riefenstahl edited the famous Nazi documentary. In such films, whatever
coherency, fluency and continuity exists, does so because of some established
approach for various shooting units, and because, in editing, points of
similarity between parts of the footage are noted and shots linked as if by
plan.

Shooting

The next step in production is the shooting period. Extensive pre-
production rehearsal is a luxury that few film directors can indulge in. It is
time-consuming and expensive to hire the actors, locations and photographers
necessary for full acting and camera rehearsals. Dry runthroughs—with
mock sets and viewfinders or empty cameras—are occasionally tried. Even
though such rehearsal may only vaguely approximate the actual shooting
set-up, it allows experiment with camera and actor blocking. But what the
director can always depend upon, whether others are available or not, is his
own imagination.

To expect to rehearse, experiment or make substantial changes during
production is usually impractical and expensive. Full crew and equipment

MEDIUM CLOSE SHOT. Ross is expecting the driver to say something
to him.

                         VOICE OFF SCREEN

              What's your name, Corporal?

THREE SHOT, OVERSHOULDER of Ross looking toward the sergeant and
the major, whose name is Blake. It is he who just asked Ross his
name.

                             ROSS

              Ross, sir . . .J. N. Ross

CLOSEUP Blake. He watches Ross with a suggestion of suspicion and
distrust.

                             BLAKE

              Maybe you'd better come along with us.

CLOSEUP Ross. He is surprised at the abrupt suggestion and the tone
of voice.

                             ROSS

              (starts to object, then stops) All right,
              sir.

Ross gets into the jeep next to the sergeant. The jeep starts to
move. The CAMERA rides as a passenger as we

                                            DISSOLVE

Fig 1͏. The dialogue script form can be less flexible in its notion sound relationships,
at least where dialogue itself is concerned, but it also tends to be more cohesive than
the two-column form. It is often treated with the master scene approach. See also
the example in Fig. 32.

are present and waiting for the real shooting to begin. More often, as a
preliminary to the shooting period, the director has a short conference with
the cameraman to give and take ideas and to establish some common ground
on which to work. The director's meeting with his actors might include discussing the basic conceptions of character with, perhaps, some line rehearsals,
and more rarely a brief walkthrough of parts of the action. For all practical
purposes, however, the moment planning is complete the director must be
prepared to plunge into shooting.

    With a crew of experienced workers, of course, the need for extensive
rehearsal lessens: they are more capable of doing their planning in the

imagination, and less likely to find that their plans are impossible to carry out in reality. But even with experience, rehearsal can be beneficial, as it allows everyone to experiment with working together as a team before the stress of the actual shooting.

Working on the Set

As head of the crew, the director sees to the shooting progress and keeps himself informed of the activities of all those working with him. He guides and funnels the talent and energy of this disparate group of individuals, some passionately involved in their work, others simply holding down a job.

For a documentary production, this group may consist of two or three people working on a very informal basis. As the size of the crew increases for a major production, the methods of work and of communication tend to become formalized and detailed. But whatever the make-up or size of the group, the director may become a focal point for both conflict and inspiration. When tensions arise, as they do in any production, the crew turns to the director for release or reaffirmation. When spirits are low, he must rouse commitment to the job in hand.

Making a Setup

Because so many things are involved in shooting even a comparatively simple scene in a film, certain procedures have come into use which, if followed, make sure that everyone concerned knows what everyone else is doing. The cameraman and actor might otherwise not really be working together, and neither may be ready when the time comes to photograph the scene.

While there is no rigid system, most shooting companies follow some method or other. Depending upon the complexity of the shooting conditions, the personal style of the director or the needs of the scene, variations can be worked out.

A shooting crew, large or small, at work on a sound stage or on location, always attracts spectators. This is true in Hollywood where such crews are at work daily, and have been for over fifty years, and it is true in Zambia, where such crews may have worked only once or twice before in the memory of the oldest local inhabitant. The process of putting something together always attracts interest. Because the machines used by the crew are strange and sometimes exotic-looking, and because society puts an aura around that figure known as an actor, the film crew is often the focus of a large crowd.

Fig. 41. A simple interior set from the "silent" days of motion picture production, actually built outdoors and lit by the sun. To the right is a 35 mm hand-cranked camera.

But to operate properly, the crew must be allowed space and relative quiet. Thus the first step in making a setup is for a member of the crew, usually the assistant director, to attempt to attain this space and quiet by controlling and limiting the audience which naturally gathers. This is especially important during location shooting where the spectators are strangers full of questions, and where the shooting crew is working under conditions foreign to them. So the assistant director calls out to "clear the set" shortly before work on the shot begins.

When the set or location has been cleared and everyone can concentrate, a briefing session follows. The director makes his plans known to the actors, the cameraman, the boom man, the script clerk and whoever else might be directly involved in the coming shot. Depending upon his personal relationship with the crew, the director may choose to speak to all of these people at once or individually. Whatever the conference method used, each of the crew members, by asking questions and getting answers, comes to an understanding of the intent and requirements of the scene.

Fig. 42. A simple interior sound stage set with a minimal crew. For a small production such as this the crew may consist of only two or three people.

Using a viewfinder or verbal descriptions, the director sets the camera viewpoint of the scene. He tells the cameraman what area is to be included in the shot. He indicates camera angle, relationship of camera to actor and lighting requirements, and discusses the actor's movements so that the lights can be set accordingly. At the same time, the director explains any camera movement planned, and, if a microphone boom is to be used, he tells the boom man where the actors will be in the set so that the microphone can be placed for a good sound recording. The director may occasionally ask the actors or their stand-ins to work with him in this process, as he roughs out the action in relation to camera angle and movement.

Just as the director has complete control over the internal time of the film (but can control external time only if he edits the film himself), so he has complete control over the internal spatial composition. To designate the exact shot he wants, he uses the same vocabulary with the cameraman as the writer used with the director. This vocabulary—made up of such words as "long shot," "low angle," etc.—while not exact, does allow a communication chain to exist which will link initial film idea to ultimate film realization

G

Fig. 43. Making a trucking shot on location, working from a car-mounted camera
platform. [Sinful Davey, *United Artists.*]

—through the intermediaries of writer, director, cameraman, and/or cutter.

The cameraman, on the basis of the director's comments, sets up a shot
which he hopes is about the angle and composition the director had in mind.
The director checks the setup before shooting begins. If he is not satisfied
with it, he changes it. When a director and a cameraman have worked together for some time, on several films, they often develop a language of their
own. Sometimes, in such a relationship, the director gives the cameraman
only the vaguest shot description. The cameraman knows what the director
wants and sets it up for him without delay.

With the camera viewpoint decided, the cameraman directs his crew
to set up the lights, and the camera operator to set up the camera. If necessary, the director may again check camera placement while the action is
rehearsed by the actors or their stand-ins.

At this point, the director and actors, and the cameraman and his crew
may separate. Often, different parts of the setup are worked on simultaneously. The director and actors may leave the set for rehearsals elsewhere,
giving the cameraman room to guide his gaffer (chief lighting technician) in
adjusting lights for visual effect and in checking the light level with a light

Fig. 44. Location shooting in Rome with a small crew. [*The Appointment*, *Metro-Goldwyn-Mayer.*]

meter. While this is going on the assistant cameraman measures the near and far points of the field with a tape measure, so that the proper focus can be set on the lens. He also sets the f/stop according to the cameraman's directions.

The director, discussing with the actors the purpose of the shot, rehearses them in such matters as line delivery, body movement and gesture. Some directors are quite explicit with their actors, going through the motions they want and pronouncing the words as they think they should be. Other directors work indirectly, by suggestion. They hope that by touching the emotions of their actors, and then gently guiding the actor's work, they will

Fig. 45. Location crews often work under difficult conditions. [The Russians are Coming, The Russians are Coming, *United Artists*.]

get the performance they want. Whether the rehearsal is long and detailed, or a short runthrough or less, depends upon the attitudes and working method of the particular director. These can be widely divergent. At one extreme, Billy Wilder says:

> I don't rehearse at all. The actors forget what we were rehearsing, I forget how I rehearsed it, absolutely impossible. I have one hour of runthrough before I start the shooting, sit around with the crew and the cast and discuss the sequence ahead of us each new day, what is to be noticed, where I'm going to do this and that. There's no such thing as my coming on the set in the morning with a piece of chalk and drawing little blueprints and saying: "He will move three steps and take the cigarette out and now he will sit on the couch." We just fool around with ideas until the scene comes to life for all of us, then I talk to the cameraman and the cutter separately about chopping the whole thing up into separate shots. Then I go in and I might do twenty takes until it's exactly right.[28]

Fig. 46. Setting up a crane shot on location. This device gives unusual mobility to the camera. [Dr. Doolittle, *20th Century-Fox*.]

Moving quite far in the other direction, Otto Preminger says:

> I rehearse just before I do the scene and I rehearse as long as necessary. There is no limit. Time is expensive and naturally in the back of one's mind; one cannot completely eliminate it, but I've educated myself just to forget it. Otherwise the whole thing becomes hurried and silly. I could make every picture ten days shorter if I could slough it. Some actors just need more time and more rehearsal and some don't. Some actors, who are basically picture personalities, cannot rehearse. They become what they call stale. Really it is because they don't quite know what they are doing.

Fig. 47. An experienced crew in action: hauling the dolly along tracks to accompany the action, while the microphone boom and shoulder mounted light (in the center) follow. Cable carriers on either side keep lines from snarling, and keep them out of the camera's view. [*Courtesy 20th Century-Fox.*]

> You've got to catch them when they are doing it best. Some actors need a lot of rehearsal and those are very good actors.[29]

Whichever of these or any other method is chosen, the actors must be ready, at the end of the rehearsal period, to go "on camera." Of this moment, George Cukor says:

> You can do all sorts of preparation but nothing can be planned out perfectly ahead of time . . . You know, you can make preparations, you can talk and you can establish a sort of friendly relationship. But when you're before the cameras with your actress you're sort of alone with your god. There you are. When the cameras start to purr it really happens. Up to then it's very polite and hopeful and cordial. You establish a relationship before but the real "working relationship" doesn't happen until you're working.[30]

During this period of preparation the assistant director works as liaison between the two units. When the sound and picture technicians are ready, he informs the director, and director and actors return to the set. The crew is now ready to "roll a scene."

The "Take"

With professionals, this enmeshing process can be quick and relatively painless as the cameraman makes last minute lighting adjustments, the camera operator practices following the movements of the actor, and the actor modifies his gesture and movement and his line delivery. During the enmeshing the director works with all members of the crew, making minor suggestions, modifying, adjusting, shaping, changing, until finally he is satisfied with what he has.

The director now calls for a "take" to be made. Up to this point the photographer, actors, wardrobe women, make-up experts and set dressers have all contributed to the physical scene, checking to make sure that everything is in order and looks as it should—the eighteenth century ballroom looks like an eighteenth century ballroom, or the foxhole looks like a foxhole. The director has kept a weather-eye on these mechanical and technical aspects of preparing a scene, and at the same time has coordinated the work and movements of the actors and cameraman. But, except in his mind, the director has never actually "seen" the shot he is going to take.

Before the camera actually "rolls," everyone must be notified that this is a "take" and not a rehearsal. In preparation for the take, the assistant director once again clears the set of all persons not immediately concerned. Bystanders, actors for other scenes, visitors and interested crew members must be warned of the approaching take, and, if necessary, asked to leave the shooting area. Not only is there danger of these people appearing either visually or audially as spurious actors in the scene, but their presence clutters the working area and distracts the working members of the crew. A maximum of concentration and a minimum of confusion are the first requirements of a good take, and they can occur only where the non-workers are separated from those involved in the immediate scene.

Once the working area is cleared, the director makes a final briefing of his actors and crew. This is the last opportunity to clear up confusions or misunderstandings and to make the crew into a single-minded working unit. From this time forward it is assumed that everyone knows, down to the last intricate detail, exactly what his job is and how to do it. If any member of the crew has doubts or reservations, this is the time to speak up.

As a final step in this preparatory phase the cameraman and sound engineer make a final check over their equipment. The cameraman checks the placement and quality of his lights, the operator checks his camera and lenses to make sure they are properly adjusted for the scene, and the sound crew checks the microphone placement for pickup and adjustments on the sound recording equipment.

During the ready check, which is the next step, the assistant director makes his final checkout of all elements of production. Although each crew member is responsible for his own particular aspect of the scene, the assistant director must see that each member has made his personal check and is in fact ready to go. Should the take be made without all members of the crew being ready, the assistant director takes blame for the oversight. Once the assistant director has gone through his final check, the director can assume that the crew is ready.

The director may call for final camera and action rehearsals which duplicate the take entirely, except that the camera and sound recording equipment is not running. During this rehearsal, the script clerk sees that the actors know of their lines, and notes details of any action needed to match another scene. This is an extremely important step because of the fragmented nature of production. The final check of script lines, action detail, wardrobe and make-up is made.

The assistant director calls for quiet on the set. The director asks the cameraman, "Ready on camera?," and the sound engineer, "Ready on sound?," and the actors, "Ready?" By the time he receives the O.K. from them the set is quiet. If the scene is being shot on a sound stage, a series of mechanical devices operate to warn people in the vicinity that a take is being made. An outsider inadvertently walking in, a loud noise or a telephone ring would ruin the take. The mechanical warning devices consist of a loud alarm bell (warning on-set and off-set persons of the imminent take), a warning light on the outside of the stage door (which is now closed and locked from the inside), and sometimes wig-wag lights which attract the attention of any passers by and warn them to be quiet.

If the crew is working on location, these devices are not available. The assistant director must rely on the cooperation and awareness of passers by, and on guards he might have posted throughout the area to warn persons in the vicinity that a take is in progress.

With a final, "quiet on the set, please," the scene is now ready for identification, or slating. Slating is done in one of several ways. The slateman may take up a position in front of the camera, holding a small board (the slateboard), on which is recorded the name of the production, the production number, the name of the director and cameraman, the scene and take number, and any other information that will identify the strip of film to laboratory workers and to the editor. The director says, "Roll'em!"—if the scene is a sound scene, the sound engineer turns his equipment from "off" to "on" and waits for it to reach operating speed, which is usually only a few seconds. From this moment on, every sound on the stage is recorded. When the equipment is in operating condition, the engineer says "Speed!" and the cameraman takes this as a cue to turn on his camera, which operates at full speed immediately. The slateman reads out the scene and take numbers from his slate, so that there will be an audible as well as a visual record of it, usually selecting only the scene and take numbers to repeat.

This last part of the ritual varies according to the equipment in use. With non-automatic equipment, the sequence of events is as described above, and is ended as the slateman brings the clapper board of the slate down with a sharp slap. The impact of the clapper is seen on the film and recorded on the sound track. The noise provides a keying system for the editor to synchronise with the image again later on. With automatic equipment, when correct sound speed is reached this turns on the camera. On other equipment the slating operation may be partially or wholly automatic using buzzers, sound blips, light flashes or other signals on the sound and image recording film.

When the scene has been slated, the slateman quickly and silently moves out of the way. The director says, "Action!," which is the signal to the actors to begin the scene.

Now all the work of the previous months, days, or hours will, or will not, come to fruition. At the word, "Action!," the actors and the cameraman begin. From this point on, the shot runs itself and whatever was planned and rehearsed is now performed.

During the scene the director must watch for everything. He must notice all sounds, all images, inflections, glances, innuendos, changes of pace. He must judge the performance and decide whether or not it is successful in terms of the total film. This is extremely difficult because he must make his decision while the take is in motion, while the action is performed and the lines spoken. Difficult as it is, he must now guard against either missing faulty details that could flaw the shot, or convincing himself that the flaws are not great enough to matter.

RETAKES

The word, "Cut!," spoken by the director, ends the shot. The sound engineer turns off the recorder and the cameraman turns off the camera. But it is not yet time to relax. In a brief followup period the cameraman indicates that everything was, or was not, "O.K. on camera," and the sound engineer does the same for sound. If this first try was a perfect one for everyone, crew and director included, then the director asks that this be circled as a "print" take on the camera log. Later, in the processing laboratory, this take is singled out for workprinting. If this is not a "circle" or "print take," the laboratory processes the film only and does not go to the trouble and expense of printing material which in all probability is not useful.

If this attempt has been satisfactory, then the director may go on to the next scene. The whole process of making another setup begins again. If the shot is not perfect, the director calls for a "retake." For a variety of reasons, it is rare that only one take of a shot is made. Many machines and men are called upon to operate perfectly during this time, and both human and mechanical failures are common. The director may not be pleased with the actor's performance, or with the way the camera moved in relation to the actors, or an actor may be dissatisfied with his job and wish to have another try at it. With the pressure of making a take, some of the spontaneity or polish of his performance may have suffered. He may "flub" a line or move awkwardly, or his timing may be off. Even if in this part the human element was perfect, some actor in the background may have performed inadequately or may have moved in a way that detracts from the shot. Even if the human element was perfect, or as nearly perfect as possible, the cameraman may announce that he boggled the panning movement of the camera, or that he tilted too far up or down. Sometimes he will feel his composition in motion could be improved and will ask for another take. The sound engineer may say that he heard some extraneous sound in the middle of the dialogue, or that the actor mumbled a line, or that he could hear the actor's feet shuffling on the floor. Even should the actors, cameraman and sound engineer each feel his part of the take was perfect, there are reasons for a retake. Some detail of matching might be faulty—the actor's cigarette may have burned down too far and not match with the scene taken seven days ago which will appear next to this one in the final film. Even assuming complete perfection of all internal and external, mechanical and human factors, the director may often still call for a second take simply because he knows that some error may have gone undetected, and that there is a better chance of having a good take if there is more than one.

The number of takes a director makes of a shot is limited by the picture's budget, the director's shooting style, and the crew's patience. Each director has his own method of work. Some work sparsely, perfecting the elements before the camera rolls. Others work on the theory that it is better to make many takes, giving the editor more choice and the performers a better chance also. A few directors who are assured of ample budgets, and can command the cooperation of their crews, might make twenty or thirty or even more takes for each shot. Other directors will be satisfied with two or three.

The number of takes varies with the type and complexity of the scene, of course, so an "average" number of takes is no guide to what actually happened on the set. One scene may be successfully recorded in two takes, another in ten. The average would be around six. In deciding when to draw the line on the number of takes made, the director must take into consideration not only such matters as budget and patience, but he must also exercise judgment in pursuing his desire for perfection. While he may feel that perfection is something devoutly to be wished, he should know it is rarely attained and that he must be satisfied with something less than an absolute imagined perfection.

Knowing when to go over the shot again, and when to stop and go on to the next shot, is a fine art and an important part of directing skill. It is the skill of knowing the capabilities and limitations of men and machines in combination, and the skill of extracting the maximum from them with the minimum loss of patience and energy.

9

The Actor

IN FILM, AN actor is any person or, in effect, any thing that moves, and is moved by, the story. It becomes a focal point of audience attention and interest, and undergoes some process of change, or change of fortune, as the story is told. Often, the actor is a human being, but objects, events and animals are equally useful—rivers, nations, cities, diseases and abstractions such as problems and revolutions have all served as actor material.

The camera lens, unlike the human eye, is impartial in its view of the world. It looks upon all that is visible with equal interest. Not being human, it does not suffer from human fallibility and human self-interest. Inanimate objects such as dishes and stairways, and events such as lightning and sunshine, are portrayed equally as well as Lassie-dogs and beautiful girls.

Giving, and taking away this sense of action, movement and life is one of the chief tools of filmic expression. Depending upon style, felt story need. and personal philosophy, much interest may be created in inanimate objects, Through their action in the story, such objects can take on meaning. And, since the lens which records their image for the audience is impartial, they can be made as important and as interesting visually as any human, even when there are humans in the scene competing for attention. On the other hand, human beings can be used as if they were properties or set dressing. They may become scenic elements, important as parts of the scene or compositional factors, but not contributing directly to story action, being of interest in themselves, or undergoing any change. Objects and persons are used in whatever way best serves the story.

CASTING

It is through the actors that the film idea becomes physical. Just as the factors of environment—sound, time and image—are designed, so are the actors, who work within and upon that environment. "Design" of actors involves primarily selection (casting) and thereafter a shaping of movement and speech so that these are in harmony with the idea and style of the film.

The intensity of an actor's personality can affect the entire nature of the film. François Truffaut says, of his use of Charles Aznavour:

> The trouble with *Shoot the Piano Player* was that I was able to do anything—that the subject didn't impose its own form. Aznavour has a marvelous comic ability—I could have made the film comic; he has great authority—I could have made the film tough. But at the beginning, I didn't know what I wanted to do—aside from a mad desire to use Aznavour, because of *La Tete Contre Les Murs*. Of course I should have waited until I knew him better.[31]

The casting problem for films is different than for the stage. With a stage play, the actors can be adapted to the characters to be played much more readily than in film. The ability to adapt the self to another is, in fact, the primary requirement of a stage actor. For example, a talented actress of thirty could portray a woman of seventy on the stage with comparative ease. There is enough distance, both aesthetic and real, between the stage actor and his audience to allow great leeway in characterization and adaptation. In casting for the stage, therefore, dramatic talent—vocal and bodily discipline plus dramatic intelligence—is a more relevant factor than physical or psychological likeness. Since, on the stage, the aim is to trigger that actor-audience communication, a phenomenon that can exist even in the absence of costume, scenery and make-up, the talent to accomplish this is of prime importance.

In film, however, the process is generally reversed. A character is adapted to the actor playing him. So intimate is the relationship between the audience and actor in film that room for illusion is appreciably narrowed. Here the actress of thirty, no matter how talented, can portray the seventy-year-old woman successfully only on extremely rare occasions, and then probably for only a few moments at a time. The importance of physical appearance and its effect on casting is described by Buñuel:

> For casting I depend mostly on my intuition about the physical requirements of the role. In *Nazarin* I needed a dwarf. We screened eight of them. The one I chose on the basis of his physical appearance turned out to have extraordinary acting ability. However, for speaking parts I much prefer working with a professional actor than with a non-actor.[32]

Casting for films thus involves determining a likeness to the conception of the character. Age, specific physical characteristics (other than height, which is of minimal importance in film), specific vocal qualities, ability to respond to suggestion, and "personality" are factors in casting for film. Of these, personality is perhaps the most important, and elusive. Psychological compatibility is as important to film casting as is physical likeness to the character being portrayed.

Personality and Character

Just as the stage actor must have that talent for vital communication with the audience, the film actor must have a talent for projecting personality, preferably the personality of the character he is playing. It is probably impossible to define just what personality in this sense is, but certainly the idea is related to the total of physical, emotional and spiritual characteristics of an individual as these are understood by others. In some way, this totality of the film actor must be similar to the character he will play. Identifiable, individualistic characteristics of an actor, unless they happen to correspond with the character, can be highly distracting and destructive of effect. In addition, other factors can enter into casting—production and financing. Satyajit Ray outlines one casting decision this way:

> I have three main reasons for casting Peter Sellers. (a) My great admiration for him: it's good to work with a real virtuoso once in a while. (b) I thought it would be fun to see him playing an Indian in an Indian film, and I thought the idea would intrigue Sellers too (I was right). (c) *The Alien* needs top technical quality, with special effects in colour, etc. Which meant processing abroad—which meant bigger cost—which called for a wider market to bring back that cost—which meant British/American distribution to exploit that market—which called for a big name in the cast to interest the distribution company—which meant Sellers.[33]

It is for reasons as diverse and highly interrelated as this that a selection is made of an actor to play a part in a film.

Although this discussion has referred specifically to the selection of human actors, the same rules apply in the selection of non-human actors—animals, events and objects. The tiger who does not look and act as if he were ferocious will not do as the man-eater. Rain, no matter how destructive in actuality, will not look destructive unless it has a certain obvious force or turbulence. Appearances and actions, more than realities, are the guide in film casting because they are the aspects of the actor that register as sound and picture. Other characteristics, no matter how suitable to the part, are useless unless they can be recorded.

Because there is less room for error in film casting (due to the fixed nature of the completed film, an actor to whom the audience does not respond cannot be replaced), selection must be done with extreme care and precision. Success in casting can determine the success of a film. Poor casting can mean failure. Any deviation from an original conception of character because of lack of actor availability or other limiting factors must be accounted for elsewhere in production. If for some reason, a person is cast who is not quite right for the part, an attempt must be made to make him seem right. Indirect means of expression must be used, rather than the direct means of the actor himself. Depending upon the particular limitations of the actor selected, heavy dialogue passages might be avoided, or closeups, or scenes requiring him to work with another actor. The actor's good points should be capitalized, and his distracting qualities minimized. But no amount of patching can really hide a poor or inept performance. Because a film, once it is finished, is a permanent event, faulty casting will forever be evident to anyone who sees it. Few other flaws in the film making process can so quickly destroy the entire film.

Care in selecting actors for minor parts is almost as important as for the major roles. "One of the biggest problems is casting bits," Alfred Hitchcock has said, in describing some of his experiences:

> They shouldn't be too familiar. I remember sitting through a recent show-ing of *Trader Horn*, and after all those perils in the wilds of Africa the travellers arrived at a trading post. Up from behind the counter pops C. Aubrey Smith. I've never heard such belly laughter![34]

There are usually a great many more roles to cast in a film than in a stage play, so this part of the process is sometimes neglected or delegated to a subordinate.

More important than familiarity is consistency in performance between major and minor players. The casting of minor parts in *High Noon*, such as the hotel keeper, the ex-sheriff and the alcoholic, added much to the overall effectiveness of the film. *The Asphalt Jungle* and *Treasure of the Sierra Madre* likewise had a depth of talent in acting. The early Alec Guinness films: *Kind Hearts and Coronets*, *The Man in the White Suit*, *Lavender Hill Mob*, were characterized by a uniformly high level of performance, even in the smaller parts. Often minor parts, particularly when they strike some emotional chord with the audience, can add immeasurably to the total acting effectiveness of the film. Such minor characters must look their parts as much as do the major characters. Occasionally the strongest impression left on a viewer by a film is a fleeting expression on the face of some silent character—an old woman, a child, the anonymous witness to an accident. Such images, however brief, convey such direct power to the audience that they somehow sum up the scene in ways that are unforgettable. Such fleeting intensity is not usually characteristic of stage performance. In film, fleeting intensity is an actor's greatest power.

INANIMATE OBJECTS AS ACTORS

If the actor is an inanimate object or an event, some directing problems are permanently solved, while others are created. If an automobile is the star of the film, the director will find the automobile always ready, willing and able to work, never in need of food, rest or flattery. But he must also do much of the automobile's acting for it, with camera and sound, by lighting, at times by animation techniques and by story construction. In dealing with the inanimate actor, the principal task is that of making the actor animate, not necessarily in the anthropomorphic sense, but so that there appears to be in it intense interest or at least liveliness, if not life. If it can be given this appearance, the job is well done.

Like human actors, inanimate actors vary in their abilities and some are naturally more interesting than others. A machine in motion, for instance, is naturally more interesting than a vase on a table. A moving storm is more interesting than a lake. In general, anything which moves or gives the appearance of motion seems to have more interest, more liveliness, to the audience than things that do not move. Therefore if there is a choice of inanimate actors, the moving, changing object is to be preferred. At times, of course, a non-moving object gives more "life" to the story than a moving one. The vase mentioned above, for instance, cannot move—it is always there in the scene. Perhaps it has never even been noticed by other actors. But perhaps it also contains the secret of the story. If the audience knows this, then the inaction of the vase, its inability to move itself, can be emotionally affective to an audience, and in this sense it can "act" and have life. This is a relatively uncommon use of the inanimate, because of the difficulty of sustaining this kind of "action" over time.

Using unmoving objects as actors creates a problem of fixing attention. An audience notices, during any one moment of a film, objects which have competed successfully with all other visually interesting scenic elements. The brightest, sharpest, most brilliantly colored and mobile—so long as these are within the limits of comfort—are noticed by the audience as it looks at a shot. During a conversation with François Truffaut, Alfred Hitchcock related a solution to a problem he had faced:

A.H. By the way, did you like the scene with the glass of milk?
F.T. When Cary Grant takes it upstairs? Yes, it was very good.
A.H. I put a light in the milk.
F.T. You mean a spotlight on it?
A.H. No, I put a light right inside the glass because I wanted it to be luminous. Cary Grant's walking up the stairs and everyone's attention had to be focused on that glass.[35]

Psychologically what is noticed is the object of greatest interest, so long as the eye is not distracted. Objects that draw attention are always a matter of concern in pictorial composition, but their use is especially critical when the actors are rather inanimate. To fix attention on the actor, to animate him, other scene elements are artificially "toned down." The inanimate actor becomes the brightest, largest, most colorful or sharpest object in view (fig. 48). If the principal actor were a drill press, for example, then other interesting scenic elements would be minimized visually: the operator of the drill press would wear subdued clothing, not a bright plaid shirt. Nor would he move elaborately or attract special camera attention. Careful selection of camera angle to exclude distracting elements and to fix attention on the principal actor, control of background activity so that it does not intrude on the principal action, manipulation of color, brightness and focus, and skillful use of camera movement and, occasionally, of moving lights, brings life and vitality to the most static object and thus attracts and holds audience interest.

NATURAL EVENTS AS ACTORS

Natural events such as rain, oceans, fire, the effects of wind may also be used as actors in a film. While it is easier to fix attention upon a man-made object because it can be picked out of an environment and isolated, it is usually more difficult to animate than a natural event. Man-made objects have a machine-like quality, a hardness and lifelessness, and human beings generally do not experience any affinity with them. Man-made objects need to be given personality and identity in order to provide the audience with some basis for identifying with them or for having an interest in them—without, of course, violating the basic nature of the object. To make a man-made object move in a human way can attract attention and create interest, but it does not convey the nature of the object itself. Rather, it makes the object into a kind of artificial human. If the purpose of the film is to tell something about the essential nature of the man-made object, this treatment will fail. A balance must be found between artificial modification of the environment (including object movement) to attract and hold attention, and a sense of and respect for the essential nature of the object itself.

Natural events are natural actors, perhaps because almost all human beings tend to accept and identify with nature more readily than they identify with the products of their own endeavor. Many people see supernatural causes behind natural events, and this magnifies their importance to an audience. Natural events usually have some movement of their own—the flow of water, the drop of rain, the color and exciting movement of fire. For all their inherent talent, however, such events embody one important problem for the director (which at the same time makes them exciting)—control. Natural events cannot be so much directed as caught by the camera. An eye and a sense of timing will make the talent of the events available, even when they cannot be directed or constructed. The simple trial and error method used in photographing human actors is inappropriate. The action and filmic appearance of the natural event must be imagined, and the photography directed on the basis of this estimate. To some extent the movement of natural events can be predicted, but the unpredictable must be taken into account, either as good fortune to be exploited, or an obstacle to be overcome. The man-made object can be adapted to the director's purpose, but he

Fig. 48. James Broughton on location during the filming of *The Bed*. The main actor in the film—the bed sitting in the background—attracted attention in a number of ways: not only was it an interesting and complex object in itself, but in one sequence it careened down a hillside under its own power. [The Bed, *James Broughton*.]

must adapt his purpose to the natural event. Such adaptation may at times involve compromise, but more often it calls for inventiveness and keen observation to detect and reveal the essential nature of the event.

Inanimate objects such as vases generally undergo no change in appearance over time and no change of location in space. Sameness and predictability means both ease of use and absence of inherent interest. As an actor, the natural event is unpredictable, continuously changing in appearance, and often in location. Experience and observation of the event may reveal patterns in the change, however, that can form the basis for an estimate of change. True, clouds cannot be told to move over a little, and fields of grain will not wave in a flowing manner on demand. But nature has a certain inertia that causes her to continue what she has been doing, and changes tend to be gradual rather than abrupt. A little investigation into the habits of prevailing winds in the example above would go a long way toward giving the director some measure of "control" over his clouds and fields of grain. Knowledge of this kind is useful whenever nature is used as an actor.

The concept of a natural event as an actor does not exclude human beings. In riots or other forms of mass hysteria, for instance, groups of human beings act on the same principles as the natural event, and can be "controlled" in much the same fashion for the purposes of filming.

ANIMAL ACTORS

As the actor becomes more inherently interesting and more animated, he becomes more intractable, unpredictable and uncontrollable. With the animal, the range of predictability is even more narrow than with natural events, though it still exists. The animal's movement is varied, innately interesting, often beautiful and skillful, sometimes expressive. The subject is continually changing. Though the animal is more interesting than the natural event, communication with it is only slightly better. At best the director cannot be certain that he can impose his will upon the will of the animal. At times, even highly trained animals balk. The dancing dog just does not want to dance and so he sits wagging his tail. Untrained animals, though domestic, almost never obey the director, and only sometimes obey their own masters. Often the directing consists of arranging the environment around the animal-actor (possible also with the man-made object but not the natural event), and then letting the animal-actor react to it as it will (something the natural event does but the man-made object does not). All of the manipulative and imaginative skill used with man-made objects is necessary with animals, together with all of the experience, adaptability and quick thinking used with natural events. In addition, there must be an attempt at communication. If the animal-actor is working in its natural habitat, the job will be easier if the shooting does not disturb the naturalness of the habitat. It is better if the script does not call for unnatural or specific actions on the part of the animal, or if a species of animal, rather than an individual, can be used as the subject.

However, animals, like events, do act in characteristic ways. Certain stimuli will usually evoke predictable responses. The house cat, if petted and well fed, will usually grow content. The domestic dog will try to please its master. The hungry lion will attack the antelope; the enraged elephant will stomp through the native village, and the frightened zebra will run across the veld. Work with animals is indirect, a manipulation of stimuli, rather than of direct dealing with response. The stimulus is provided and the camera and sound recording equipment so arranged that it records the response to the stimulus given. The arrangement is important. Poorly arranged equipment acts as a spurious stimulus and distracts the animal into giving unwanted responses.

In proper context, such animal responses will in turn stimulate an audience interpretation appropriate to the action. Audiences read meanings into the picture (although they believe they read meanings from the picture), and thus the animal-actor can appear to give a specific response, when in

Fig. 49. Some animals take very naturally to "acting" though the director cannot be certain that he can generate the desired response. [Dr. Doolittle, *20th Century-Fox.*]

reality the animal is reacting to something quite different. A rabbit startled by a loud noise, for instance, can in editing be made to look as if it were running from a pursuing dog. Applying an off-screen stimulus obtains the necessary response. In editing, the director can suggest that the stimulus was some factor in the story.

Babies and very small children may be handled as other animals, though often they are less manageable than animals because a mature animal has a self-discipline which is lacking in children. Of course, the older the child becomes, the more it can be handled as if it were a human being.

Human Actors

All of the most useful characteristics of man-made objects, natural events, and animals as actors are implicit in the human actor—as well as some of the less advantageous qualities. While the human actor is more interesting and animate than the man-made object, some human actors do not have the object's dependability. The human actor can be placed in a desired environment, but his reaction to this environment is not always predictable. A strange environment will cause the human actor to react in much the same way that an animal reacts to a strange environment. Though humans do not have to be given life, as man-made objects do, the actor's personality must be shaped to the personality of the character being portrayed. Audiences identify easily with human actors, but this identification can carry spurious emotions with it. Audiences can sometimes have violent feelings against, as well as for, human actors. In theory human actors can be controlled by communicating with them. Between two persons of strong feeling and conviction—such as a director and an actor—that can be a problem. The expression a director wants on an actor's face, for instance, is something which cannot be readily described. To tell an actor to "look sad" helps him little because there are thousands of ways to "look sad." For this reason the director will sometimes use the technique of stimulus-response, describing or suggesting stimuli, guiding the actor's thinking toward the desired response, rather than attempting to specify the physical reaction. The interaction between director and actor can be very subtle, as George Cukor notes:

> But, you know, you influence people in a very curious way. An interesting thing happened, for instance, with *A Star is Born*. When Judy Garland finished doing the scene in her dressing-room, in which I thought she was remarkable, I said to her, "Well, that's rather like Laurette Taylor." And Marguerite Taylor, who later wrote a book about her mother, saw the same resemblance. Judy had never seen Laurette Taylor, but I was a great admirer of Laurette, and unconsciously I suppose that I must have passed something of her on to Judy. And that, very often, is the way one stimulates an actor's imagination. At the same time we were shooting *Camille* my mother had just died, and I had been there during her last conscious moments and I suppose had a special awareness. I may have passed something on to Garbo, almost without realising it. You don't tell her how to say "I'm strong," but somehow you find yourself creating a climate in which she can say it that way.[36]

In working with human actors, the keenness and timing used with natural events is brought into play, because human actors have much of the mercurial nature of natural event. An actor may give a superlative performance—just what the director wanted—once for each shot (if the director is lucky). Unless the actor is "on camera" at that moment, the only people who will ever enjoy it are the crew members. For the purposes of the film, the performance may as well not have existed. Human actors have a different, and far less useful kind of inertia than natural events. Theirs is an emotional inertia, their governors are their feelings at the moment rather than the physical environment of the natural event. Human actors are more predictable in general, but less predictable in detail, than other kinds of animate actors.

THE ACTOR'S CONTRIBUTION

So far, the human actor has been discussed as if he had no will of his own, as if it were only his presence and his response, and not his understanding, which gave value to his performance. Of course, this is not strictly true. The actor who neither understands the film idea, nor has a feeling for the character he is playing, is probably doing a lesser job than he would if he knew what his work was all about. Even a skilled actor may need help in finding out the exact nature of his work. Jean Renoir describes one method he used to direct actors:

> Quite late I discovered a marvelous thing which I owe to Louis Jouvet and Michel Simon, who used to apply it on the stage. It was well known up to the romantic period, and it's called the Italian method—*à l'italienne*. You sit down around a table with the actors, and you read the dialogue exactly as though you were reading the telephone directory: no expression, absolutely blank. You forbid them to give any expression, and you must be very severe, because any actor instinctively wants to give an expression before knowing what it's all about. You read a scene about a mother witnessing the death of her child, for instance. The first reaction of the actress playing the mother would probably be tears. We're surrounded by clichés, and for many actors it's as though they had a little chest-of-drawers, with an answer to a question in each drawer. . . . But if you read the lines without any expression, this forces the actor to absorb them; and all of a sudden—you see them spark. One of the actors has a kind of feeling which is going to lead him towards an interpretation of the part which is not a cliché. It will be his own interpretation, having nothing to do with what was done before.[37]

Above all, as in other kinds of acting, the human film actor must work for credibility, that quality which allows an audience to believe in the character, rather than the actor. An actor, Bresson says, cannot be himself:

> He must be another. This brings about an odd circumstance: this apparatus, which is the camera, takes everything. . . . That is to say, it takes the actor who is himself and another at the same time . . . there is phoniness . . . the result is not true. Through the cinema you must make contact only with those things which are true . . .[38]

To obtain that sense of "truth," different directors use different techniques. Otto Preminger:

> I believe firmly that an actor can do things much better when he believes that he invented them. I never want to have an actor feel that he's directed. As a matter of fact, if there are two possibilities and the one the actor suggests is, in my opinion, a little less effective than the one I would suggest,

I let him do it his way because I feel I will get something in exchange. It becomes easier; it's more right for him, even if it could be improved.[39]

But, more than with other dramatic media, it is true that the actor is an object to be manipulated, it is true to say that the actor does, or can, have little will of his own. This is due partly to the peculiar nature of the medium itself, and partly to the conditions of the typical shooting situation.

On the stage there is an appreciable qualitative difference between the human, living being and "dead" objects such as scenery or costumes. Dead objects have almost no means of coming to life on the stage. Their function is forever contributory to the more important function of the human actor himself. The direct communication of living being with living being which is possible in a theatrical performance energizes the stage actor (and audience), vivifying his performance and lending lifelike quality to the action which takes place. Settings, property, costumes, make-up, sound effects and lights solidify and enhance his performance, but the focus of attention always remains on the actor. This concentrated attention does not stray from the human beings on stage, unless, of course, the play or performance itself is dull. When the human beings leave the stage, which is never for very long, the story of the play remains momentarily in suspension until they appear again. With the film, however, the human actor must be prepared to yield the stage to the other kinds of actors just discussed. Since objects, events and animals can, and often do, assume the acting function in certain scenes, sequences and sometimes for an entire film, the human actor tends to be of less relative interest to the film spectator. "Dead" objects in a film are not naturally inanimate objects, as on the stage, but objects that the director is not presently using to tell his story. Attention is given to the whole image because of this and because of the two dimensional nature of film, in which an actor has no more "reality" than a chair. In a film, he is a two dimensional object just as the chair is, and since the chair can be made to move as much as he can, then the human actor can assume no innate superiority over it.

That vivid communication between living beings which is natural to the theatrical performance is replaced in film with another kind of communication. In one way it is a more encompassing one because it can extend to such things as storms and trees and amoeba, while it is at the same time more specific because of the power to fix attention which is characteristic of film.

In general, then, the actor's "presence," in a psychological as well as physical sense, more than his understanding, lends value to his performance. If the actor understands the whole script with all of its subtleties and innuendoes, appreciates its structure and knows how the cameraman and editor will lend their skills to telling the story, so much the better. But it is quite possible in film making to be a successful actor without ever having read the script.

What is necessary in the human actor is his complete presence at the moment of shooting: total attention, absolute concentration, full knowledge of the immediate intensive situation, and the ability to work within the technical demands of film making. The film actor has no way of knowing how his work is being received through the picture and sound recording machines —they do not cough, laugh or applaud as audiences do. He must rely heavily on the director: during shooting, the director is the only person who has a complete sense of continuity, and thus the actor relies upon him for guidance in matters of balance, consistency and emphasis. Unlike the stage actor who, night after night, goes through the entire story in continuity, the film actor must be prepared to perform any action in any sequence and with any intensity. His is a confused world of effect unrelated to cause, and he can only operate in such a world because the director is there to help him. At times a director may underrate his own usefulness to the actor. Lindsay Anderson says:

> Acting at its best is a creative, fully expressive art; and I think that the tendency today to regard actors as unfortunately necessary pieces of furniture, to be manipulated and pushed around by the director, is very mistaken. When I read in a notice of *This Sporting Life* a phrase like "Anderson has 'managed to extract' powerful performances from Richard Harris and Rachel Roberts," I can only smile. This is an extraordinarily false idea of how such collaborations work. In fact the Frank Machin of the film is Richard Harris' creation—and a vital contribution to the whole personality of the picture. To work *with* artists of this calibre is enormously stimulating—much more so than trying to restrict them to the limits of one's own imagination.[40]

The director is not only the actor's mirror and his audience, but his alter-ego, his other self through which he can have some sense of what he is doing at the moment, and of how this moment fits with another moment. Most of the memory work performed by the stage actor is, in film, provided by the director. A sense of continuity, over-all rhythm and specific knowledge of the camera's reception of the image of the actor are other acting duties performed by the director. To the director goes much responsibility, as well as credit, for the acting performance.

NON-ACTORS

On occasions, non-actors, persons who have had no previous acting experience, or persons with acting experience on the stage, in radio or on television, are used in a film. The initial task in dealing with all such non-actors is to find some basis of communication, some way of describing needs and desires to persons who do not speak the language of film.

The process begins with the non-actor's point of view or background of experience, which will establish a basis for understanding. From this, the non-actor can be brought to some realization of the needs of the film. With actors who have had experience in another medium, it would be to the director's advantage to know something about that medium and to be aware of the training in methods and systems in the actor's history. This is the starting point. If the individual has had no acting experience whatsoever, then the starting point becomes the individual's understanding of what is to be accomplished in the scene. "In my first film no one was an actor, except for one or two very small parts," relates Bernardo Bertolucci,

> and so my work reduced itself to this: having seen that actor, at dinner, laugh in a way that I liked, I would say to him: "Try to laugh as you did last night." That is, to refer the performance always to something of their own, never to something abstract. To always take, as a point of reference, their way of moving, of laughing, of speaking.[41]

It would be a mistake to believe that non-actors always, or even usually, give "bad" performances, that they are incapable of portraying on film any deep or complex emotion. Fine performances have been rendered by non-actors under the guidance of a responsive, sympathetic director wise enough to provide enough coverage so that when the film is put together the performance can be used to its best advantage.

Herbert Kline's *Forgotten Village* is told entirely by non-actors, yet he uses a story structure which is not unlike that of a fictional film. The film, a remarkably successful example of this type of documentary, achieves its aims in several ways. First, those who were selected to play parts in the film were persons who had had experiences similar to those in the film. Second, no dialogue was used. Third, the actors appeared in their natural environment. And fourth, the story was about a *group* of people and thus the camera was never called upon to focus its attention on one person to any extent. There-fore the problem of sustaining action did not seem to occur. Most of the work of directing the actors consisted of encouraging them to do what they ordinarily would, without looking at the camera. They were not called upon to give any philosophical or abstract dimension to their performances. All such suggestions were provided by the narration and the music. Sequences in which a larger dramatic action occurred, such as the sickness or the death of a child, were built out of fragments, skillfully cut together to seem a unified scene. Occasionally a bit of planned gesture was used to suggest an emotion, such as when the mother bites a corner of her robe when she is worried about her child. Reaction shots were almost always taken separately from the shots which provided the motivation, and were later cut in, in somewhat the way a stimulus-response would be suggested in cutting a sequence with animal actors.

Much of what appears to be acting in films is actually the product of the effects produced by the selection of a particular camera angle, by lighting, music and the context provided with editing. Often these techniques alone can give the audience the illusion that the actor is experiencing emotion and change. Skill and discipline in expressive physical motion and expressive production of sounds are admirable in any actor, but deficiencies in either or both of these elements does not necessarily result in poor film acting. Sometimes, in a film, nothing else is required but that the actor look like himself— if he is clumsy and inarticulate, the footage may still be useful because many of the undesirable and unnecessary parts of the performance can be deleted in editing.

There is one great limitation in the use of persons without previous acting experience, and this is in the lip-sync or dialogue film. Without training in the techniques of delivering memorized or rehearsed material, in character, as if it were spontaneous, the non-actor, as a general rule, fails. Only on rare occasions can a non-actor deliver more than a few lines in sequence without their sounding memorized, and without destroying, in his concentration on the lines, all the sense of spontaneity and emotional value that the performance should have. If the non-actor can be allowed to use his own words, and if he can be sufficiently conditioned to the presence of the camera and sound recording machinery so that he loses his self-consciousness, better results will be achieved.

Relaxation of artificiality can be promoted in several ways: care in the selection of people with whom to work, placing the focus of concentration upon the feelings of the non-actor rather than upon the record that is being made of those feelings, and assurance that all imperfections can be removed easily and that continued immediate perfection is not required. This latter assurance is probably most valuable in working with non-actors. Few persons outside of the film production field realize that sustained performance is irrelevant to the making of a film. Once the non-actor realizes that he is not required to give such a sustained performance, that he need catch the feeling for only brief moments and need not artificially stretch out this feeling— something the trained actor is skilled in and accustomed to doing—then the non-actor gains confidence in his own capability.

Whenever non-actors are to be used in dialogue sequences, extra cover shots should be planned in such a way that they can be used to shore up weak parts of the performance and give it a body and variation it might not otherwise have. Of course there is always the alternative of later dubbing in the voice of a professional over a picture of a non-actor, but this is an expensive and time-consuming process, one difficult to do well, and should be considered only when other means have failed.

FILM ACTING TECHNIQUE

The effectiveness of film acting, whether it is performed by an inanimate object or a human being, is largely dependent upon how well the work is performed for the camera and sound recorder. The production of sound must always be production in relation to the characteristics of the sound recorder; action is in relation to the camera. Unless these sounds and actions are adapted to the peculiar characteristics of the film equipment, they will fail to reach their audience.

DIALOGUE

Anyone with literary or dramatic training is aware of the differences between dialogue in life and dialogue on the stage. Though dramatic dialogue often seems to duplicate that of life speech, in fact it is carefully constructed to lead from one story event to the next, and to guide the audience's emotions and attitudes concerning the events. Film dialogue performs a similar function, but its delivery is in an entirely different manner, and during transmission to the audience, it can be manipulated, displaced, edited and distorted according to the needs of the story.

Dialogue, like action, is delivered out of continuity in the film process; again the actor must rely upon the director's sense of continuity to keep within the vocal range of the shot immediately preceding and immediately following the one on which he is working. In addition, the actor must keep this vocal range within the limits of the sound recording machines, and within limits acceptable to film audiences. Should he wish to shout, he need physically raise his voice only partially. The character of the sound produced and his facial expression, more than volume, will convey the idea of a shout; volume or intensity of sound can be artificially boosted later if desired. A whisper can be more lifelike than the familiar stage whisper which is designed to reach the last row in the balcony. If it is too soft, or too loud, in film the volume can, within limits, be adjusted accordingly. Other distortions in the actor's voice—resonating tones and vocal qualities—can, again within limits, be modified by the sound recording equipment. Dynamics and tone quality are thus controllable to a degree not available in stage speech. But in such matters as enunciation, diction and pronunciation, the film actor must be as nearly in character as possible. There are no electronic means of modifying these. If a stage actor "flubs" a line one night, he can correct this the next night, but the film scene, once recorded, becomes a permanent work.

Since it is difficult for the human being to hear his own voice objectively, and impossible to hear it as others do, the responsibility of guiding the vocal performance of the actor falls upon the director. Sometimes, in large budget pictures, a person is assigned to coach the actors on their delivery of lines. This "dialogue director" does no direction of the actions of the actors. More often, however, the principal director has the job of coaching and coaxing the actors to give him the vocal performance necessary. While recording the scene, the director listens carefully to make sure that his actors have given the needed delivery. Technical flaws are noted by the sound engineer, and modifications of speech content by the script supervisor. But it is the director's responsibility to note dramatic flaws. Fortunately, the magnetic recording system allows the director to listen to the vocal performance immediately after it is given. Thus, by occasionally asking the sound engineer to play back the scene just recorded, the director has a way of checking his own subjective feelings.

Gesture and Movement

The actor's gesture and movement is affected by his relationship to the camera and by the characteristics of lenses, as well as the demands of continuity and of dramatic communication. Unlike vocal qualities, which can to some extent be modified after recording has taken place, the actor's every gesture and movement is recorded unchangeably on film. The only "correction" is deletion in editing. To a playgoing audience, an extraneous gesture, a nervous mannerism, or a mistake may in the flow of events go unnoted. In a film, such errors are not only glaringly magnified, they are made permanent. Every action, like every line, must be performed perfectly. Again, any change in timing, any correction and modification, all have to take place before the camera starts to operate.

The stage actor who turns to films discovers that the comparatively large gesture and broad movement of the stage has few uses in film work, where facial expression and small, intimate movement is important. The actor "tones down" his movements to suit the requirements of the medium, especially when the photographer is recording his work in closeup. Often only the detail of gesture, rather than a whole movement, is selected to express the inner psychological state of the character. In *Belle de Jour*, the heroine's hands and feet are used to show her agitation as she approaches her initial contact with the house of prostitution. Her hands are shown in closeup nervously moving along a marbled surface; her feet, also in closeup, take a few steps, stop, turn, turn back and then move forward again. Such selection of detail concentrates audience attention on the single, most expressive gesture.

The film actor must also learn to synchronize his movements with camera movements and to deliver his gestures with a precision not demanded of him on stage. If it is necessary for him to stand up slowly on a certain line, he will have to do it the same way as each take is made. If he does not, but stands up too quickly or on the wrong line, the photographer may not be able to move the camera quickly enough to keep him in frame. If he speaks the line before or after the movement, the shot may not match the one preceding or following and the actor may find his scene on the cutting room floor. While recording the scene, the director watches the actor's movements carefully to make sure that the effect he wants is coming across to the camera. Technical flaws in camera movement and framing are the concern of the cameraman. The director is concerned with tempo, communication of idea, characterization and continuity.

THE DIRECTOR AS AUDIENCE

The director is the film actor's sole audience while he is performing. Only the director is concerned with the total effectiveness of this particular shot within itself and as it relates to the other parts of the film. It is to the director that the actor must turn for reaction, for guidance, for a mirror of himself, for some indication of how he looks from "out front," which, in this case, is located within the camera and sound recorder. Many actors find the film medium a difficult one in which to work because they feel the lack of the presence of a living audience. Stage actors modify and shape their performances each night to suit the characteristics of the particular audience. The film actor has no such resources. What he does must suit everyone who sees the film, at all times and in all places. Matters of timing, emphasis and line delivery—so fluid and immediate for the responsive stage actor—must not only be worked out in detail for the film actor, but must be performed with absolutely fixed precision in the complete absence of the intended audience.

Because the actor depends upon the director to be his audience, a close working relationship should develop between actor and director. If he is wise, the director will capitalize upon this dependence to help establish a bond of common purpose and understanding between them. Nicholas Ray says this about his method of working with his actors:

> I give a great deal of importance to the actor because he's the medium of expression and, if you can reach him properly, he can contribute. With some actors it's difficult to even find enough imagination and talent within them to just live up to your expectation. So your relationship with them has to be perhaps even more patient. I try to maintain a close, intimate relationship with them because one way of learning or being able to tap their resources is to learn something about them. Knowing how they have reacted to other pressures, other stimuli in the past, provides you with a clue to how you might get spontaneous reactions from them during the making of the film.[42]

In this way the director can shape the actor's performance to his design, without so limiting him that the actor feels he is contributing nothing to the film. Not all directors, of course, feel this way, but many do. The actor should be free to offer suggestions and ideas which he thinks might improve his work. The director should encourage these suggestions. When they are good, he can incorporate them into his design. Even when he cannot use them, he has given the actor the opportunity to voice his views and to feel he is actively participating in shaping the film. Attitudes to this vary widely among directors and even with one director while shooting a single film. A comment by Bresson points to an underlying dilemma in this intimate blending of what can be the highly creative work of a talented individual:

> I do not want the actor to express himself. What he gives me, he gives me without knowing. It is I who must express myself.[43]

Occasionally an actor's idea may be unsuitable for the particular situation at hand, but may form the basis for action in another scene in another part of the picture. A wise director makes maximum use of good ideas from any source. And, he makes use of the actor's interest in doing a good job. Donald Siegel devised this method:

> In order to gain some time I always invite the cast over to my house to have a rehearsal—secretly, of course—the studio doesn't know anything about it, to avoid worries about the actors asking to be put on salary, which they never do.[44]

The film actor must be willing to accept the director's judgment as final. Once the stage actor is on the stage in front of his audience, he is really more or less independent of the stage director. He can, and often does, subtly modify his performance to better suit his own understanding of the part and his own capabilities. In film, the director simply calls for another take if he does not agree with the actor's performance. But sometimes a director takes a different approach, as Kurosawa describes in speaking of *Drunken Angel*:

> Shimura played the doctor beautifully, but I found that I could not control Mifune. When I saw this, I let him do as he wanted, let him play the part freely. At the same time I was worried because, if I did not control him, the picture would be quite different from what I had wanted. It was a real dilemma. Still, I did not want to smother that vitality. In the end, although the title refers to the doctor, it is Mifune that everyone remembers.[45]

The film actor cannot tell what portion of his work will be used; only with the final film does he know which of his actions and words were retained, and which deleted, to obtain the total effect. Working thus somewhat blindly, the actor accepts the director's decisions and goes on to the next scene.

Every director has his own method of "handling," or being the audience to, his actor. Of the comment that he seemed to have the ability to elicit outstanding acting performances from the women who appeared in his films, George Cukor said:

> Well, I think that most of these ladies are very practical minded and expect you to deliver the goods. They have to feel that what you're telling them

makes sense. This is very important. After you establish a rapport with them you can tell them the most devastating things. They don't care as long as they trust your judgment and have confidence in you. They don't care as long as they feel that you're watching them very sharply and sympathetically. You can say anything to them as long as you make them feel that they will eventually get it. You don't treat them like hopeless cases, you see. You can say awful things to them because you believe they will eventually get it . . . and they know that you believe.[46]

This mutual striving to achieve the best possible result, the confidence that it will be achieved, is in many cases the way an outstanding result is achieved. Some directors treat all actors the same way in all situations; others vary their techniques according to the personality of the actor and the particular problem being treated. Directors can be dictatorial and autocratic, or informal and relaxed in their approach. Whatever approach the director elects to use in treating his actors, he must remember that so far as they are concerned his value to them is directly related to his ability to be their audience.

CHARACTERIZATION

Some aspects of characterization have already been defined before the actual shooting begins. The details of costuming are worked out with the production designer. Costume is selected and shaped to express the inner state of being, and outer circumstances, of the person in the film. A conception of the character's actions and voice has been formed; this was one of the bases for casting. The balance of concern is with characterization—specifically, with what occurs during that moment in which all the planning and estimates, the conceptions and guesses, are reduced to the reality of action in the shooting situation, and are recorded by the film making machinery. Of this moment in film making, Cukor says:

Rehearsals are just meant for going through the mechanics of the thing. In the actual being before the camera something must be discovered; there must be an electricity there that can only come the first time something is done. Before, you just go through the motions and let yourself go when your time comes . . . When you are before the camera things should "happen." Good people will vary it every time, for every take . . . make it fresh, give little changes each time . . . If you have too much rehearsal it becomes mechanical.[47]

The way in which the costume is worn and used, the detail of gesture, behavior and mannerism, the vocal inflection, the tempo of movement, the carriage and posture, the personal idiosyncrasies which may be used to characterize the individual—all these, while possibly planned roughly in advance and created directly in response to the needs of the story, are principally inventions of the moment, and they can arise as much from the skills and talents of the actor as from the director. Cukor continues:

> I never tell them what they should do. I coax, persuade, push sometimes. But it's important to let them discover reactions and feelings in the character they're playing. Everything is not perfectly laid out ahead of time and on the set I'm not a dictator. There must be a pleasant happy atmosphere.[48]

Character in film can be suggested with the selection of clothes and objects (hand properties) with which the actor surrounds himself, and by the distinctive manner of his using these clothes and objects. Together they form the external signs of character, suggest personal history, present status and emotional state of the character. The nervous playing with hand-strengthening balls by the commander throughout *The Caine Mutiny* told more about the insecurity of his feelings and the state of his mind than facial expression or vocal intonation. The movement of a character within a scene, his psychological movement within, his reactions, his consciousness of the world about him, his thoughts and feelings, his attitude toward objects in his environment and toward the environment itself—all reveal character. Not only what he uses, but how he uses it reveals his character. In *Open City*, the priest, Don Pietro, enters a shop in which statuary is sold. He comes upon two statues standing side by side, one of a saint, the other of an unclothed woman. Alone with them momentarily, he gazes at first absentmindedly at the two, and then, becoming increasingly aware of the unclothed nature of the nude, he turns the female statue so that she faces away from the saint. He looks at the statues for a moment in satisfaction, and then realizes that still the situation has not been resolved. He then turns the saint's statue away from the woman, so that now the two statues are facing away from one another. How deeply such a search for characterization can affect both actor and director is apparent in Carl Dreyer's comment:

> What interests me—and this comes before technique—is reproducing the feelings of characters in my films. That is, to reproduce, as sincerely as possible, the most sincere feelings possible.
> The important thing for me, is not only to catch hold of the words they say, but also the thoughts behind the words. What I seek in my films, what I want to obtain, is a penetration to my actors' profound thoughts by means of their most subtle expressions. For these are the expressions that reveal the character of the person, his unconscious feelings, the secrets that live in the depths of his soul. This is what interests me above all, not the technique of the cinema.[49]

There is no formula or list of items which can be used to determine if all appropriate means for portraying character have been exhausted. The most useful way of approaching the problem, at least from the film's point of view, is to develop a complete conception of all aspects of the character being played, both internally and externally, and to let the specific movement or sound emerge directly from that conception. This process will assure both the actor and the director that the means used to externalize character are affective, appropriate and accurate.

<h2 style="text-align:center">REHEARSAL</h2>

Although there may be an opportunity to rehearse actors before the shooting begins, such rehearsal is rarely the extensive period of time associated with theatrical work, where weeks and often months of preparation precede performance. In film, rehearsal usually includes discussion of characterization and story analysis, but only rarely can the director work with an actor on the set, and with the equipment to be used, for more than a short time. A few directors rehearse their actors in mock sets before shooting begins. But in general, the rehearsal time available is when the camera and sound crews are setting up their equipment, and the scenery and wardrobe

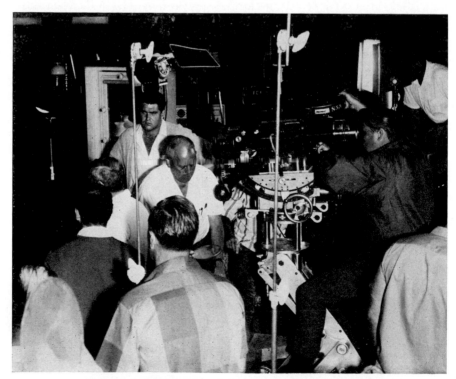

Fig. 50. A director at work in his normal environment.
[Dr. Doolittle, *20th Century-Fox.*]

departments are making their adjustments. Once these have been set, the director must return to the set with some understanding between himself and the actors as to what they are to do.

Just before shooting, the director gives the actors his final instructions, and there is a runthrough during which the camera goes through its actions and the sound engineer checks to make sure that the recording equipment has been placed properly. During this runthrough, the director often monitors the action through the camera viewfinder, although he may wish to concentrate his attention upon the performances of the actors without equipment interference. In any event, the number of these runthroughs is usually quite limited because production costs are high. For each moment that the director hesitates and deliberates, not only his salary and the actor's salary, but the salaries of all the members of the shooting crew, together with space and equipment costs, are consuming the budget consigned to the film at a frighteningly rapid rate.

10

Directors and their Public

A FILM EXISTS IN the audience's mind, the images thrown upon the screen and the sounds fed through the speakers being only the stimulus to that response. This response is the ultimate goal, the basis for the design. The film ends there where it begins.

But in any enduring or static sense, "an audience" does not exist. Responding to a question about an audience understanding him, Fellini said:

> How can I worry about something completely unknown? Anyway what does the word "audience" mean? Who are they? It is a monster without any collective conscience or identity, and so it is impossible to be conditioned by their wants. If you pay attention to all that, you put yourself in a very humiliating and subservient position: that of a slave to a very mysterious boss, a boss who doesn't know what he wants. It's the worst position for a man to find himself in, that of serving. It is up to you, as an artist, to be the boss. How could I possibly be concerned with the specific demands of people all over the world . . . I just say something that I like to say, and because I am a normal man, I think that my problems and likes and dislikes, my fears and hopes, should interest other normal people. . . . The "audience" is in the final analysis nothing but a creation of the filmmakers. It is corrupt because it has been violated . . . People have become used to a certain approach: they have become used to being emotionally violated. When a film comes along which doesn't do that, they "don't understand."[50]

Every audience is different, and any audience, upon assembling, though it were composed of identical individuals as in the last assembly, has been changed and is changing as the result of life experience. More than that, a film audience is not organic, but a group of individuals in a social, listening–viewing situation, loosely brought together out of felt need for, or interest in, some element which they expect to find in the film being projected. These needs and interests, out of which any particular audience is created, vary, both within and among individuals, from a purely psycho-physical interest in things that move to an equally basic search for meaning, for ways of bringing order out of the conflicts of life. Whether stockholders in a meeting, family and friends in the living room, students in a classroom or habitués of the local art house, they seek to be informed, enlightened, persuaded, reassured, pleased and moved—in short, to be entertained, to receive something of psychological value in return for their investment of time and attention. Taking a different meaning for the word "entertainment," but holding the same value for film as a medium of exchange, Orson Welles said:

> The biggest mistake we have made is to consider that films are primarily a form of entertainment. The film is the greatest medium since the invention of movable type for exchanging ideas and information, and it is no more at its best in light entertainment than literature is at its best in the light novel.[51]

An audience seeks to encounter those things within themselves and their lives which affect the pleasure or pain of their existence. They seek, in their struggle to live with themselves, nature and other people, knowledge and values which relate to life problems. The process has been called one of "escape," and the concept is useful if it is understood that what human beings desire when they attend a film (or any work of art, for that matter) is not the usual connotation—an escape from reality—but an escape *to* reality. Every audience member brings to the film an unenunciated anticipation that the gap between passionate individual interest—sex, violence, power, action— and social necessity will be bridged in a way that will prove individually meaningful.

Meaning and Message

What does the audience find? The question is an important one. It is answered differently for different films, for viewers take from the theatre a conglomerate of their own personalities and their perceptions of the filmic experience. Some films which seemingly have no reason to exist other than attracting a dollar to the box office carry material which in some way promises to alleviate the enduring human burden of living, either by distraction into some fanciful realm where all things become possible, including, by implication, the solution of real problems, or by descending into an equally fanciful world where violence itself becomes the solution. For, willfully or not, purposefully or not, all films carry meaning. And this meaning, there sometimes by design and sometimes by accident, is carried both explicitly, in the events of the film, and implicitly, in the treatment given these events. Of his film *Grande Illusion*, Jean Renoir says:

> . . . if you want to persuade the public to accept a new point of view, to share in a discovery, you have to play the part of the prostitute, to put on a

bit of makeup in order to attract . . . you have to be a little bit dishonest, you have to give something the public can follow, and the easiest thing is the action. You must take a popular plot. For instance, I am sure that initially *La Grande Illusion* was so successful because it was an escape story. The escape story has nothing to do with my film. But it is a mask, a disguise, and this disguise made *Grande Illusion* a big money maker.[52]

The most trivial seeming farce imparts some point of view about human life. The most adventurous spy thriller offers values and criteria for standards of human conduct which communicate themselves to the audience regardless of its awareness of, or perhaps even agreement with, these values. These implicit meanings are often more important than the explicit "message." In the stockholders' meeting, the tone of confidence and authority is as important as the balance sheet. In the classroom, the sense of logical understructure is as important as methods of solving equations. And in the living room and art house, value systems expressed by characters tell as much, and sometimes more, than the literal outcome of the story. What is seen, what is remembered, what becomes part of conscious and subconscious thought is beyond ordinary awareness. The most affecting elements are impressions profoundly and yet so subtly made that they become consciousness itself, part of the storehouse of human experience which is the individual.

Escape and Reality

In viewing a film, audience awareness is sharpened. Those sensuous (and social) impressions which predominate serve to make "raw" the area of awareness stimulated. The audience leaves the viewing situation to confront the same life as before, but different elements within that life now engage its attention. Essential meaning in a film lies in these impressions as well as in the stories being told. They are the peculiarly cinematic phenomena with which the director works.

But if the audience seeks escape to reality, it will often find it, in film as in life, masked by superficiality. What appears on the screen as reality is, of course, nothing more than illusion and nothing more than a rapid succession of shifting light patterns. And although these patterns may at times appear more intense, more provocative, more brilliant, even more meaningful than the drab, meaningless continuum that life often seems, neither the representation nor the experience offered by the representation can be confused with reality itself. So profound is the film experience, so complete its influence, so comprehensive its appeal to the senses and the emotions, that film makers, as well as their audiences, sometimes confuse film and reality, believing in some way that film, by virtue of its supposed objectivity, can reveal objective reality in ways no other art form does or can. Whatever it is, film is not reality, although in some cases, it is true, the two may come very close to blending: where the subject matter of the film is in itself a fad or form of mass hysteria, a mass illusion or delusion that flares for a short time. In a sense, Richard Lester found himself on this fine line:

> I don't really have any desire for any of my films to go into time capsules. And I expect *Hard Day's Night*, which I haven't seen for a year, to be absolutely dreadful now. Because it was of that period, of the pop explosion.[53]

A grasp of "reality" is tenuous at best, no more clearly definable or separable than film itself. Film can no more be looked at as "reality," and believed in its entirety, than reality can be looked at and believed in its entirety. The feeling of having a grasp on existence is illusionary: the tenuousness is real. It is better neither to accept all experience as "real" in a concrete or actual sense, nor to judge that anything that is not concrete or easily grasped, is not real. Actually, all films are fiction in that they are fabrications, humanly subjective views of some segment of life, projected as being more or less typical of that segment. The film maker begins with certain of the raw materials of life— time, space and sound—selecting, expanding and contracting, accelerating and decelerating, augmenting and diminishing in both large and small ways, channeling these stimuli into the recording machines that will ultimately make some form of his perceptions available to his audience. The process is one of making subjectively perceived and recorded fragments which are then altered and restructured in sequence for effect. As soon as two shots are joined in any kind of continuity, structure begins. With successive shots, the element of time enters, and with time, story. Out of these three elements of detail of action, structure and time comes the resultant film which, hopefully, has been so made as to convey meaning to its audience.

The relationship of this process to the life reality from which it springs begins, of course, with the conception of the film idea. The random, chaotic, out-of-focus character of life begins to be focused, or channeled, with the conception. This focusing continues through the director's work as he creates and selects the details from life reality which will fit into his structural pattern. As Peter Brook puts it:

> It all leads back to the central problem, which is that of finding ways of giving a denser impression of reality. We've been prisoners for years of a naïve simplification of what realism means—hence the British cinema view that it is all a matter of art direction, something to be achieved by being more honest than the Americans in the amount of rain that beats upon your heroine. . . . Part of the fiction that has to be exploded concerns the myth that the director's hand must be permanently visible. This becomes an unreality as in *Marienbad*, and then a consistent style becomes an unreality. Now all the methods of freeing camerawork have brought us closer to a surface realism . . .[54]

H

And Carl Dreyer says:

> . . . The artist must describe inner, not outer life. The capacity to abstract
> is essential to all artistic creation. Abstraction allows the director to get out-
> side the fence with which naturalism has surrounded his medium. It allows
> his films to be not merely visual, but spiritual. . . . Every creative artist is
> confronted by the same task. He must be inspired by reality, then move
> away from it in order to give his work the form provoked by his inspira-
> tion.[55]

The goal is to touch that inner sense of personal reality in the individuals
of that abstraction called "the audience." In the numberless studies of so-
called "mass audiences," they have been questioned, analyzed, labeled,
channeled, categorized and questioned again. Their needs, wants, desires,
possessions and thoughts have been listed, tabulated, punched into cards and
fed into machines which promise to tell them what and who they are, and to
tell others when and what they will buy. What such studies do, and must
ignore for the sake of the information they create (and, through use of this
information, what they degrade for their own ends), is the individuality of
human nature, the distinctiveness of human experience, the unduplicatable
combination of inheritance and environment which makes every individual
unique. Not only does the notion of mass audience assume identity rather
than diversity among individuals, it tends to minimize the fact of choice on
the part of individuals as they select what media, and what presentations
within those media, to which they will expose themselves. Through feedback
of the information these studies create, they play a large part in limiting the
choice available to the individual, and form an ever-shrinking helical trap.

Hopefully film can at times escape. Jean Renoir suggests:

> We are obliged to please too many people, because it's the condition of the
> job. If you start out with the idea of pleasing everyone, however, of course
> you end up satisfying no one. One has to start with the idea of achieving a
> certain objective, uncovering a certain truth, and if the mass public accepts
> it, so much the better.[56]

The film maker can address his work to the individual, rather than to the
abstract "public." That individual, during production, is himself. Buñuel
comments that "I make films for only a few friends, and of course to please
myself."[57] Although Howard Hawks appears at first to challenge this idea,
his conclusion argues otherwise:

> I have no desire to make a picture for myself. There has never been a
> picture so good the public didn't care to see it. I like to make comedies
> because I like to go into a theater and hear people laughing—the more
> laughter the better I feel. I have no desire to make a picture for my own
> pleasure. Fortunately, I have found that what I like, most people also
> like, so I only have to let myself go and do what interests me.[58]

The film maker creates films for all those with his convictions, his perceptions, his log of experience, his projection of himself upon the world. Fred

Zinnemann commented simply that "A director should do what he is excited about."[59] In this the director is like other artists who create for "others like himself;" his efforts differ only in the matter of economic necessity. There must be enough like himself alive and of an age and with the economic resource to see his film, who are aware of the film, who are given sufficient physical proximity to enable them to see it, and who, in the end, do. Creating for some audience of the future is, for the film maker, futility. Just as the events of the film are always "now," so must the film maker's audience be now, an audience which exists, a group of individuals who will pay to see and to hear what he believes.

RESPONSE

From the audience, the director learns his most valuable lessons. He gains clues to what will work, what will evoke the response, how to extend it, to manipulate and guide it. The director observes audiences and their reactions, he learns to understand what moves them in order that he may learn to create what moves them. He studies their laughter, their moments of quiet, their tears and the movements of restlessness which may signify loss of attention. He senses the excitement of their tension, the relief of their relaxation. He observes the causes of these effects in the works of others and of his own. Ultimately, he develops a rapport with audiences which enables him to reach them through the technical procedures which comprise film making, bombarding their eyes and ears with critically planned stimuli, to achieve communication of his ideas.

The director is, in fact, an audience himself. When he looks at his potential subject, he becomes audience. He is part of the humanity he wishes to contact and for which he creates. In searching himself, he will find others. With himself, as with others, he brings to the film indirectly all to which it refers or which is relative, whether the film is a fictional mystery drama or a searching documentary. His purpose in this is, in some way, to convey more than the facts of a news story, more than the abstract generalizations of a sociologist or historian, more than the moral judgments of a clergyman, but to convey the truth of man as a totality, as man, to make his subject known in terms comprehensible, intellectually and emotionally, to others.

WORKING ATTITUDE

Pressure is a condition under which the director works, the pressure of too little time, too little money, too much ego, too many technical limitations. For every minute that the shooting company is at work, relatively large sums of money are being spent for salaries, equipment costs, set costs, and all the other costs which enter into the production scheme. To handle pressure, the successful director employs a blend of strength and flexibility, concrete visualization and ability to change, good organization with responsiveness to the moment, toughness and sensitivity. He knows when another rehearsal or another take with its extra expenditure of time and money is essential to success, and when the shot he has in the can, even though it may not perfectly match his imagined scene, is the best that can be done for the film. To accomplish this, he must be able to think quickly and decisively under pressure. Many decisions must have already been made before shooting begins; great numbers of others must be made every hour of the working day. They must be made with purpose, and a sense of confidence. He learns not only to perform his own work under difficult conditions, but to use these conditions to secure the best possible performances from his actors and from all members of his shooting crew. To achieve the most within the limitations, he uses both tact and tactic in dealing with actors and crew: tact to engage the cooperation of all involved, tactic to work around obstacles or misunderstandings which erupt in the shooting situation.

This production mental set, as it might be called, the frame of mind with which the director enters upon his work, requires the same combination of concentration and awareness that is required of an actor performing on a stage. The director's total concentration on the job in hand is essential. But he must never become so immersed in the immediate demands of the situation that he forgets his ultimate goal—his mental image of the finished film. He must not be so tense and concerned that he fails to rebound from errors of his own making and errors made by those around him. Nor must he be so subjectively involved that he fails to recognize, meet and dissolve crises as they occur, or so defensive that he fails to compensate for the weaknesses both of himself and of others. Finally, he should not be so preoccupied that he loses his ability to turn problems into solutions, and to know the difference between those disasters which are disaster, and those which, with but slight manipulation, can become blessings.

He must be a salesman. His enthusiasm and conviction that the film is a good one, and one worth making, must be communicated to all members of the crew, most of whom—at least in the beginning—are simply reporting for work and have little initial interest or involvement in what is going on. But for the purposes of the film they must become a shooting unit, a group of individuals each of whom performs his own task to the ultimate of his ability and in doing so creates an atmosphere that through a positive mutuality enables others to equal or surpass their own best past performance.

Types of Director

Because the work of directing is so personal, there are probably as many types of directors as there are directors. Each has his own way of working with people to enable them to accomplish the work that needs to be done. Any one director may change this from time to time as his personal philosophies change, or as he sees the need to change because he is working with differing groups of people. Some directors play the dictator on the shooting set, stating their desires and ordering people about with little apparent patience for their shortcomings or their problems. Other directors ask for suggestions from the shooting crew, make suggestions to members of the crew and try to maintain a feeling of free interchange of ideas among set workers. Still other directors maintain a kind of free command of the situation. They start the process of taking scenes and thereafter keep all the members of the crew working together without actually asking them to do anything specific. The size and complexity of a film can affect a director's working method. Of working with large budget films, Jean Renoir says:

> I get far too much pleasure out of doing the odd jobs on a film to want to get tied up in an undertaking where one becomes a kind of general, with a whole staff at one's disposal. The general doesn't have any fun; the really entertaining thing is to be a corporal giving riding lessons to half a dozen men, teaching them how to hang on to a horse. That's where the fun is. [60]

There are countless ways of handling the job of directing, and there are times when some dictatorial directors become quite receptive to dictation from others, or when the receptive director becomes dictatorial. Whatever kind of interpersonal relationship seems to work with a group, that is the proper relationship to establish. Mutual experience seems to be helpful in creating a productive crew situation. Hitchcock says:

> I have a team who were with me on earlier pictures, and by now we have a sort of telepathic communication that sets us right. [61]

Personal Qualities

Because of the need to work with people, both actors and crew, and to get work from them, the qualification most important to the director is probably that of responsiveness. He must be responsive to those around him and must sense when they are having difficulty performing their work and try to find out why. Often he is the one who suggests a solution, or gives the worker a sense of perspective which allows him to find his own solution. The director must be responsive as well to the constant change in situation. As the man in charge of the shooting company, he must be aware of changes in working conditions, of fatigue, boredom or tension in his workers. Finally, responsiveness to dramatic values in life and in the material with which he works provides him with the imagination and resource necessary to keep him in touch with his audience. A keen interest in people and a feeling for human problems and perplexities are invaluable, both in making it possible for him to gather impressions of life, and in using these impressions as the materials of his work. His ability to make something of value out of the artificialities of production depends largely upon his response to life, upon his memory of response. Of the kind of responsiveness he feels is necessary to the director, J. P. Melville says:

> The most important quality needed by a film director—or as I prefer to say, a film creator (*un créateur de cinema*)—is the ability not to work through his intellect, otherwise he ceases to create a spectacle. He must also have a feeling for observation, memory, psychology, and a fantastically acute sense of sight and sound. He must have the instinct of a showman. A film is a spectacle, just like the circus or the music-hall; when it's well done, it becomes a work of art.[62]

The great store of feelings the director has, comes to work for him as he shapes the blocking of a scene, advises an actor to raise his voice on the last line, suggests that detail or gesture which makes the scene live, chooses the most telling angle and composition, or asks the cameraman to pan slowly at first and then move quickly to the point of attention. Such decisions and technical manipulations are shaped not only out of the need to solve an immediate technical problem, however compelling that might be, but out of the director's dramatic and filmic sense and out of his sense of human value. In rehearsal the director must know what he wants. And when the scene is shot, he must know if he got it. All this is accomplished with response. He cannot be the impartial observer, the disinterested passerby—unless he wishes to risk having his audience react in a similarly indifferent way. When he reads the story, he responds to it. When the actors and the crew attempt to carry out his ideas, he responds to their work. Until the film in completed form is projected for its first audience, *he* is the audience, the whole audience. If he does this part of his job well, he will find that the members of the crew will come to think of him as a source of reaction, a way to measure what they have done. When he is dissatisfied, they know that what they have done is not enough; his satisfaction tells them the story is being told.

UNDERSTANDING THE MEDIUM

Second only to responsiveness is the qualification of knowledge, especially knowledge of writing, camera work and cutting. To read a script intelligently and be able to understand what it is trying to do, there must be understanding that, if some elements of the script seem vague or hazy, it is because the writer struggles constantly with the problem of expressing in unequivocal words, events and ideas which are equivocal and non-verbal in nature. Of the script for *Accattone*, Pasolini said:

> The truth is antecedent to any technique. If you read the scenario of *Accattone* you will find all the elements of the film. The scenario already covered everything and I invented or improvised nothing while shooting, outside of small and irrelevent details; that is to say I followed the scenario very carefully, though it had been outlined in a rather approximate manner, a bit like a sketch. Nevertheless, when I drafted the scenario I already

had in mind what I was to do and would have done when shooting. Obviously, between scenario and film there is a qualitative jump.[63]

The importance of each word must be weighed in trying to form a whole image of the film idea. And finally, there must be a sense of what to follow in the script and what not to follow, a sense of what will "play" and what will seem artificial.

The writer depends upon this sense of the dramatic in the director. He depends upon his talent for visualizing in concrete terms scenes which the writer has only imagined. Just as the method of working with actors may vary tremendously from director to director, so the director's relationship with the script is different for different directors. John Boorman, in speaking of film scripts and the writers of film scripts, says:

> Well, I think my attitude to writers is very equivocal, because I feel that if a guy's too good, I'm a bit nervous, because I don't really want to be a handmaiden to a writer. I just want to use writers, I just want to squeeze them, exploit them, steal their ideas, and then discard them . . . when I read a very very good script, I get terribly depressed, because what you're doing then is just making somebody else's work.[64]

On the other side, Fred Zinnemann says:

> The writer makes his greatest contribution at the beginning of the picture —my function is to translate the treatment into visual terms. I work very closely with the writer.[65]

That the director should have a knowledge of photography is obvious, since one of his principal companions throughout the shooting period will be his cameraman. A comment Anthony Mann made regarding landscape compositions is appropriate to most photographic concerns of the director:

> You look for them, of course, and you keep on looking, and you are always amazed at what you can find. This is the director's art, it's what he sees, and nobody else sees it like him, because every one of us is different and each one of us would see it differently. We see it through our own eyes and through our own feelings of blood and energies and all our experience. This is the exciting thing, when you are able to capture what you saw on film because you have a great cameraman. Not all cameramen can see what you see, and not all cameramen can capture what you feel.[66]

But unless the director knows the technical characteristics of camera work and film, he will not recognize where such techniques must be stretched in order to accomplish his aim. Were he ignorant of camera work, he would constantly be demanding setups that could not be physically performed. Mental calculations must always be close to the practical, to devising ways of doing things which have some probability of being accomplished in reality. With a technical knowledge, he knows how far he can go. In actual shooting, this is sometimes further than the cameraman himself realizes. If the director has an inadequate command of the technical characteristics of camera and film, he cannot tell the cameraman how to obtain the required shot. Then he finds himself working within the cameraman's personal and professional limitations. Richard Lester:

> You learn to work under pressure, to make intuitive decisions on the spot. It's a lot easier—and faster—if you know what your lenses can do, know exactly how to get an effect and can communicate that information to your cameraman. You learn when to be firm, when to be flexible.[67]

If the director creates uneditable footage—material that does not match, has little sense of rhythm or action, with gaps in the story, or other faults—he will have little choice during cutting but to distort the original intent. The director without a knowledge of how a film is cut is in a particularly vulnerable position, since cutting is the last and final process in making a film. Editing is a realistic process. The work must be done with what is there. A shot cannot, after all, be wished into existence.

The director's aim is not only to provide himself with workable footage, but to take advantage of the cutting process itself in telling his story. He must know how the various editing techniques affect the internal rhythms of his scenes, how time can be condensed, passed or extended, how visual and audial relationships can be established or changed, how spatial relationships can be manipulated, how portions of the action can be emphasized or de-emphasized, how structure is created and what effect transitional devices will have on the total impression of the film.

Though seldom the case, all workers in film should in some degree know something about what all other workers in film do to carry out the film idea. For the director, complete knowledge is a necessity. Without it, he cannot begin the first step of performance of his job.

> When I started out in films, you know, the director had to do almost everything himself. He practically developed the film himself; and of course it was tremendously exciting. Then all these technical preoccupations shut us up in our own little world, just as the old time craftsmen were enclosed in the world of their particular craft . . .[68]

Thus has Jean Renoir spoken of some of his feelings about directing. He continues:

> The New Wave directors know their craft; but there are a tremendous number of directors around who know absolutely nothing about the technical problems of their job. They really haven't the first idea about photography, or about what happens when you develop a film, or about sound recording. The director simply comes along and says "I want such and such a scene," and the technicians do it for him. So people now have their general ideas, their artistic ideas, and the artisan has given way to the artist. And this is something to regret, because great art is made by artisans and not by artists.[69]

As he looks back upon the work which, a few weeks ago, seemed ultimately right, the director begins to detect its flaws, to see its weaknesses. For these errors he takes all responsibility, and from them learns his craft. Even for those errors which were beyond his control, he takes the blame, because part of his craft is to surmount such errors, so that they will not flaw the final product. If they are visible and, if he has failed to mask or divert the effect they have, then he has only partially succeeded. What counts in the final work of art is not the effort that was made, or not made, it is not the valor or expense of the try, but the result.

And, when he is successful in all this, what happens? Richard Fleischer tells it this way:

> The trouble is, not only are you no better than your last picture, but you are practically indistinguishable from it. While I was directing *Fantastic Voyage* back in Hollywood, if I got offered one science fiction subject I got two dozen. Now I'm directing a musical for the first time in my life. I'm not halfway through it, no one has seen anything I've done, but already I've been offered three major musicals after I finish this. It's terrifying, when you come to think of it . . .[70]

*   *   *   *   *

Since the early days of the Lumières and Porter, films and the world audience for which they are made have changed. Now, workers in business suits leave automated factories in the afternoon, drive down jammed superhighways to seemingly secure, well-heated, well-gadgeted tract homes. Trips to the moon are no longer fantasy, or even science fiction. Although great train robberies still occur, the railroad as a major means of human transportation has been replaced by jets. Films have changed too. No longer are they haphazard, poorly exposed pictures of movement but now smooth, colorful, tuneful, well turned-out products. The picture frame is wider now, and the world it looks at appears to be more complex and more worrisome than what seems, when viewed in retrospect, to be the simpler days of the 1890s and early 1900s. Audiences and the world and films have changed, but these changes have not been fundamental. It would be accurate to say that solutions to man's problems have changed, but the problems remain the same. The problem of the enervating monotony of work remains, though factories are now called offices or industrial complexes or laboratories. The problem of new external worlds to conquer remains, though it now takes man into sea and space instead of to western frontiers. Poverty, ignorance, hypocrisy, war—all are with us, and man still struggles with the passions that have been within him since human life began.

It is to these universal elements, and especially to the problem of "humanness," that the film director addresses himself. As he does so, he assumes some measure of responsibility in shaping the nature of his audience as it carries on man's struggle with his first enemy, and his only friend.

Notes

1. Higham, Charles. "Meet Whiplash Wilder," *Sight and Sound* 37 (Winter 1967/68), p. 21.
2. Johnson, Albert. "The Tenth Muse in San Francisco," *Sight and Sound* 25 (Autumn 1955), p. 104.
3. Bragin, John. "A Conversation with Bernardo Bertolucci," *Film Quarterly* XX (Fall 1966), p. 39.
4. Milne, Tom. "Jean-Luc Godard and *Vivre sa Vie*," *Sight and Sound* 32 (Winter 1962/63), p. 10.
5. Perkins, V. F., and Shivas, Mark. "Interview with King Vidor," *Movie* (July/August 1963), p. 9.
6. "Thoughts on My Craft," *Sight and Sound* 25 (Winter 1955/56), p. 128.
7. Mitry, Jean. "John Ford," *Interviews with Film Directors*, ed. Andrew Sarris (New York: Bobbs-Merrill, 1967), p. 159.
8. Madsen, Axel. "Lang," *Sight and Sound* 36 (Summer 1967), p. 112.
9. "The Art of Sound," *Film: A Montage of Theories*, ed. Richard Dyer MacCann (New York: E. P. Dutton & Co., 1966), p. 39.
10. Cameron, Ian, and Perkins, V. F. "Hitchcock," *Movie* (January 1963), p. 4.
11. Ritchie, Donald. "Kurosawa on Kurosawa," *Sight and Sound* 33 (Summer 1964), p. 111.
12. Cameron, Ian; Shivas, Mark; Mayersberg, Paul, and Perkins, V. F. "Richard Brooks," *Movie* (Spring 1965), p. 6.
13. Von Sternberg, Josef. "More Light," *Sight and Sound* 25 (Autumn 1955), p. 72.
14. Robinson, David. "'thank God—I am still an atheist' Luis Buñuel and Viridiana," *Sight and Sound* 31 (Summer 1962), p. 118.
15. Fenwick, J. H., and Green-Armytage, Jonathan. "Now You See It: Landscape and Anthony Mann," *Sight and Sound* 34 (Autumn 1965), p. 188.
16. "Interview with Otto Preminger," *Movie* (November 1962), p. 20.
17. *Ibid.*
18. Houston, Penelope, and Milne, Tom. "An Interview with Peter Brook," *Sight and Sound* 32 (Summer 1963), p. 111.
19. Marcorelles, Louis. "A Conversation with Jean Renoir," *Sight and Sound* 31 (Spring 1962), p. 81.
20. Montagu, Ivor. *Film World* (Baltimore, Maryland: Penguin Books, 1964), p. 288.
21. Fenwick and Green-Armytage, *op. cit.*, p. 186.
22. Weinraub, Bernard. "'A Funny Thing' in Madrid," *The New York Times*, November 7, 1965, II, p. 11.
23. *Loc. cit.*
24. *Loc. cit.*
25. *Op. cit.*, p. 129.
26. *Ibid.*
27. Bogdanovich, Peter. "Interview with Donald Siegel," *Movie* (Spring 1968), p. 5.
28. Higham, *loc. cit.*
29. Cameron, Ian; Shivas, Mark, and Mayersberg, Paul. "Otto," *Movie* (Summer 1965), p. 16.
30. Overstreet, Richard. "George Cukor," *Interviews with Film Directors*, ed. Andrew Sarris (New York: Bobbs-Merril Company, 1967), pp. 91–92.

31. Ronder, Paul. "François Truffaut—An Interview," *Film Quarterly* XVII (Fall 1963), p. 9.
32. Aubry, Daniel, and Lacor, J. M. "Luis Buñuel," *Film Quarterly* XII (Winter 1958), p. 8.
33. Malik, Amita. "In the Picture: Satyajit Ray and *The Alien*," *Sight and Sound* 37 (Winter 1967/68), p. 20.
34. Johnson, Albert. "In the Picture: Echoes from *The Birds*," *Sight and Sound* 32 (Spring 1963), p. 66.
35. Truffaut, François. *Hitchcock* (New York: Simon and Schuster, 1967), p. 103.
36. Gillett, John, and Robinson, David. "Conversation with George Cukor," *Sight and Sound* 33 (Autumn 1964), p. 191.
37. Nogueira, Rui, and Truchaud, François. "Interview with Jean Renoir," *Sight and Sound* 37 (Spring 1968), p. 62.
38. Greene, Marjorie. "Robert Bresson," *Film Quarterly* XIII (Spring 1960), p. 7.
39. *Loc. cit.*
40. Cowie, Peter. "An Interview with Lindsay Anderson," *Film Quarterly* XVII (Summer 1964), p. 14.
41. Bragin, *op. cit.*, p. 41.
42. Apra, Adriano, *et. al.*, "Interview with Nicholas Ray," *Movie* (May 1963), p. 17.
43. Greene, *op. cit.*, p. 6.
44. Bogdanovich, *op. cit.*, p. 4.
45. Ritchie, *op. cit.*, p. 110.
46. Overstreet, *loc. cit.*
47. Overstreet, *op. cit.*, p. 93.
48. *Ibid.*
49. Delahaye, Michael. "Carl Dreyer," *Interviews with Film Directors*, ed. Andrew Sarris (New York: Bobbs-Merrill, 1967), p. 112.
50. Bachmann, Gideon. "Interview with Federico Fellini," *Sight and Sound* 33 (Spring 1964), p. 84.
51. "The Third Audience," *The Cinema of Orson Welles*, ed. Peter Cowie (New York: A. S. Barnes & Co., 1965), p. 176.
52. Nogueira and Truchaud, *op. cit.*, p. 61.
53. French, Philip. "Richard Lester," *Movie* (Autumn 1965), p. 7.
54. Houston and Milne, *op. cit.*, p. 113.
55. *Op. cit.*, pp. 128–29.
56. Marcorelles, *op. cit.*, p. 82.
57. Aubry and Lacor, *loc. cit.*
58. Becker, Jacques; Rivette, Jacques, and Truffaut, François. "Howard Hawks," *Interviews with Film Directors*, ed. Andrew Sarris (New York: Bobbs-Merrill, 1967), p. 195.
59. Johnson, "The Tenth Muse in San Francisco," p. 104.
60. Marcorelles, *op. cit.*, p. 82.
61. Johnson, "In the Picture: Echoes from *The Birds*," p. 66.
62. Nogueira, Rui, and Truchaud, François. "A Samurai in Paris," *Sight and Sound* 37 (Summer 1968), p. 119.
63. Miller, L. C., and Graham, M. "Pier Paolo Pasolini: An Epical-Religious View of the World," *Film Quarterly* XVIII (Summer 1963), p. 34.
64. Farber, Stephen. "The Writer in American Films," *Film Quarterly* XXI (Summer 1968), p. 7.
65. Johnson, "The Tenth Muse in San Francisco," p. 110.
66. Fenwick and Green-Armytage, *op. cit.*, p. 188.
67. Bluestone, George. "Lunch with Lester," *Film Quarterly* XIX (Summer 1966), p. 14.
68. Marcorelles, *op. cit.*, p. 82.
69. *Ibid.*
70. Arkadin. "Film Clips," *Sight and Sound* 35 (Autumn 1966), p. 203.

Film References

The following list of films refers to film titles mentioned in the text. The country of origin, date and director are noted. It is included for reference purposes only, and is not intended to be a recommended list of films.

Accattone (Italy, 1961), Pier Paolo Pasolini
Alien, The (India, 1969), Satyajit Ray
All Quiet on the Western Front (USA, 1930), Lewis Milestone
All These Women (Sweden, 1964), Ingmar Bergman
Asphalt Jungle, The (USA, 1950), John Huston
Battle of San Pietro, The (USA, shot in Italy, 1944), John Huston
Beauty and the Beast, The (France, 1945), Jean Cocteau
Belle de Jour (France, 1967), Luis Buñuel
Blackboard Jungle, The (USA, 1955), Richard Brooks
Born Free (USA, shot in Africa, 1966), James Hill
Bridge on the River Kwai (England, 1957), David Lean
Caine Mutiny, The (USA, 1954), Edward Dmytryk
Camille (USA, 1937), George Cukor
Captain's Paradise, The (England, 1953), Anthony Kimmins
Carnet de Bal, Un (France, 1937), Julien Duvivier
Casablanca (USA, 1942), Michael Curtiz
Chronique d'un Eté, Un (France, 1961), Jean Rouch and E. Morin
Citizen Kane (USA, 1941), Orson Welles
City, The (USA, 1939), Ralph Steiner and Willard van Dyke
Connection, The (USA, 1960), Shirley Clarke
Dr. Doolittle (USA, 1967), Richard Fleischer
Dr. No (England, 1962), Terence Young
Dr. Strangelove or: How I learned to stop worrying and love the bomb (USA, 1963), Stanley Kubrick
Dolce Vita, La (Italy, 1959), Federico Fellini
Don Quixote (USSR, 1957), Gigory Kozentsev
Drunken Angel (Japan, 1948), Akira Kurosawa
Easy Street (USA, 1917), Charles Chaplin
8½ (Italy, 1963), Federico Fellini
Exterminating Angel, The (Mexico, 1962), Luis Buñuel
Forgotten Village (USA, shot in Mexico, 1941), Herbert Kline
Fox, The (USA–Canada, 1968), Mark Rydell
Giant (USA, 1956), George Stevens
Goldfinger (England, 1964), Guy Hamilton
Gold Rush, The (USA, 1925), Charles Chaplin
Graduate, The (USA, 1967), Mike Nichols

Grande Illusion, La (France, 1937), Jean Renoir
Great Expectations (England, 1947), David Lean
Great Train Robbery, The (USA, 1903), Edwin S. Porter
Group, The (USA, 1965), Sidney Lumet
Hard Day's Night, A (England, 1964), Richard Lester
Henry V (England, 1945), Laurence Olivier
High Noon (USA, 1952), Fred Zinnemann
Jazz Singer, The (USA, 1927), Alan Crosland
Juliet of the Spirits (Italy, 1965), Federico Fellini
Kind Hearts and Coronets (England, 1948), Robert Hamer
Knack, and how to get it, The (England, 1965), Richard Lester
Lady in the Lake (USA, 1946), Robert Montgomery
Last Year at Marienbad (France, 1961), Alain Resnais
Lavender Hill Mob (England, 1951), Charles Crichton
Lawrence of Arabia (England, 1962), David Lean
Letter from an Unknown Woman (USA, 1948), Max Ophuls
Lifeboat (USA, 1944), Alfred Hitchcock
Litho (USA, 1961), Cliff Roberts
Lord of the Flies (England, 1962), Peter Brook
Lunch Hour at the Lumière Factory (France, circa 1895), Lumière Brothers
M (Germany, 1932), Fritz Lang
Maltese Falcon, The (USA, 1941), John Huston
Man in the White Suit, The (England, 1952), Alexander Mackendrick
Metanomen (USA, 1967), Scott Bartlett
Mondo Cane (Italy, 1963), Gualtiero Jacopetti
Nazarin (Mexico, 1958), Luis Buñuel
Never on Sunday (Greece, 1960), Jules Dassin
Night and Fog (France, 1955), Alain Resnais
Occurrence at Owl Creek Bridge, An (France, 1964), Robert Enrico
Odd Man Out (England, 1947), Carol Reed
Open City (Italy, 1945), Roberto Rossellini
Orpheus (France, 1949), Jean Cocteau
Pacific 231 (France, 1949), Jean Mitry
Passion of Joan of Arc, The (France, 1928), Carl Dreyer
Petulia (England–USA, 1968), Richard Lester
Pink Panther, The (USA, 1968), Blake Edwards
Place in the Sun, A (USA, 1951), George Stevens
Plaisir, Le (France, 1951), Max Ophuls
Planet of the Apes (USA, 1968), Franklin Schaffner
Primary (USA, 1960), Richard Leacock
Queen of Spades, The (England, 1948), Thorold Dickinson
Quiet One, The (USA, 1948), Sidney Meyers
Rains Came, The (USA, 1939), Clarence Brown
Rashomon (Japan, 1950), Akira Kurosawa
Red Desert, The (Italy, 1964), Michelangelo Antonioni
River, The (India, 1951), Jean Renoir
Ronde, La (France, 1950), Max Ophuls
Rope, (USA, 1948), Alfred Hitchcock

Shoot the Piano Player (France, 1960), François Truffaut
Some Like It Hot (USA, 1959), Billy Wilder
Song of Ceylon (England, 1935), Basil Wright
Spellbound (USA, 1945), Alfred Hitchcock
Star is Born, A (USA, 1954), George Cukor
Stray Dog (Japan, 1949), Akira Kurosawa
Streetcar Named Desire, A (USA, 1951), Elia Kazan
Sunset Boulevard (USA, 1950), Billy Wilder
Testament of Orpheus (France, 1959), Jean Cocteau
Tete Contre Les Murs, La (France, 1958), Georges Franju
Third Man, The (England, 1949), Carol Reed
This Sporting Life (England, 1963), Lindsay Anderson
Throne of Blood (Japan, 1957), Akira Kurosawa
Time Out of War, A (USA, 1954), Denis and Terry Sanders
Titan, The (USA, 1949), Richard Lydford
To Kill a Mockingbird (USA, 1963), Robert Mulligan
Trader Horn (USA, 1931), W. S. Van Dyke
Treasure of the Sierra Madre (USA, 1948), John Huston
Trip to the Moon, A (France, 1902), George Méliès
Triumph of the Will (Germany, 1936), Leni Riefenstahl
Very Nice, Very Nice (Canada, 1962), Arthur Lipsett
Viridiana (Mexico, 1961), Luis Buñuel

Directors
and Their Principal Films

THE FOLLOWING LIST of directors refers to persons mentioned in the text. The country of origin or principal work, dates of birth and death, and representative films are mentioned. The films mentioned are not inclusive nor have they been selected for their quality, but rather as a fair sample of the kinds of work done over a period of time.

Anderson, Lindsay (1923–   ) English
   Critic, theater worker: associated with "free cinema" movement. Films: 1963 *This Sporting Life*, 1966 *The White Bus*, 1968 *If*; shorts: 1953 *Thursday's Children*, 1953 *O Dreamland*, 1957 *Every Day Except Christmas*.
Antonioni, Michelangelo (1912–   ) Italian
   Made documentaries in early forties, features starting 1950. Films: 1950 *Cronaca di un Amore*, 1960 *L'Avventura*, 1960 *La Notte*, 1961 *L'Eclisse*, 1964 *Red Desert*, 1966 *Blowup*, 1969 *Zabriskie Point*.
Bergman, Ingmar (1918–   ) Swedish
   Director Royal Dramatic Theatre, Stockholm, Swedish Film Institute. Films: 1945 *Crisis*, 1950 *Summer Interlude*, 1952 *Summer with Monika*, 1957 *Wild Strawberries*, 1963 *The Silence*, 1968 *Shame*.
Bertolucci, Bernardo (1941–   ) Italian
   Pasolini's student and assistant. Films: 1962 *La Commare Secca*, 1964 *Prima della rivoluzione*, 1969 *Il Sosia*.
Boorman, John (1933–   ) English
   Works in USA, from British television. Films: 1965 *Having a Wild Weekend*, 1967 *Point Blank*, 1968 *Hell in the Pacific*, 1969 *Rosencrantz and Guildenstern Are Dead*.
Bresson, Robert (1907–   ) French
   Studied painting, former assistant to Rene Clair. Films: 1945 *Les Dames du Bois de Boulogne*, 1950 *Le Journal d'un Cure de Campagne*, 1959 *Pickpocket*, 1965 *Au Hasard Balthazar*, 1967 *Mouchette*.
Brook, Peter (1925–   ) English
   Works in theater and films. Films: 1953 *Beggar's Opera*, 1960 *Moderato Cantabile*, 1962 *Lord of the Flies*, 1967 *Marat/Sade*, 1968 *Tell Me Lies*.
Brooks, Richard (1912–   ) American
   Works also as writer. Films: 1952 *Deadline USA*, 1955 *Blackboard Jungle*, 1958 *Cat on a Hot Tin Roof*, 1960 *Elmer Gantry*, 1964 *Lord Jim*, 1966 *The Professionals*, 1967 *In Cold Blood*.
Buñuel, Luis (1900–   ) Spanish
   Works in many countries, wherever he can without official interference. Films:

1938 *Un Chien Andalou* (with Dali), 1930 *L'Age d'Or*, 1950 *Los Olivados*, 1952 *Robinson Crusoe*, 1958 *Nazarin*, 1961 *Viridiana*, 1962 *The Exterminating Angel*, 1967 *Belle de Jour*.

Chaplin, Charles (1889–) English
Worked in United States, now lives in Switzerland, started under Sennett. Films: 1918 *Shoulder Arms*, 1923 *A Woman of Paris*, 1931 *City Lights*, 1936 *Modern Times*, 1940 *The Great Dictator*, 1947 *Monsieur Verdoux*, 1966 *Countess from Hong Kong*.

Clair, Rene (1898–) French
Has worked in USA, journalist, actor, early sound films noteworthy. Films: 1924 *Entr'Acte*, 1927 *The Italian Straw Hat*, 1930 *Sous les Toits de Paris*, 1931 *Le Million*, 1932 *A Nous la Liberté*, 1945 *And Then There Were None*, 1956 *Les Grandes Manouvres*, 1965 *Les Fêtes Galantes*.

Cocteau, Jean (1899–1963) French
Novelist, essayist, playwright, poet. Films: 1930 *Le Sang d'un Poete*, 1945 *La Belle et la Bête*, 1949 *Orphée*, 1959 *Le Testament d'Orphée*.

Cukor, George (1899–) American
Started as stage director, "woman's director," long Hollywood career. Films: 1931 *Tarnished Lady*, 1933 *Dinner at Eight*, 1937 *Camille*, 1944 *Gaslight*, 1949 *Adam's Rib*, 1954 *A Star is Born*, 1960 *Heller in Pink Tights*, 1964 *My Fair Lady*.

Dreyer, Carl (1889–1968) Danish
Journalist, script writer, editor. Films: 1919 *The President*, 1928 *Passion of Joan of Arc*, 1931 *Vampire*, 1943 *Day of Wrath*, 1954 *Ordet*, 1964 *Gertrud*.

Eisenstein, Sergei (1898–1948) Russian
Teacher and theorist of film. Editing important. Films: 1924 *Strike*, 1925 *Battleship Potemkin*, 1927 *October*, 1929 *General Line*, 1931 *Que viva Mexico*, 1938 *Alexander Nevsky*, 1941–46 *Ivan the Terrible, I and II*.

Enrico, Robert (1931–) French
Began as editor and assistant. Films: 1962 *Montagnes Magiques*, 1963 *La Belle Vie*, 1965 *Les Grandes Gueules*, 1966 *Les Aventuriers*, 1967 *Tante Zita*, 1968 *Ho*.

Fellini, Federico (1920–) Italian
Began as cartoonist, assistant to Rossellini. Films: 1953 *I Vitelloni*, 1954 *La Strada*, 1955 *Il Bidone*, 1957 *La Notti di Cabiria*, 1959 *La Dolce Vita*, 1963 *8½*, 1965 *Juliet of the Spirits*.

Fleischer, Richard (1916–) American
Son of cartoonist Max Fleischer. Films: 1948 *So This is New York*, 1952 *The Narrow Margin*, 1954 *20,000 Leagues Under the Sea*, 1955 *Violent Saturday*, 1959 *Compulsion*, 1967 *Dr. Doolittle*, 1968 *Boston Strangler*.

Ford, John (1895–) American
Long successful Hollywood director. Films: 1924 *The Iron Horse*, 1939 *Stagecoach*, 1940 *The Grapes of Wrath*, 1946 *My Darline Clementine*, 1952 *The Quiet Man*, 1966 *Seven Women*.

Godard, Jean-Luc (1930–) French
Film critic with *Cahiers*, "new wave" director. Films: 1959 *A Bout de Souffle*, 1960 *Le Petit Soldat*, 1962 *Vivre Sa Vie*, 1964 *Bande a part*, 1965 *Alphaville*, 1966 *Made in USA*, 1967 *Weekend*.

Griffith, David Wark (c. 1880–1948) American
Pioneer and innovator in all aspects of film. Films: 1915 *Birth of a Nation*, 1916

Intolerance, 1919 *Broken Blossoms*, 1920 *Way Down East*, 1922 *Orphans of the Storm*, 1930 *Abraham Lincoln*.

Hawks, Howard (1896–   ) American
Action and comedy films. Films: 1928 *A Girl in Every Port*, 1930 *The Dawn Patrol*, 1932 *Scarface*, 1938 *Bringing up Baby*, 1948 *Red River*, 1967 *El Dorado*.

Hitchcock, Alfred (1899–   ) English
Worked in US since 1940, "the master of suspense." Films: 1926 *The Lodger*, 1929 *Blackmail*, 1935 *Thirty-nine Steps*, 1940 *Rebecca*, 1943 *Shadow of a Doubt*, 1951 *Stranger on a Train*, 1958 *Vertigo*, 1960 *Psycho*, *The Birds*.

Kline, Herbert (1909–   ) American
Editor of "New Theatre and Film." Films: 1938 *Crisis*, 1939 *Lights Out in Europe*, 1941 *Forgotten Village*, 1947 *My Father's House*.

Kurosawa, Akira (1910–   ) Japanese
One of few Japanese directors known in West. Films: 1950 *Rashomon*, 1954 *Seven Samurai*, 1957 *Lower Depths*, 1957 *Throne of Blood*, 1962 *High and Low*.

Lang, Fritz (1890–   ) Austrian
Many films in USA, studied art in Vienna. Films: 1922 *Dr. Mabuse*, 1924 *Metropolis*, 1931, *M*, 1944 *Woman in the Window*, 1952 *Rancho Notorious*, 1953 *Big Heart*.

Leacock, Richard (1921–   ) American
Born in England, brother of Philip Leacock, associated with "cinema verité." Films: 1960 *Primary*, 1961 *Football*, 1962 *David*, 1963 *Chair*, 1963 *Jane*.

Lester, Richard (1932–   ) American
Works in England, from television. Films: 1964 *A Hard Day's Night*, 1965 *Help*, 1965 *Knack*, 1966 *Funny Thing Happened on the Way to the Forum*, 1968 *Petulia*.

Lubitsch, Ernst (1892–1947) German
Much work in Hollywood, sophisticated sex films, "Lubitsch Touch." Films: 1932 *Trouble in Paradise*, 1938 *Ninotchka*, 1940 *That Uncertain Feeling*, 1945 *Cluny Brown*.

Mann, Anthony (1906–1967) American
Actor, stage manager and director, action films. Films: 1947 *T-Men*, 1949 *Reign of Terror*, 1950 *Winchester 73*, 1954 *Glenn Miller Story*, 1957 *Men in War*, 1961 *El Cid*, 1967 *Dandy in Aspic*.

Méliès, George (1861–1938) French
Magician, pioneer, fades, double exposures. Films: 1901 *Indiarubber Head*, 1902 *Trip to Moon*, 1911 *Baron Munchausen*.

Melville, J. P. (1917–   ) French
Stage work as well as films. Films: 1947 *Le Silence de la Mer*, 1948 *Les Enfants Terribles*, 1955 *Bob le Flambeur*, 1961 *Leon Morin*.

Ophuls, Max (1902–1957) German
Worked in Germany, France, USA, camera fluidity, tracking shots. Films: 1935 *Divine*, 1948 *Letter from an Unknown Woman*, 1950 *La Ronde*, 1951 *Le Plaisir*, 1954 *Earrings of Madame De*, 1955 *Lola Montes*.

Pasolini, Pier Paolo (1922–   ) Italian
Noted for use of non-actors, novelist, poet. Films: 1961 *Accattone*, 1962 *Mamma Roma*, 1964 *Gospel According to St. Matthew*, 1969 *Edipoke*.

Preminger, Otto (1906–   ) American
Born in Austria but production mainly in USA, theater work also. Films: 1944 *Laura*, 1946 *Fallen Angel*, 1947 *Forever Amber*, 1960 *Exodus*, 1962 *Advise and Consent*, 1963 *Cardinal*.

Ray, Nicholas (1911–   ) American
    Writer, stage director, radio producer. Films: 1947 *They Live By Night*, 1955 *Rebel without a Cause*, 1961 *King of Kings*, 1962 *55 Days to Peking*.
Ray, Satyajit (1922–   ) Indian
    Commercial artist, one of few Indian directors known in West. Films: 1954 *Pather Panchali*, 1956 *Aparajito*, 1959 *World of Apu*, 1958 *Music Room*, 1960 *Goddess*.
Renoir, Jean (1894–   ) French
    Son of Auguste Renoir, brother of Pierre Renoir, worked on stage, much work in USA also. Films: 1926 *Nana*, 1931 *La Chienne*, 1934 *Toni*, 1937 *La Grande Illusion*, 1939 *La Regle du Jeu*, 1951 *The River*.
Resnais, Alain (1922–   ) French
    Former editor, short documentaries. Films: 1955 *Night and Fog*, 1959 *Hiroshima Mon Amour*, 1961 *Last Year at Marienbad*, 1962 *Muriel*, 1965 *La Guerre est Finie*.
Rossellini, Roberto (1906–   ) Italian
    Technician, editor, writer, neo-realist. Films: 1945 *Open City*, 1946 *Paisan*, 1949 *Stromboli*, 1959 *General Della Rovere*.
Siegel, Donald (1912–   ) American
    Editor, montage director. Films: 1946 *The Verdict*, 1954 *Riot in Cell Block 11*, 1956 *Invasion of Body Snatchers*, 1962 *Hell is for Heroes*, 1964 *The Killers*, 1968 *Madigan*.
Truffaut, François (1932–   ) French
    Critic, "new wave." Films: 1957 *Les Mistons*, 1959 *The 400 Blows*, 1960 *Shoot the Piano Player*, 1961 *Jules et Jim*, 1966 *Farenheit 451*, 1968 *Bride Wore Black*, 1969 *Stolen Kisses*.
Vidor, King (1894–   ) American
    Journalist, long time Hollywood director. Films: 1925 *Big Parade*, 1928 *The Crowd*, 1937 *Stella Dallas*, 1947 *Duel in the Sun*, 1956 *War and Peace*, 1959 *Solomon and Sheba*.
Von Sternberg, Joseph (1894–   ) Austrian
    Worked mostly in Hollywood, light and camera work important. Films: 1925 *Salvation Hunters*, 1927 *Underworld*, 1930 *Blue Angel*, 1934 *Scarlet Empress*, 1935 *Devil is a Woman*.
Warhol, Andy (c. 1930–   ) American
    Works in all arts, "pop" movement, began "The Factory." Films: 1963 *Sleep*, 1964 *Eat*, 1965 *Vinyl*, 1965 *Screen Test*, 1966 *Chelsea Girls*, 1968 *Lonesome Cowboys*.
Welles, Orson (1915–   ) American
    Actor-director-producer, radio, theater, films. Works all over world. Films: 1941 *Citizen Kane*, 1942 *Magnificent Ambersons*, 1946 *Stranger*, 1951 *Othello*, 1955 *Confidential Report*, 1957 *Touch of Evil*, 1962 *The Trial*.
Wilder, Billy (1906–   ) Austrian
    Works principally in USA. Co-scripts films. Films: 1945 *Double Indemnity*, 1945 *Lost Weekend*, 1950 *Sunset Boulevard*, 1959 *Some Like It Hot*, 1960 *The Apartment*, 1966 *Fortune Cookie*.
Zinnemann, Fred (1907–   ) Austrian
    Works principally in USA and England. Films: 1948 *The Search*, 1950 *The Men*, 1952 *High Noon*, 1953 *From Here to Eternity*, 1965 *Behold a Pale Horse*.

Select Bibliography

BOOKS

THE LIST BELOW suggests the kinds of books which are useful to those interested in film directing. There is, in addition to a small core of books on practical film production, an increasing number of books by and about individual directors and films.

Baddeley, W. Hugh. *The Technique of Documentary Film Production*, Hastings House, Publishers, 1963.

Benoit-Levy, Jean. *The Art of the Motion Picture*, Coward-MacCann, Inc., 1946.

Boleslavsky, Richard. *Acting: The First Six Lessons*, Theatre Arts, n.d.

Clark, Frank P. *Special Effects in Motion Pictures*, Society of Motion Picture and Television Engineers, Inc., 1966.

Eisenstein, Sergei. *Film Form*, edited and translated by Jay Leyda, Harcourt, Brace and Company, 1949.

Eisenstein, Sergei M. *The Film Sense*, translated and edited by Jay Leyda, Harcourt, Brace and Company, 1947.

Fielding, Raymond. *The Technique of Special-Effects Cinematography*, Hastings House, Publishers, 1965.

Geduld, Harry M., ed. *Film Makers on Film Making*, Indiana University Press, 1967.

Gordon, Jay E. *Motion-Picture Production for Industry*. The Macmillan Company, 1961.

Grierson, John. *Grierson on Documentary*, edited and compiled by Forsyth Hardy, with American notes by Richard Griffith and Mary Losey, Harcourt, Brace and Company, 1947.

Halas, John, and Manvell, Roger. *The Technique of Film Animation*, Hastings House, Publishers, 1968.

Huntley, John, and Manvell, Roger. *The Technique of Film Music*, Hastings House, Publishers, 1968.

Lewin, Frank. *The Soundtrack in Nontheatrical Motion Pictures*, reprint from the Journal of the Society of Motion Picture and Television Engineers, Vol. 68, No. 3, March 1959.

Lindgren, Ernest. *The Art of the Film*, 2nd ed., The Macmillan Company, 1963.

Lawson, John Howard. *Film: The Creative Process*, 2nd ed., Hill & Wang, Inc., 1967.

MacCann, Richard Dyer. *Film: A Montage of Theories*, E. P. Dutton & Co., Inc., 1966.

Macgowan, Kenneth. *Behind the Screen*, Delacorte, 1965.

Manvell, Roger, ed. *Experiment in the Film*, The Macmillan Company, 1951.

Pudovkin, V. I. *Film Technique and Film Acting*, translated by Ivor Montagu, Lear Publishers, Inc., 1949.

Reisz, Karel, and Millar, Gavin. *The Technique of Film Editing*, Hastings House, Publishers, 1968.

Ruesch, Jurgen, and Kees, Weldon. *Nonverbal Communication: Notes on the Visual Perception of Human Relations*, University of California Press, 1966.

PERIODICALS

The periodicals listed below have consistently informative articles about the various aspects of film making of interest to film directors.

American Cinematographer Magazine
Cahiers du Cinèma (also published in English)
Film Comment
Film Culture
Film Facts
Film Quarterly (formerly Hollywood Quarterly)
Films and Filming
Films in Review
International Film Guide (updated yearly)
Movie
Sight and Sound
Variety

Glossary

THE GLOSSARY INCLUDES those terms used in the book which are not fully explained in the text, which are used throughout the text, or which may be unfamiliar terms. Those terms appearing in parentheses, ( ), refer to words used interchangeably with the principal reference word. Terms in italic refer to words defined in the glossary.

ACTION. Movement, change, progression, *becoming*.

ACTOR. Any person or thing which moves, and is moved by, the *story*, which becomes a point of audience attention and interest, and which undergoes some process of change, or change of fortune, during the story telling: includes inanimate objects which can be given the appearance of motion without anthropomorphism.

ALL-INCLUSIVE TRACK. See *non-selective track*.

APPARENT TIME. Illusory or synthetic time; see *external*.

ART DIRECTOR. See *production designer*.

AUDIAL DESIGN. Creating timed sound tracks for use with timed moving images.

"BECOMING," QUALITY OF. Sense of potentiality; that feeling for time continuum in which events are understood as emerging from previous events and leading into still other events; see *being*.

"BEING," QUALITY OF. Having value independent of relationship to a continuum; individual; unique; see *becoming*.

BLOCK. A method of planning for shooting; fitting action and camera movement together.

BOOM. A long armed support for a camera or a microphone; see *crane shot*.

BRIDGING SHOT. A *transitional* shot intended primarily as a connection between two shots, scenes or sequences within the film.

CAMERA-AS-CAMERA. A type of *subjective* camera in which the camera is not specifically identified with a character in the action, but is frankly a camera present when the action is being performed.

CAMERAMAN (*director of photography*). The person or persons given responsibility for photographing the motion picture, including lighting, camera operation and camera effects.

CANNED. See *stock*.

CENTER OF ATTENTION. That element or area of a shot to which audience attention is attracted.

CHANGE OF ANGLE. A spatial device to maintain a sense of visual flow when constructing a continuous action out of many strips of film; also important in maintaining temporal *continuity*.

CHARACTERIZATION. The total of devices or methods used by an actor to portray a human being other than himself.

CHEATING. Creating scenes synthetically, without sets or actors; may involve *optical effects*, animation, laboratory tricks, miniatures or model shots; also deceptive editing for effect.

CIRCLE TAKE. See *print take.*

CLEAN ENTRANCES AND EXITS. Rolling the camera before the *action* begins and continuing to photograph until after the action ends.

CLOSEUP (close shot). Relative term describing a shot in which the subject occupies all or almost all, of the frame area.

CODA-EFFECT. Effect of return, recall or duplication, where audience attention is drawn to the fact that perception of and feeling about the action has changed because of what has been experienced since the first action was viewed.

COMPLETE SCORE. A musical *score*, either *stock* or *composed*, running the entire length of the film; see also *through composed.*

COMPOSED MUSIC. Music written and recorded especially for the film, as differentiated from *stock* or "canned" music.

COMPOUND CAMERA MOVEMENT. A combination of two or more *simple camera movements*, such as combining a tilt and a pan; such combinations also compound the effects of the movements.

CONTINUITY. Those properties within individual shots which allow them to be related to other shots; also, the sequence of relationships obtained when the shots have continuity.

CONTINUITY GIRL. Script clerk; see *script supervisor.*

CONTRAPUNTAL SOUND. Sound having rhythm, meaning or direction running counter to the picture.

COVERAGE. Photographing or recording enough material of a scene or sequence.

CRANE SHOT. A shot using a camera mounted at the end of a long arm or boom, thus enabling the entire camera to move vertically and horizontally in relation to its subject, as well as swinging toward, away or around in an arc.

CROSSFADE. Fading one sound out while simultaneously fading another sound in; the audial equivalent of a *dissolve.*

CUT. Change of shot made in editing by abutting two lengths of film with a simple splice; see also *transition.*

CUTAWAY. A shot occurring in the same time segment as the *master scene*, but in a different location.

CUTTING. In editing, the process of making a *continuity* out of sounds and photographed images.

DEAD OBJECTS. Objects which the director is not presently using to tell his *story.*

DEPTH OF FIELD. A lens characteristic; the amount of space or depth in the scene, measured in feet from the camera, which will be in sharp focus when photographed; as, from five to fifteen feet.

DIALOGUE DIRECTOR. In large budget films, a person assigned to coach the actors on delivery of their lines; ordinarily does no direction of the *action.*

DIRECTOR OF PHOTOGRAPHY. See *cameraman.*

DISSOLVE. A *transitional* device in which a *fade out* is exactly *superimposed* over a *fade in*, thus giving the visual effect of one scene "dissolving" into another.

DISTORTION LENS. A lens used on the camera or in printing which in some way distorts or modifies the photographic image; see also *fish eye* and *split.*

DOLLY. A small wheeled platform on which a camera and tripod can be mounted and which enables a dolly shot to be made, a movement toward, away, around or along side of the *action* being photographed.

DRAMA. See *story*.

DRY RUNTHROUGH. A pre-production rehearsal from which one or more of the elements of set, camera or actors is missing; going through the action but not filming it.

DYNAMIC COMPOSITION. In film, composition tending toward movement, change, pro-progression and "*becoming*."

DUB (*re-record*). Properly, the process of combining sound tracks; in sub-dubbing, the final combination goes through several steps—the sub-dubs—before final dubbing; also commonly, though incorrectly, used to mean *post-syncing*.

EDITING. The whole process of assembling component shots of a film into their final order and cutting them to their final length. Also applied to soundtracks.

EFFECTS. See *optical effect, special effect, sound effect*; "effects" can apply to any one of these more completely descriptive terms.

ESTABLISHING SHOT. A *shot* which establishes or shows the spatial relationships between objects or actors, usually, but not always, on a relatively large scale.

EXTERNAL. An apparent, illusory or synthetic effect between, or over, two or more shots; time, motion or composition which is a composite of the time, motion or composition of the individual shots; synthesized time, motion or composition, considered in context. See also *internal*.

FABRICATED ENVIRONMENT. An image of a setting built up in the audience's mind through selection of details of existing locations, so photographed and cut together that they seem an actually existing place.

FADE IN. A transitional device in which the picture appears gradually from a blank screen; it can be achieved in printing or, more rarely, in the camera.

FADE OUT. A transitional device in which the picture disappears gradually into a blank screen; it can be achieved in printing or, more rarely, in the camera.

FIELD (*location*). Any place away from a sound stage where the film is shot.

FISH-EYE LENS. A lens which photographs its image as if reflected from a shiny hemispherical surface; see *distortion lens*.

FLUB. A mistake.

FOCUS IN. A *transitional device* in which an image, first out of focus, then comes into focus.

FOCUS OUT. A *transitional device* in which an in-focus image is thrown out of focus.

FORMAL FRAME. The standard aspect ratio of a particular film, which remains constant through the film; see also *informal frame*.

FRAME RELATIONSHIP. A spatial device; actors and objects must maintain a consistent relation to the audience's only real point of reference, the frame of the picture.

FREELY ASSOCIATED TRACK. A type of selective track in which the sound/picture relationship is based on intended meanings, rather than the illusion of synchronization.

FREEZE FRAME. A visual effect in which the moving picture seems to stop its motion in the midst of the shot.

HARD FOCUS. A photographed image in sharp focus; outlines are hard edged.

HARD LIGHT. A quality of light which causes hard or sharp edged shadows to be thrown.

HEAD. The beginning of a shot.

HIGH ANGLE. A camera position from which the camera looks down upon its subject.

IDEA. Film as conceived in written, visual or imagined form.

ILLUSORY TIME. Apparent, or synthetic time; see *external*.

IMPROVISED SCORE. A musical score composed at the time of its recording.

INFORMAL FRAME. A framing provided by composing pictorial elements within the frame; varied continuously throughout the film; see also *formal frame*.

INSERT. A shot designed for insertion, during cutting, at whatever point in the action appears best; it has the same tension, tempo and feeling as the *master scene* and occurs in the same location; it is a detail shot, a smaller or different portion of the main scene.

INTERCUT. Any shot cut into a *master scene*.

INTER-FRAME RELATIONSHIPS. Relationships extending across two or more shots.

INTERNAL. Within any one shot; time, or motion, within any one shot; internal composition, composition within the frame.

INTERPRETIVE MUSIC. Music occurring without reference to any visible source.

INTERPRETIVE SOUND EFFECTS. Sound effects occurring without reference to any visible source.

INTRA-FRAME RELATIONSHIPS. Relationships within one frame.

JUMP CUT. Abutting two shots of the same action which were photographed without a change of angle having been made between them.

LIP SYNC. Sync dialogue; see *synchronous dialogue*.

LIVE. Unrehearsed or "on the spot;" without interruption; done in the field; opposite of *stock* or canned material.

LOCATION. A place or setting, usually away from a sound stage.

LONG FOCAL LENGTH LENS. A telephoto lens: with 35 mm equipment, a lens with a focal length of about 100 mm or greater; with 16 mm equipment, a lens with a focal length of about 50 mm or longer.

LONG SHOT. A relative term describing a shot in which the subject occupies a relatively small part of the frame area.

LOOP. A length of film, the ends of which have been spliced together, forming a continuous loop.

LOW ANGLE. A camera position in which the camera looks up at its subject.

MASS. In film, apparent object size.

MASTER SCENE or master shot. A method of organizing the shooting so that continuous actions are recorded in longer segments, with inserts, cutaways and cover shots being added later.

MASTER SHOT. See *master scene*.

MASTER PRINTING TRACK. See *master track*.

MASTER TRACK. Final, completed *mixed* sound track for a film.

MATCHING. Consistency in all matters of picture and sound; see also *continuity*.

MEDIUM ANGLE. A camera position in which the camera looks more or less directly at its subject across intervening space; assumed to be desired unless excluded by the terms *high angle* or *low angle*.

MEDIUM SHOT. A relative term describing a shot in which the subject and the background occupy approximately equal area in the frame.

MIX. See *rerecord, dub*.

MOTIVATED MUSIC. Music which could reasonably be expected to occur in the scene being viewed.

MOTIVATED SOUND. Sound which could reasonably be expected to occur in the scene being viewed.

MOVING SHOT. A shot in which the camera moves.

NARRATION. A non-synchronous monologue speech occurring on the sound track in the absence of any visible source.

NG. No good, e.g., an N.G. take.

NON-ACTORS. Persons who have had no previous film acting experience.

NON-SYNCHRONOUS MONOLOGUE. See *narration*.

NON-SELECTIVE TRACK. A sound track that attempts to be complete in choice of sound; including all sounds both within the camera's view and outside it.

NORMAL ANGLE. See *medium angle*.

NORMAL FOCAL LENGTH LENS. A lens so named because it seems to record images much as the human eye sees them, at least more so than do the other extremes of focal length; with 35 mm equipment, a 50 mm lens; with 16 mm equipment, a 25 mm lens.

OBJECTIVE CAMERA. Use of camera which puts the audience in the position of an unseen but interested observor of the scene who is in an ideal position to witness the action.

ONE SHOT. A shot containing one person.

OPTICAL EFFECT. Usually refers to a *transitional* device made in the printer; e.g., *fade, dissolve, wipe*; sometimes called simply "opticals."

OUT OF FOCUS. A photographed image in which all lines and objects appear very soft or fuzzy.

OVERCRANKING. Shooting (slow motion) with a camera speed greater than projection speed so that the final action will seem to move more slowly than in reality; see also *undercranking*.

OVERLAPPING. Repetition of segments of action or speech for convenience in cutting; allowing sound from one shot to extend beyond the cut or other transitional device to the succeeding shot.

OVER THE SHOULDER (overshoulder). A shot containing at least two actors, one of which is only partially visible in the close foreground.

PANNING, also panorama or pan shot. A simple camera movement in which the camera is pivoted horizontally.

PARTIAL SCORE. Music, either stock or composed, for parts of a film.

PICKUPS. Redoing parts of the narration track for either technical or aesthetic reasons.

POINT OF VIEW SHOT (POV). A shot in which the camera takes the point of view of a character or object in the scene; see *subjective* camera.

POST PRODUCTION RECORDING. See *post recorded* and *post syncing*.

POST RECORDED. Effects, music or speech recorded after the picture has been photographed.

POST SYNCING. A process of recording lip-sync dialogue after the picture has been photographed; see also *dubbing*.

PRE RECORDED. Sound effects, music or speech recorded before the picture is photographed.

PRESENCE. The sense of being there, active, contributing; acting awareness; sound proximity.

PRINT TAKE or *circle take*. A take thought to be perfect and which is singled out for workprinting after processing.

PRODUCTION DESIGNER. The person or persons given responsibility for design and layout of the physical visual elements of a film—set, costume, properties, make-up and sometimes lighting. Also known as art director.

PULL BACK. A *dolly* away from the subject.

RAW STOCK. Motion picture film which has as yet not been exposed; after exposure, it is said to have a latent image; when this is developed, the film is referred to as original, or sometimes negative.

REACTION SHOT. A shot which shows reaction or response to another *action*.

READ. Understood.

READING (OF LINES). An actor's interpretation of dialogue or narration.

REESTABLISHING SHOT. Similar to *establishing shots*, except that reestablishing shots appear later in the scene or sequence as reminders to the audience.

RERECORD. A process in which the individual elements of the master track are individually modified and corrected, and, in some timed relationship, are combined into the *master track*.

RETAKE. Additional attempt to photograph a scene with the same setup, duplicating action as closely as possible.

REVERSE ANGLE. A shot in which the actors seen in the previous shot seem to have changed position without explanation; the camera angle which achieves such an effect.

ROOM SOUND. The characteristic quality of "silence" offered by a particular acoustical situation.

SCENE. Setting, location or environment; also, two or more *shots* which seem to make a relatively definable unit.

SCORE. Musical accompaniment to picture; may be *complete* or *partial*.

SCREEN DIRECTION. Consistent movement of an object or actor in relation to the frame, creating audience association.

SCRIPT. See *idea*.

SCRIPT CLERK. A continuity girl or *script supervisor*.

SCRIPT SUPERVISOR. The person or persons given responsibility to note and check details of action, property, set and lines for the purposes of *matching*.

SECOND TAKE. See *retake*.

SEQUENCE. Two or more scenes which seem to make a relatively definable unit; also, the order of events.

SETTING. Environment, atmosphere and mood acting upon the action which occurs within its boundaries; space in which to work.

SHOT. A discrete length of film; a photographed shot is a *take*; an edited shot is that uninterrupted length of film, regardless of length, between any two transitional devices.

SHORT FOCAL LENGTH LENS or *wide angle lens*. With 35 mm equipment, a lens with a focal length less than 50 mm, usually about 25 mm or less; with 16 mm equipment, a lens with a focal length less than 25 mm, usually about 15 mm or less.

SHOT-BY-SHOT APPROACH. A method of organizing the shooting of a film in which each shot is planned precisely and photographed exactly as it will appear in the final film, allowing for such overlapping and coverage as will be necessary to join the shots in continuity; see also *master shot* approach.

SILENCE. Absence, or relative absence of sound; in film, rarely absolute.

SILENT SCENE. A scene which will be silent in the final film.

SIMPLE CAMERA MOVEMENT. A camera movement in one dimension.

SIZE OF SHOT. The relative size of the subject in relation to the frame.

SLATING. Identification of sound or picture film.

SOFT FOCUS. A photographic image with softened definition.

SOFT LIGHT. A quality of light which causes soft edged shadows to be thrown.

SOUND EFFECTS. All sounds from any source, but in film usually subdivided into speech, music and all other sounds (effects).

SOUND FILTERS or audial filters. Devices used in sound recording to modify sound quality through differential passing of various sound frequencies; high pass filters tend to remove lower frequencies; low pass filters tend to remove higher frequencies.

SOUND PERSPECTIVE. The quality of sound, a combination of volume and location in space, giving the impression of relative distance of sound source.

SPATIAL DESIGN. Composition of timed moving images for use in a *continuity* of shots and sounds.

SPECIAL EFFECTS. Out of the ordinary photographic effects, usually achieved, at least in part, optically in the laboratory or on the set.

SPLIT OR MULTIPLE IMAGE LENSES. A type of *distortion lens* which can split or multiply the number of images of the subject, usually in a regular pattern.

SPOT COMPOSED. A musical score, usually of several parts, composed for specific sections or "spots" in a film.

STATIC, STATIC FILM COMPOSITION. A situation in which the *dynamic* factors are momentarily in balance.

STATIC SHOT. See *static film composition*.

STILL. A still photograph taken during production for publicity or record purposes; also used sometimes to describe shots in which the camera does not move.

STILL SHOT. A shot in which the camera does not move.

STOCK. "Canned" sound effects or music derived from tapes or discs, usually recorded or composed apart from the film and adapted to it by means of *cutting* and *re-recording*; opposite of *live*.

STORY. Drama, or an event of interest to human beings.

STORY BOARD. A set of pre-production sketches of all or part of the action of a film which implies the nature of the action, the set, set dressing, make-up, properties, costume, lighting, camera angle, camera movement and actor movement.

STRUCTURE. A quality inherent in any *story* which has meaning.

STYLE. A quality in a film which emerges from the way in which a director typically solves problems.

SUBJECTIVE CAMERA. Use of camera which seems to involve the audience within the scene in place of a character; opposite of *objective camera*.

SUPERIMPOSITION. A visual or audial effect in which two or more pictures or sounds simultaneously appear on the screen or the sound track.

SUSPENSE. Artificial stretching of time and attention to achieve temporary psychological stress.

SWISH PAN. A fast pan, accomplished by moving the camera so quickly that the image resulting is blurred; in editing this blur is juxtaposed to the succeeding shot with a cut, giving the impression that the camera has "swished" away from the subject to another; used as a transitional device.

SYMBOL. Highly condensed and potentially efficient ways of conveying meaning.

SYNCHRONOUS SOUND (sync sound). Sound recorded at the time its source is being photographed; usually referring to synchronous dialogue.

SYNCHRONOUS DIALOGUE. Lip-sync or sync sound; see *synchronous sound*.

SYNTHETIC MATERIAL. Special effects material created, usually without sets or actors, for inclusion in a film.

TAIL. The end of a shot.

TAKE. Making a shot on picture and/or sound film.

TELEPHOTO. See *long focal length lens*.

THROUGH COMPOSED. A musical score, usually one extended piece, for an entire film.

TILT. A *simple camera movement* in which the camera is pivoted vertically.

TIME DESIGN. Composition of timed *action* and timed sound for use in a *continuity*.

TONAL VALUE. The amount and distribution of light in relation to shadow and darkness; independent of the concept of color, or hue.

TOTAL COMPOSITIONAL AREA. All that the camera photographs at any particular moment, regardless of distance from or relationship to the camera.

TRACK. A sound track.

TRANSITION, TRANSITIONAL DEVICE. Any method of going from one shot to the next.

TRACKING SHOT. A moving camera shot in which the camera is mounted on a wheeled platform that moves on rails laid especially for the shot.

TRUCKING SHOT. Similar to the *dolly*, but the trucking shot is normally more extensive in area and movement; almost always moves with the subject and maintains the same camera-subject distance.

TWO SHOT. A shot containing two persons; with more persons, the shots become "three shots," "four shots," or "group shots."

UNDERCRANKING. Shooting with a camera speed less than projection speed so that the final action will move faster than in reality; see also *overcranking*.

VARIABLE FOCAL LENGTH LENS. See *zoom lens*.

WIDE ANGLE LENS. A *short focal length lens*.

WILD. Sound of any kind recorded *non-synchronously*.

WIPE. A *transitional* device in which one image replaces the next as if one photograph were slid on top of all or part of another; there are many patterns of wipes available; an *optical effect*.

ZOOM, ZOOM LENS. A lens which can be adjusted to any focal length on a continuous scale from wide angle to telephoto; when the focal length settings are changed within a *shot*, the magnification of the image changes, producing a zoom shot or an ersatz *dolly*.

Index